THE WORLD BIBLIOGRAPHICAL SERIES

This series, which is principally designed for the English speaker, will eventually cover every country in the world, each in a separate volume comprising annotated entries on works dealing with its history, geography, economy and politics; and with its people, their culture, customs, religion and social organization. Attention will also be paid to current living conditions – housing, education, newspapers, clothing, etc.– that are all too often ignored in standard bibliographies; and to those particular aspects relevant to individual countries. Each volume seeks to achieve, by use of careful selectivity and critical assessment of the literature, an expression of the country and an appreciation of its nature and national aspirations, to guide the reader towards an understanding of its importance. The keynote of the series is to provide, in a uniform format, an interpretation of each country that will express its culture, its place in the world, and the qualities and background that make it unique. The views expressed in individual volumes, however, are not necessarily those of the publisher.

VOLUMES IN THE SERIES

Djibouti

WORLD BIBLIOGRAPHICAL SERIES

General Editors:
Robert G. Neville (Executive Editor)
John J. Horton

Robert A. Myers   Ian Wallace
Hans H. Wellisch   Ralph Lee Woodward, Jr.

John J. Horton is Deputy Librarian of the University of Bradford and currently Chairman of its Academic Board of Studies in Social Sciences. He has maintained a longstanding interest in the discipline of area studies and its associated bibliographical problems, with special reference to European Studies. In particular he has published in the field of Icelandic and of Yugoslav studies, including the two relevant volumes in the World Bibliographical Series.

Robert A. Myers is Associate Professor of Anthropology in the Division of Social Sciences and Director of Study Abroad Programs at Alfred University, Alfred, New York. He has studied post-colonial island nations of the Caribbean and has spent two years in Nigeria on a Fulbright Lectureship. His interests include international public health, historical anthropology and developing societies. In addition to *Amerindians of the Lesser Antilles: a bibliography* (1981), *A Resource Guide to Dominica, 1493-1986* (1987) and numerous articles, he has compiled the World Bibliographical Series volumes on *Dominica* (1987) and *Nigeria* (1989).

Ian Wallace is Professor of Modern Languages at Loughborough University of Technology. A graduate of Oxford in French and German, he also studied in Tübingen, Heidelberg and Lausanne before taking teaching posts at universities in the USA, Scotland and England. He specializes in East German affairs, especially literature and culture, on which he has published numerous articles and books. In 1979 he founded the journal *GDR Monitor*, which he continues to edit.

Hans H. Wellisch is Professor emeritus at the College of Library and Information Services, University of Maryland. He was President of the American Society of Indexers and was a member of the International Federation for Documentation. He is the author of numerous articles and several books on indexing and abstracting, and has published *The Conversion of Scripts* and *Indexing and Abstracting: an International Bibliography*. He also contributes frequently to *Journal of the American Society for Information Science, The Indexer* and other professional journals.

Ralph Lee Woodward, Jr. is Chairman of the Department of History at Tulane University, New Orleans, where he has been Professor of History since 1970. He is the author of *Central America, a Nation Divided*, 2nd ed. (1985), as well as several monographs and more than sixty scholarly articles on modern Latin America. He has also compiled volumes in the World Bibliographical Series on *Belize* (1980), *Nicaragua* (1983), and *El Salvador* (1988). Dr. Woodward edited the Central American section of the *Research Guide to Central America and the Caribbean* (1985) and is currently editor of the Central American history section of the *Handbook of Latin American Studies*.

VOLUME 118

Djibouti

Peter J. Schraeder

Compiler

(With the assistance of Erick J. Mann)

CLIO PRESS
OXFORD, ENGLAND · SANTA BARBARA, CALIFORNIA
DENVER, COLORADO

British Library Cataloguing in Publication Data

Schraeder, Peter J.
Djibouti. — (World bibliographical series, V. 118).
1. Djibouti (Republic) – Bibliographies
I. Title   II. Series
016. 96771

ISBN 1-85109-084-3

Clio Press Ltd.,
55 St. Thomas' Street,
Oxford OX1 1JG, England.

ABC-CLIO,
130 Cremona Drive,
Santa Barbara,
CA 93117, USA.

Designed by Bernard Crossland.
Typeset by Columns Design and Production Services, Reading, England.
Printed and bound in Great Britain by
Billing and Sons Ltd., Worcester.

*To Diane Clay and Judy Calix
for all the hard work and good cheer.*

Contents

Contents

Introduction

About the bibliography

The Republic of Djibouti, formerly known as the Côte Française des Somalis (French Somali Coast) and the Territoire Français des Afars et des Issas (French Territory of the Afars and Issas), became one of Africa's newest states on 27 June 1977, when it achieved independence from France. Unlike the majority of African countries, Djibouti constitutes a 'mini-state' that, over the years, has been described as a 'cross-roads' at the intersection of Africa, the Middle East and Asia, the 'hell of Africa' due to its often inhospitable climate, and the 'eye of the cyclone' – a reference to the country's special role as an island of stability in the troubled region of the Horn of Africa. In many respects, these references point out the unique nature of a country that, at the time of writing, has enjoyed less than a decade-and-a-half of independence.

The limited duration of Djibouti's period of independence, however, does not mean that the country has been ignored within the scholarly literature devoted to the Horn of Africa. Among the twenty-two categories into which the following 409 annotated works are divided, several have historically generated a great deal of interest among scholars. For example, Djibouti's role as the coastal end-point of the Djibouti–Addis Ababa railway has fostered a tremendous number of travellers' accounts, as well as works on the evolution of transport within the country. Similarly, the internal politics, foreign relations, and general history of the country – so crucial to a complete understanding of regional conflict and co-operation in the Horn of Africa – have also been areas of traditional interest among scholars. More surprising, perhaps, is the vast number of works within the fields of geography and earth sciences. These works were spawned by Djibouti's geographical location at the triple juncture of the Red Sea, Gulf of Aden and East African rift systems, a position which has made the country a veritable treasure trove of volcanic and geothermal activity. Other topics of growing interest to scholars, particularly in the aftermath of Djibouti's independence, continue to include the periodic refugee burden imposed on this small country as a result of regional conflict and drought (see 'Migration and Refugees'); the harmful physiological and social side-effects of substantial local usage of a narcotic known as 'khat' (*catha edulis*; see 'Social Conditions, Health and Welfare'); the Djiboutian government's attempts to replace an almost total dependence on imported energy and foodstuffs by developing local energy and agricultural potential (see 'Energy' and 'Agricultural Development'); and the importance of regional and international development co-operation, most noted by the establishment in Djibouti City of the headquarters for the Intergovernmental Authority on Drought and Development (IGADD; see 'International Development Co-operation').

The primary purpose of this annotated bibliography, therefore, is to introduce the interested reader to the limited, albeit growing, field of Djiboutian studies. As is the case in all such endeavours, the bibliography inevitably builds upon the preliminary archival explorations of numerous scholars and research institutes. Among these are W. Sheldon Clarke, the first US chargé d'affaires accredited to Djibouti who also compiled the first general English-language bibliography dealing with Djibouti (see *The Republic of Djibouti – an introduction to Africa's newest state and a review of related literature and sources*, q.v.); the Documentation Center of Djibouti's French Cultural Center which compiled the first general French-language bibliography dealing with the country (see *Bibliographie de la République de Djibouti*, q.v.); and Virginia Thompson and Richard Adloff, two Africanists who wrote the first general English-language book devoted to exploring Djiboutian society, politics and international relations (see *Djibouti and the Horn of Africa*, q.v.). These and other excellent works will be complemented by the scheduled publication in 1991 of two book-length studies on Djibouti: a massive bibliography compiled by W. Sheldon Clarke of French- and English-language works on Djibouti, inclusive of newspaper articles, locally-produced Djiboutian political pamphlets, and numerous unpublished papers and reports; and a general introduction to Djiboutian society and politics written by Adrian Fozzard as part of the well-received Westview Profiles/Nations of Contemporary Africa series.

Due to Djibouti's common cultural, ethnic, religious, political and language ties with its two larger neighbours, Ethiopia and Somalia, an equally important starting point for a full understanding of the nascent field of Djiboutian studies is the vast body of scholarly works subsumed under the broad titles of Ethiopian and Somali studies. For example, both Harold Marcus (q.v.), a noted US historian of

Ethiopian studies, and Mohamed Khalief Salad (q.v.), a respected scholar within the field of Somali studies, have compiled bibliographies dealing with Ethiopia and Somalia, respectively, which are useful starting points for studies specifically focusing on Djibouti. Similarly, the volumes devoted to Ethiopia and Somalia as part of the Scarecrow Press's African Historical Dictionaries series are also of great benefit (see *Historical dictionary of Somalia* and *Historical dictionary of Ethiopia*, q.v.). Indeed, several of the works cited throughout the pages that follow constitute general works which, although primarily focused on either Ethiopia or Somalia, contain information or passages of direct relevance to Djibouti.

Individuals intent upon utilizing this volume as an introduction to either brief, or more extensive, forays into the field of Djiboutian studies should be aware of two caveats. First, although the majority of works cited are in the English language, summaries of approximately eighty French works have been included throughout the text, particularly for categories lacking sufficient English-language materials (such as 'Ethnicity and Population' and 'Constitution and Legal System'). Those seeking a more comprehensive introduction to French-language works should first consult the above-noted bibliography published by the Documentation Center of Djibouti's French Cultural Center, as well as the forthcoming volume by W. Sheldon Clarke. Second, despite this bibliography's primary focus on relatively 'easy-to-find' books and journal articles, several citations constitute 'hard-to-find' publications more dependent on inter-library loan services. Among these are publications of various agencies of the Djiboutian government; donor organizations, such as the US Agency for International Development (USAID); private institutes, such as the Arlington, Virginia-based Volunteers in Technical Assistance (VITA); and regional organizations, such as IGADD.

Acknowledgements

Before proceeding with this general introduction to Djibouti, it is important to acknowledge those individuals and organizations which, although not responsible for any remaining deficiencies or omissions, greatly facilitated various stages of the research process. First, special thanks are due to the Africa Bureau of the US State Department which provided the author with an internship at the US Embassy in Djibouti in 1987. It was while serving in this capacity that I began compiling and annotating the initial citations of this volume. While working in Djibouti City, both the French Cultural Center and the US Embassy facilitated my initial archival forays. Among those who

Introduction

were most helpful were Chargé d'Affaires, John-Egan McAteer, Administrative Assistant, Kathie Snider, and Mohammed Ogaz, a Djiboutian national who introduced me to numerous personalities within Djibouti City. In Washington, DC, special thanks are reserved for the highly efficient staff in the Africa Division of the research arm of the Library of Congress. Their computer-generated lists of holdings on Djibouti and special searches greatly facilitated a six-week stay during 1989 devoted to compiling and annotating resources. In Chicago, Illinois, my status during 1989 and 1990 as a Visiting Scholar with the African Studies Program at Northwestern University facilitated access to the extensive Africana holdings of the Melville Herskovitts Library of African Studies. In this regard, special thanks are due to Akbar Virmani, assistant director of the African Studies Program, and Hans Panofsky, senior specialist on Africana holdings at Northwestern University. Finally, my current position as Assistant Professor in the Department of Political Science at Loyola University of Chicago has provided me with an exceptionally collegial and supportive workplace. Among those who contributed to the final product were Bonnie Juettner, my graduate research assistant who helped edit the index to the bibliography, and administrative assistants Judy Calix, Diane Clay, and Mary-Margaret Kelly, each of whom typed various portions of successive drafts of the manuscript. Last, but not least, is Erick J. Mann, my undergraduate research assistant who is listed on the title page. Erick provided an invaluable service by tracking down and preparing initial summaries of roughly thirty entries required to complete the bibliography, preparing the initial draft of the index, and helping to respond to various editorial queries. His sharp mind and excellent archival skills will serve him well as he pursues his graduate studies in African history. To Erick and everyone else who helped along the way, I extend a heart-felt thank-you!

Geography[1]

Located in the Horn of Africa, Djibouti comprises a land area of 23,200 square kilometres (approximately the size of Massachusetts or Wales). Despite its small size, historically the country has generated a large degree of international interest due to borders with its larger neighbours of Ethiopia (420 kilometres) and Somalia (80 kilometres), as well as its strategic location straddling the Straits of Bab-el-Mandeb. With a coastline of approximately 370 kilometres ranging from Ras Doumeira in the northeast to Loyada in the southeast, Djibouti commands the southern entrance of the Red Sea and access to the Gulf of Aden and the Indian Ocean. This coastline is broken by the extremely large and picturesque Gulf of Tadjoura. In addition to Djibouti City, which constitutes both the capital and major port, the major urban areas include Ali Sabieh, Dikhil, Obock and Tadjoura.

The topography of Djibouti is most noted for a largely barren, flat landscape composed of black volcanic rock. The harsh beauty of these plains is broken by the basaltic range north of the Gulf of Tadjoura where mountains range from 800 to 1,750 metres in height. The highest geographical point of the territory is the Moussa Ali mountain range (2,063 metres above sea-level), whereas the lowest point is Lake Assal at 155 metres below sea-level. The other major inland body of water is Lake Abbé, located on Djibouti's southwestern border with Ethiopia. Although there are a number of subterranean rivers, the country is completely devoid of any permanent, above-ground rivers.

Despite the relatively harsh landscape, there is an abundance of flora and fauna. In the northern portion of the country, one finds the ancient Day Forest and a variety of tree species, such as jujube and euphoria, fig-trees and wild olives, holly, juniper and mimosa. To the south and southwest of the Gulf of Tadjoura, the vegetation is similar to that found in other arid regions of Africa, and includes acacia and doum palm trees. Among the types of fauna are a wide variety of birds (the migration routes of many species traverse Djibouti and the Red Sea), numerous types of antelopes and gazelles, more limited numbers of carnivores (such as cheetahs) and scavengers (such as hyenas), as well as monkeys, squirrels and warthogs. Perhaps most spectacular is the extremely rich diversity of marine life found along Djibouti's coastline and coral reefs, a factor which has made the country a special point of interest to international scuba-diving associations.

The average annual rainfall is 128 millimetres and is usually spread over no more than twenty days. Different regions of the country, however, receive varying amounts of rain. For example, the coastal regions receive between 60 to 70 millimetres of rainfall per annum, while the northern portions of the country receive between 120 and 140 millimetres. The rainy season lasts between January and March, with the majority of precipitation falling in quick, short bursts which result in periodic flash floods, devastating those areas located at sea level, as exemplified by the flood of April 1989 that killed eight and destroyed the dwellings of approximately 150,000 people in Djibouti City.

The often torrid climate, which has earned the country the nickname of the 'hell of Africa', varies between two major seasons.

Introduction

The cool season lasts from October to April and typifies a 'Mediterranean' climate in which temperatures range from twenty-three and thirty degrees celsius with low humidity. The hot season lasts from May to September. In addition to the dry, sand-filled *khamsin* winds which push temperatures from a low of thirty degrees celsius to a stifling high of forty-five degrees celsius, this time of year is also noted by days in which humidity approaches 100 per cent. Among the coolest areas of the territory is the high-altitude Day Forest in which temperatures as low as twelve degrees celsius have been recorded.

One of the most spectacular aspects of the country is its international reputation as a geological treasure trove. Located at a triple juncture of the Red Sea, Gulf of Aden and East African rift systems, the country hosts significant seismic and geothermal activity. In November 1978, for example, a volcanic eruption near Lake Assal created the Ardoukoba volcano – complete with spectacular lava flows – that attracted the attention of volcanologists worldwide. Of particular interest was the tremendous seismic activity which accompanied the eruption and, subsequently, led to the widening by more than a metre of the plates between Africa and the Arabian peninsula.

People

Djibouti is an ethnically diverse country where population statistics are subject to controversy and range from conservative estimates of roughly 300,000 to official Djiboutian government estimates of 500,000.[2] Despite a rather high population growth rate of three per cent per annum, the average population density for the entire country is only estimated at roughly thirteen inhabitants per square kilometre. This latter statistic masks the crucial distinction that, unlike most African countries, the majority of the population (some say as much as eighty per cent) lives in the urban centres, with the capital of Djibouti City serving as the largest urban agglomeration (roughly sixty-five to seventy-five per cent). The process of urbanization, specifically tied to the growth of the port city of Djibouti City and the construction of the Djibouti–Addis Ababa railway, constitutes an important transformation of a society that historically was largely pastoral in nature.

As indicated by the pre-independence name of the French Territory of the Afars and Issas, these peoples comprise the two dominant ethnic groups which historically inhabited the territory. The Issas constitute the largest ethnic group (roughly thirty-three per cent of the population) and inhabit the southern one-third of the country below the Gulf of Tadjoura and east of the Djibouti–Addis Ababa railway. Divided by the arbitrary imposition of colonial borders, the Issa people spill over into both Somalia and Ethiopia where they number 50,000 and 230,000, respectively. The Issas constitute but one subgrouping of the Somali peoples who inhabit Djibouti, Kenya, Ethiopia and, of course, Somalia.

The Afars, also known as the Danakil, constitute the second largest ethnic group (roughly twenty per cent of the population) and inhabit the northern two-thirds of the country above the Gulf of Tadjoura and west of the Djibouti–Addis Ababa railway. Also divided by ill-conceived colonial boundaries, the Afars spill over into the southern portion of Ethiopia's province of Eritrea and extend southward as far as the Ethiopian town of Nazreth in numbers that surpass 600,000. The combined Ethiopian and Djiboutian territory inhabited by the Afar peoples, due to its elongated, triangular shape, is often referred to as the 'Afar triangle'.

The remainder of Djibouti's population is divided among five major groups, largely living in Djibouti City, which were not historically indigenous to the area. The Gadaboursis (fifteen per cent) and Isaaks (13.3 per cent), who are also subgroupings of the Somali peoples that inhabit the Horn of Africa, migrated from northern Somalia during the twentieth century. They were attracted by work associated with the construction of the Djibouti–Addis Ababa railway and the expansion of the port at Djibouti City. Arabs and, particularly, Yemenis constitute a third major group. Largely working in the commercial sector of Djibouti City, they constitute approximately six per cent of the overall population. A fourth group, comprising approximately four per cent of the population, includes a large number (roughly 10,000) of French and other European nationals who work at nearly all administrative levels of the Djiboutian government. Of particular significance are the nearly 3,500 French troops and family members (a total of 6,000 persons) maintained by the French government on Djiboutian territory since independence in 1977. Finally, fluctuating numbers of refugees and illegal economic migrants from both Ethiopia and Somalia have periodically comprised upwards of ten to fifteen per cent of the country's population at any given time. This final grouping has strained the limited capacities of the Djiboutian government and, therefore, has contributed to often acrimonious political debates and international controversy.

In addition to sharing a common nomadic tradition that places a high value on livestock and virtues of bravery and individualism, a strong adherence to the Islamic faith, and an oral tradition that places singers and poets in high esteem, the two dominant ethnic groups – the Afars and the Issas – have maintained strong social networks that form the basis of everyday life, especially within the rural areas. The Issas maintain an especially egalitarian form of social organization based on clan membership in which all 'men' are considered equal and each has the right to voice his opinion concerning the affairs of his clan. As such, decisions are arrived at through consensus. The Issas are divided into two major clan families, each of which is further subdivided into several sub-clans. The Abgal clan family, which accounts for three-quarters of all Issas in the Horn of Africa and two-thirds of those living in Djibouti, includes the following four sub-clans: Yonis-Moussa, Saad-Moussa, Mamassan and Ourweiné. The Dalol clan family, which accounts for only one-fourth of all Issas and roughly one-third of those living in Djibouti, is similarly divided among four sub-clans: the Fourlaba, Horoneh, Walaldon and Wardick. The spiritual head of all the Issa clans resides in Ethiopia and is known as the Ogaz.

Despite a similar emphasis on clan membership as the basis for everyday life, the Afars maintain a hierarchical form of social organization that derives from traditional chiefdoms and sultanates, such as the still extant Tadjoura, Raheita and Aussa sultanates. Decisions and debate among the Afars, unlike among the more egalitarian Issas, are more the reserve of recognized leaders and the heads of clans. For example, historically the sultans of Afar sultanates made decisions based on the advice of viziers and councils composed of the heads of sub-clans and notables. In this regard, there is an important distinction between the so-called 'noble' Asaihimera ('red') clans and the less prestigious Adohimera ('white') clans.[3] Among the five major sub-clans represented in Djibouti are the Adarassoul and the Debné, both of which are prevalent in the Dikhil region; the Adail and Badoita-Mela, which are located in the region of Obock; and the Hassoba, which is representative of the Tadjoura region.

Despite the strong adherence of the vast majority of both the Afars and the Issas, as well as the Isaaks, Gadaboursis and Arabs to the Islamic faith, several Christian denominations are also represented in Djibouti. The Roman Catholic Church, with an estimated 9,000 members, is, perhaps, the most active, successfully winning over several hundred converts from the local population. Among the other churches represented in Djibouti are the Anglican Communion, the Protestant Church and the Greek Orthodox Church.

Finally, although Somali and Afar are the predominant maternal languages of the majority of Djiboutians, the official national languages are French and Arabic. Indeed, fluency in French is essential for those with political aspirations in this former French colony. French is also the means of instruction in primary and secondary schools (there are no colleges or universities within the country), although Arabic is taught as the first language at both of these levels. The Djiboutian government obviously believes that education in either Afar or Somali, unlike French and, to a lesser degree, Arabic, will work against the goal of creating a uniquely 'Djiboutian' personality and citizenry. Language is clearly viewed as an important means for promoting national integration among the various ethnic groups. Moreover, instruction in Afar, even if desired, is hampered by the fact that the language still lacks an accepted written orthography (whereas an official written orthography for Somali was chosen by the government of Somalia in 1972). As of the 1987-88 academic year, approximately 26,200 students were enrolled in primary schools, while a little over 6,300 students were attending secondary schools.

History

Historical records clearly demonstrate that the Horn of Africa was known to ancient seafarers and geographers. As demonstrated by the *The periplus of the Erythraean sea* (q.v.), accounts were being made of the trade and peoples inhabiting the coasts of the Red Sea and the Indian Ocean as early as the first century AD. For the region currently known as Djibouti, one finds references to the port of Tadjoura as early as the seventh century in the *Géographie d'Idrisi*. One century later, one finds references to the Afar peoples of the region in the writings of Ibn Said, an Arab geographer. Similarly during the ninth century, Ibn Battuta, another Arab voyager, described the existence of Somali peoples inhabiting the coastal regions ranging from Zeila to Mogadishu.[4]

The Arabs largely dominated the trading of the Horn of Africa prior to the nineteenth century except for a period of competition with the Portuguese that reached its height during the sixteenth century. A highly sophisticated caravan trade system linked coastal trading centres, such as the Djiboutian port of Tadjoura and Somalia's coastal city of Zeila, with the inland plateau region of what currently constitutes Ethiopia. The caravan traders were forced to pay transit fees to the Afar sultanates and Issa leaders who controlled the region. Whereas on the inland journey such goods as imported cloth, salt slabs from Lake Assal and, more significantly, firearms were carried, such goods as coffee, wax, hides, perfumes and, most importantly, slaves were carried on the coastal journey.[5] For example, it has been documented that, as early as 1839, the Ethiopian empire was even importing several 'small cannon' in return for one female slave for each camel required for transportation.[6]

It was specifically at the beginning of the nineteenth century that imperial competition among European powers and growing French interests in the Horn of Africa gradually contributed to the establishment of a French colony at Obock. In 1862, a treaty was signed in Paris between the French government and Afar chiefs that ceded the port of Obock and adjoining territories to France. This treaty was favoured by French commercial interests hoping to unlock the possibilities of Franco–Ethiopian trade. After a short period of official neglect, the French government commissioned the Mesnier Company in 1883 to create a coaling station at Obock capable of supporting French colonial expansion and wars, particularly in Indochina and Madagascar. The growing importance of Obock in French imperial thinking was marked by the appointment in 1884 of Léonce Lagarde as commander and, three years later, as the first of twenty-two French governors to administer this small colony. Governor Lagarde ensured the consolidation of the French presence in the Horn of Africa by signing a variety of treaties and protectorate agreements with Afar leaders. These treaties acquired rights of passage and protection for French caravan trade, as well as adding additional territories to the growing French colony.

The new colony of Obock turned out to be less than ideally situated for an expansion of trade with Ethiopia, particularly in the context of the construction of a railway from the coast into the hinterland. In addition to Obock's inability to handle heavy tonnage shipping, the mountainous region north of the Gulf of Tadjoura made the construction of a railway impracticable. As a result, French eyes turned to the less mountainous, Issa-inhabited territory south of the Gulf of Tadjoura. In a move that would forever transform the politics and economics of the region, in 1885 the French government signed a treaty with Issa leaders that traded French protection of the region from other foreigners for favoured access to Issa territory. Stimulated by the movement of French commercial interests from Obock to the southern side of the Gulf of Tadjoura, in 1888 Governor Lagarde transferred the French colonial administration to what would become known as Djibouti City – an act which became official in 1892. In 1896, the new title of the French colony – the French Somali Coast – reflected the importance that France attached to its new relationship with the Issas at the expense of traditional French ties with the Afar peoples to the north.

Originally a barren area devoid of any permanent dwellers, Djibouti City grew by leaps and bounds as a result of the construction of the Djibouti–Addis Ababa railway and the subsequent expansion of the port. The concept of the railway reached fruition in 1894 when Emperor Menelik of Ethiopia authorized the establishment of the Imperial Company of Ethiopian Railroads. Two years later, the French government approved the building of a railway from Djibouti City that would cross the approximately 100 kilometres of French territory that lay within Issa-inhabited territory. Among the milestone dates in the project were the commencement of construction in 1897, achievement of the Djiboutian–Ethiopian frontier in 1900, and the completion and opening of the Djibouti City–Addis Ababa link in 1917. As the railway line continued to prosper, the traditional caravan trade routes declined, both Tadjoura and Zeila were replaced as important coastal trading centres, and Djibouti City became a magnet for individuals seeking their fortunes.

French administration of Djibouti underwent several consecutive changes in the aftermath of the Second World War that slowly, but surely, led to pressures for self-governance and, ultimately, independence in 1977. In 1946, a Representative Council was created that was partly elected and, for the first time, included personnel from the local, indigenous population. Among the various functions of the Council were voting on the territorial budget and passing legislation dealing with some local matters. In addition, elections were held for a deputy and a senator that were allowed to take part in the French parliament. In 1956, the French *loi-cadre* (enabling act) transformed the Representative Council into a Territorial Assembly and created a Government Council that included a president who served as governor, a vice-president from the local, indigenous population, and ministers.[7]

The first test of Djiboutian desires for independence came in 1958 when, along with French citizens and other overseas territories, Djibouti voted on the constitution of the Fifth Republic. In a referendum in which voters had the option of choosing independence or a new form of autonomy within a restructured French community, nearly seventy-six per cent of all votes cast (11,733 out of a total of 15,914 registered voters) favoured continued association with France. An important factor guiding the 'yes' vote was Afar fears that independence meant ultimate annexation and, therefore, domination by the soon-to-be independent Republic of Somalia. By 1958 it was already clear that the British and Italian Somaliland territories would achieve independence and unify as part of a 'Greater Somaliland' movement. Moreover, Somali politicians were pressing for the inclusion of the three other 'lost' portions of the Somali nation that had wrongly been divided by colonial conquest. Among these were the Northern Frontier District in British-controlled Kenya, Ethiopia's

Ogaden region and, most importantly, French-controlled Djibouti (or at least that southern portion inhabited by Somali Issas). As a result of this referendum and growing Somali pressures for French abandonment of Djibouti, France initiated a conscious policy that began to favour their traditional Afar allies politically at the expense of previously growing French–Issa ties.

Growing pressures for Djiboutian independence during the 1960s led to a second referendum in 1967 concerning Djibouti's status within the French community. The idea for a referendum emerged in 1966 when, during a visit to Djibouti by French President, Charles de Gaulle, independence demonstrations turned into riots that officially left four dead and seventy wounded. Similar to the 1957 referendum, nearly sixty-one per cent of the electorate (22,523 out of a total of 37,257 votes cast) voted 'yes' for continued association with France. Votes were cast largely along ethnic lines, with the vast majority of Afars voting 'yes' and the vast majority of Issas voting 'no'. Most importantly, however, France was accused by both Somalia and disgruntled Djiboutians of Somali heritage for manipulating ethnic cleavages – most notably by expelling thousands of Somalis prior to the referendum – to ensure continued Afar dominance of the Djiboutian political scene and, thus, continued association with France. Indeed, in a move that subtlely underscored the growing French tilt toward the Afars, the name of the territory was changed in 1967 from the French Somali Coast to the French Territory of the Afars and Issas. The significance of this carefully crafted French policy was emphasized when Ali Aref and his Afar-based Regroupement Démocratique Afar (RDR; Afar Democratic Reassembly) won twenty-six out of thirty-two seats in the 1968 elections for the Chamber of Deputies.

Events during the 1970s, however, forced France to reassess its tilt toward the Afars and, ultimately, cede independence to its last colony in Africa. First, the Organisation of African Unity (OAU) and other non-governmental bodies, such as the France-based Collective of Christians for Self-Determination of Overseas Departments–Overseas Territories (DOM-TOM), were pressing for independence. Second, the dramatic rise of Somali immigration, inclusive of those individuals who had earlier been expelled from the territory, was leading to greater Afar–Issa ethnic conflict. Third, the Afar-based government of Ali Aref was losing domestic support in favour of the Somali-dominated official opposition party, the Ligue Populaire Africaine pour l'Indépendance (LPAI; African Popular League for Independence). Fourth, the territory was increasingly being subjected to attacks by Somali government-supported guerrilla groups. Finally, the unfolding revolution in Ethiopia led by Mengistu Haile Mariam, a self-proclaimed African-Marxist, raised fears of Djibouti's absorption by the new leadership in Ethiopia.[8]

The net result of these combined pressures was a referendum held on 19 March 1977 in which the vast majority (94.5 per cent) of those who took part (79,789) overwhelmingly voted for independence. Three months later on 27 June 1977, the French Territory of the Afars and Issas achieved independence as the Republic of Djibouti. In a significant change in the pro-Afar policies that dominated French political thinking in the post-1958 period, the first independent government reflected an important shift in internal Djiboutian politics: Hassan Gouled Aptidon, an Issa Somali and leader of the LPAI, became the first president of the republic, and Ahmed Dini, an Afar and secretary-general of the LPAI, assumed the position of prime minister.

Political and administrative structures

Djibouti is a republic that, fourteen years after independence, still lacks a formal constitution. As a result, the office of the president – which is responsible for choosing the prime minister – enjoys wide powers. Yet, according to an electoral law passed by the National Assembly in February 1981, the president is elected by universal suffrage for a period of six years and may serve no more than two terms. Another electoral law passed in October 1984 specifies that, in the event that the office of the president falls vacant, the head of the Supreme Court shall assume the presidency for no less than twenty and no more than thirty-five days, during which period a new president is to be elected. Neither of these two laws as of 1991 have been put to the test.

The National Assembly is the legislative arm of the Djiboutian government and is comprised of sixty-five members who are presided over by a prime minister. They are elected for a period of five years by universal suffrage. According to the National Mobilization Law passed by the National Assembly in October 1981, Djibouti is a single-party political system in which the only legal party is the state-endorsed Rassemblement Populaire pour le Progrès (RPP; Popular Assembly for Progress). As such, only those members approved by the RPP are allowed to present themselves as part of a single-party slate during election periods.

The judicial arm of the Djiboutian government is divided into three separate court systems: customary courts, sharia courts and a judicial system patterned after that of France. The customary court system maintains a trial level in Djibouti City and the four major towns of Ali Sabieh, Dikhil, Tadjoura and Obock, as well as an appellate level in Djibouti City. These courts are responsible only for civil matters. The sharia court system deals with family matters that fall under the jurisdiction of the Islamic faith. Although presided over by a cadi, this system is similar to the customary court system in that it includes both trial and appellate levels.[9]

The third realm of legal activity in Djibouti is the heavily French-influenced judicial system. The Supreme Court, created in 1979 and composed of a five-judge panel, constitutes the top court of appeals for this system. Its jurisdiction includes appeals from both the customary and sharia court systems. Among the other courts in this system are: the Judiciary Court, composed of various tribunals, such as the Criminal Court and its responsibility for all violations of the penal code; the Council of Administrative Litigation, which deals with all law matters and litigation dealing with the Djiboutian government; the Safety Tribunal of the Republic, responsible for handling all crimes related to the security of the state, such as espionage and treason; and the Superior Court of Justice, which tries public employees for illegal acts committed while carrying out their official duties, such as corruption and embezzlement.[10]

Djibouti's army and security forces fall under the direct control of the president as commander-in-chief. The Djiboutian National Army numbers approximately 2,600 soldiers, including a 900-strong infantry commando regiment; a 200-strong armoured company; an 800-strong frontier commando unit; and a 300-strong gendarmerie force. In addition, security forces, which fall under the realm of the Minister of the Interior, number approximately 1,400, inclusive of 1,200 members of the National Security Force. These Djiboutian forces are buttressed by nearly 3,500 French soldiers stationed throughout the country who fall under the command of the Commanding Officer of French Forces in Djibouti. Although the majority (2,757) of these soldiers are associated with the French Army, including the 13th Demi-Brigade of the French Foreign Legion, the French Air Force (840 personnel) and Navy (134 personnel) also are represented. Djibouti constitutes one of the last, remaining French bases on African soil.[11]

Finally, the country is divided into five major administrative *cercles* (districts). In addition to the municipality of Djibouti City, the four major districts include Ali Sabieh, Dikhil, Tadjoura and Obock.

Domestic politics

The Djiboutian political scene has been dominated since independence by President Hassan Gouled Aptidon, a veteran Issa politician

(Mamassan clan) who is reported to be eighty years old. President Gouled led Djibouti to independence under the auspices of the Somali-dominated LPAI, the ethnic nature of which he attempted to overcome by the creation of a national party (the RPP) capable of attracting both Issas and Afars alike. Although receiving an overwhelming number of votes cast in presidential elections held in 1981 (84.66 per cent) and 1987 (87.42), in both contests he was the only choice offered to the electorate. As noted above, an electoral law passed in 1981 limiting presidents to two, six-year terms means that President Gouled is scheduled to give up the reins of power in 1993.

Similar to many African leaders, President Gouled has overseen the strengthening of a single-party system increasingly subject to his personal control and restrictive of popular debate. As a result, numerous opposition parties and political movements have been banned over the years. Among these are the Front de Libération de la Côte des Somalis (FLCS; Liberation Front of the Somali Coast), an Issa-supported movement created in 1963 and based in Mogadishu, Somalia; the Mouvement pour la Libération de Djibouti (MLD; Movement for the Liberation of Djibouti), an Afar-based movement established in 1964 and based in Dire Dawa, Ethiopia; the Parti Populaire Djiboutian (PPD; Djiboutian Popular Party), a predominantly Afar-based political movement created in 1981; the Mouvement Populaire de Libération (MPL; Popular Movement of Liberation), an Afar-supported movement based in Ethiopia that reportedly resumed activities in 1988; and the Front Démocratique pour la Libération de Djibouti (FDLD; Democratic Front for the Liberation of Djibouti), an Afar-supported movement created in 1979 through a merger of the MPL and the Union Nationale pour l'Indépendance (UNI; National Union for Independence).

The so-called 'winds of change' sweeping Eastern Europe and the Soviet Union during the late 1980s and the early 1990s have led to increased demands for multiparty politics throughout Africa, inclusive of Djibouti. For example, Mohamed Moussa Kahin, former director of planning and economic adviser to President Gouled, clandestinely formed the Mouvement pour l'Unité et la Démocratie (MUD; Movement for Unity and Democracy), an organization committed to the introduction of a multiparty system in Djibouti. Kahin's actions were especially significant as he represents the first member of President Gouled's clan to openly break with the government.[12] Similarly, Aden Robleh Awaleh, an Issa of the Yonis-Moussa clan, who fled Djibouti in order to avoid life imprisonment amidst charges of political destabilization, formed the Mouvement Nationale Djiboutien pour l'Instauration de la Démocratie (MNDID; Djiboutian

Introduction

National Movement for the Installation of Democracy). Most importantly, in a move designed to unify the opposition in its quest for a multiparty political system, both the MNDID and the FDLD formed a joint organization known as the Union des Mouvements Démocratiques (UMD; Union of Democratic Movements) in January 1990. The UMD claims that it is seeking to 'unite all ethnic groups and different political pursuasions within the country' so as 'to put an end to the chaotic situation which the people of Djibouti are in due to their tribal and obscurantist regime'.[13]

As demonstrated by the membership of the above-described political parties, ethnicity has played an important role in Djibouti's post-independence politics. In an unwritten power-sharing agreement worked out prior to independence and maintained ever since, the office of the president is occupied by an Issa and the office of prime minister is occupied by an Afar. Among the Afar politicians who have occupied the office of prime minister include Ahmed Dini (1977-78), Abdallah M. Kamil (1978), and Barkat Gourad Hamadou (1978-present). Indeed, despite the restriction on multiparty debate within Djibouti, President Gouled has carefully sought to maintain an ethnic balance within the country that caters for all major ethnic groups. For example, President Gouled's Cabinet has always included one representative each from the Isaak, Gadaboursi and Arab groupings within the country, as well as a mixture of the remaining positions that ensured one more Afar than Issa. Toward this end, the first independence cabinet included seven Afars and six Issas, whereas the 1982 cabinet included six Afars and five Issas. Care is also taken to ensure proportional representation of the various clans within each ethnic group, such as the equal sharing of positions between the Abgal and Dalol clan families of the Issa ethnic group.

Ethnic politics also play a role in elections governing membership in the National Assembly. Under a power-sharing agreement worked out prior to independence and maintained by President Gouled, the sixty-five-seat National Assembly is divided along ethnic lines. Whereas Issas and others of Somali origin (Gadaboursis and Isaaks) are guaranteed a plurality of thirty-three seats, the Afars are apportioned the slightly smaller number of thirty seats. Finally, the Arab portion of the population is guaranteed two seats. A major complaint of Afar opposition candidates concerning this arrangement is that the single slate of candidates presented to the public is chosen and approved by the Issa-dominated RPP and, therefore, ensures Afar candidates who potentially are more beholden to President Gouled than to their own people. In any case, the slate of candidates presented to the voting public in the 1982 and 1987 legislative elections was overwhelmingly approved by margins of ninety and eighty-seven per cent, respectively.

Despite the conscious efforts of President Gouled to maintain some degree of ethnic balance within the government, the Afars have increasingly felt slighted by the Issa-dominated régime. As noted earlier, the Afars largely dominated the pre-independence political scene in Djibouti, a fact that was changed by independence and the accession to power of President Gouled. Indeed, since 1977, real power has resided in the hands of the Issas who have increasingly dominated the civil service, the armed forces and the RPP. Issa domination is favoured by the simple facts that they constitute the largest ethnic group and that their power base, Djibouti City, is the political and economic centre of the country. As a result, many Afars feel that those among them, such as Prime Minister Hamadou, who have accepted positions with the Gouled government, are corrupt and inept officials who merely serve as 'window dressing' for an Issa-dominated government rather than serving the legitimate needs of their own people. One of the key Afar opponents of the current régime is Ali Aref, a member of the Hasabo clan from Tadjoura who was one of the French-favoured leaders of the territory prior to 1977.

An important aspect of Djibouti's delicately balanced political system is the often disruptive impact of external and, particularly, regional events on inter-ethnic relations. This problem obviously stems from the simple fact that, while many Djiboutian Afars feel a special affinity for their counterparts in Ethiopia, as well as often strong feelings for and against the central governments that have held power in Addis Ababa, many Djiboutian nationals with ethnic ties to Somalia have been captivated by the thought of Djibouti becoming part of a 'Greater Somalia' in which all Somalis in the Horn of Africa would become part of a Somali state. During the 1977-78 Ogaden War between Ethiopia and Somalia, for example, these affinities were manifested by Djiboutian nationals taking arms against each other through clandestine movements supported by both Ethiopia and Somalia. In the latest manifestation of this phenomenon, the ongoing Somali civil war between the government of Maxammad Siyaad Barre and a host of guerrilla movements committed to his overthrow spilled over during 1989 and 1990 into the Djiboutian capital. Specifically, violent ethnic fighting broke out in Balbala, a large shanty town on the outskirts of Djibouti City, between the Gadaboursi and Issa communities. This conflict arose because Gadaboursis living in Somalia, who tend to side with the Siyaad government and are found in the Somali military, had taken part in repression targetted against Issas in northern Somalia who, in turn, tend to support the Somali National Movement (SNM), a guerrilla movement seeking to overthrow the Somali government.[14] In all such

Introduction

cases, President Gouled has not hesitated to exert pressure on targetted ethnic groups considered to be a threat to the security of the state. Yet, such actions have not approached the severity of reprisals that have generally been the norm in either Somalia or Ethiopia.

Perhaps the most debated political topic, however, is the question of who will succeed President Gouled if he steps down as required in 1993 or, for some unforeseen reason, is incapacitated earlier and unable to carry out his regular duties. As of 1991, there is no clear successor and President Gouled himself has avoided grooming a replacement. In a best-case scenario marked by President Gouled's voluntary step-down from office upon completing his second term in 1993, the personal blessing of the president as head of the RPP and founding 'father' of the country would be crucial to the success of any potential successor. In a worst-case scenario marked by the death of President Gouled while still in office, the rise of violent inter-ethnic conflict, especially between the dominant Afar and Issa ethnic groups, as well as military intervention in the political process, would become distinct possibilities. If handled in a reasonably orderly process, however, it would appear that two overriding factors would set the parameters of choosing a political successor. First, any potential candidate would undoubtedly have to be an Issa, a reflection of the dominant and growing role of the Issa ethnic group within the post-independence political system. Second, the candidate would then have to be able to muster support among all the ethnic groups within the country. This qualification is due to the lack of any ethnic group having a clear majority within the Political Bureau of the RPP, or that body which would bear the responsibility for choosing a presidential successor (assuming, of course, that the single-party system remains in force at the time of presidential transition). In any case, President Gouled, who has obviously fared far better than either of his two immediate neighbours, will be a tough act to follow.

Foreign relations

President Gouled has carefully crafted Djibouti's foreign policy according to four major goals: (1) continued close relations with France and the West in general; (2) strengthening of the Arab link; (3) neutrality in the Ethiopian–Somali conflict; and (4) promotion of regional cooperation and development. It is precisely because of the success of these policies that Djibouti has been referred to as the 'eye of the cyclone', or a centre of calm in the troubled region of the Horn of Africa.

Despite President Gouled's desire to maintain cordial relations with the Soviet Union, the People's Republic of China (PRC) and the so-called 'radical' Arab states and organizations, such as Iraq, Libya and the Palestine Liberation Organisation (PLO), Djibouti's first and foremost foreign policy objective remains continued close relations with France and the West in general. For anyone who visits Djibouti, the continued influence and importance of the French link is unmistakable. In addition to over 3,500 French soldiers and associated family members whose incomes provide a large infusion of foreign currency into the local economy, over 400 French *'coopérants'* are active at nearly all levels of government administration and the educational system. Indeed, it has been estimated that the combination of direct and indirect French expenditure accounts for nearly fifty per cent of Djibouti's gross domestic product (GDP).[15]

The continued strength of Franco–Djiboutian ties does not mean, however, that this relationship has been without problems. Budgetary shortfalls and perceived fiscal mismanagement in Djibouti during the latter half of the 1980s have led to French demands for closer scrutiny and control of the national economy. Most importantly, as of 1989 France imposed a form of 'conditionality' in which continued aid was tied to budgetary reform in three major sectors of financial expenditure within the Djiboutian government: defence, the port and the presidency. Needless to say, such demands have led to local complaints – most notably among politicians opposed to President Gouled's perceived overly 'cosy' relationship with Paris – of French violation of Djiboutian sovereignty.[16] Nonetheless, in one apparent example of Djiboutian acceptance of French demands, the Djiboutian Council of Ministers passed a decree in July 1990 that altered the organization and financial management of the Djiboutian Armed Forces.[17]

A second, and related, goal of Djibouti's foreign policy has been the strengthening of traditional links with the moderate Arab world, most notably Saudi Arabia. This basic tenet of Djiboutian foreign policy derives from the historically important role of Islam in traditional Djiboutian society, the country's geographical location at the crossroads of the Middle East and Muslim north Africa and, perhaps most importantly, the role of the oil-rich Arab countries as significant sources of financial aid. During the 1970s and early 1980s especially, Arab aid was specifically focused on the exclusion of any further Soviet penetration of the region at least partially through the maintenance of a pro-West régime in Djibouti. In this regard, a subtle division of labour occurred in which French military forces were expected to provide the military 'muscle' should any disturbances arise, while financial resources would be provided by the oil-rich countries of the Middle East. Among the various actions taken by President Gouled in order to play the so-called 'Arab card' were the proclamation of Islam as the official religion of the state, joining the Arab League and largely adhering to its major proclamations since independence, and restricting previously closer ties with Israel, such as refusing to handle Israeli shipping at Djiboutian ports.[18]

The third major foreign policy goal of Djibouti has been to maintain strict neutrality in the Ethiopian–Somali conflict. As a mini-state which serves as one of Ethiopia's economic lifelines to the outside world and which has been the target of Somali campaigns for unification within a pan-Somali state, regional conflict between its larger neighbours is an ever present concern. During the 1977-78 Ogaden War, for example, actions taken by both Somali and Afar guerrilla groups disrupted the functioning of the Djibouti–Addis Ababa railway and plunged Djibouti into economic chaos. Although reopened in 1978, this action clearly demonstrated the negative impact that fighting among its larger neighbours could exert on the stability of the country. Indeed, several political analysts predicted just prior to 1977 that Djibouti would not last very long as an independent entity. Obviously proving these pundits wrong, President Gouled has carefully sought to maintain a balance between his two larger neighbours by aggressively asserting Djibouti's status as a sovereign state which favours neither Ethiopia nor Somalia. Toward this end, President Gouled has overseen the signing of peace and friendship treaties with both Ethiopia and Somalia, the initiation of border consultations on a semi-regular basis, and the pursuit of specialized economic accords, such as the creation of an independent railway company in 1985 to handle ongoing problems associated with the Djibouti–Addis Ababa railway.

The Ethiopian–Somali dispute, however, is but one of many regional conflicts that have taxed the foreign policy reserves and ingenuity of the Gouled régime. As discussed below, ongoing civil wars in both Ethiopia and Somalia, as well as migrations caused by cycles of drought and famine, have contributed to varying and, often large, numbers of Somali and Ethiopian refugees on Djiboutian soil. In the case of Somalia, the intensification of that country's civil war in 1989-90 has strained Djiboutian–Somali relations as members of the Somali Armed Forces sought and received political asylum in Djibouti over the strenuous objections of the Siyaad government.[19] Across the Red Sea, civil war during the first month of 1986 in South Yemen (which, as of 1990, has united with North Yemen) led to the evacuation of over 7,000 foreign residents from Aden to Djibouti

City. Even the crisis initiated by Iraq's illegal invasion and annexation of Kuwait in 1990 has reverberated in Djibouti. According to the Djiboutian weekly newspaper, *La Nation* (q.v.), the Gulf crisis has cost Djibouti nearly $US 218 million in such areas as decreased shipping revenues and higher prices for oil.

A final major foreign policy goal of the Gouled régime has been the promotion of regional cooperation and development. Fully aware that Djibouti's long-term economic fortunes are inevitably intertwined with the economic health of its much larger neighbours, President Gouled has been the fiercest proponent of IGADD, a regional organization with headquarters in Djibouti City whose membership includes Ethiopia, Somalia, Uganda, Kenya, Sudan and Djibouti. The purposes of IGADD are threefold: to provide member governments with a forum for exchanging information on plans for countering drought and desertification; to facilitate the formulation of joint development projects that will benefit the region; and to provide a mechanism for collectively presenting project requirements to the international donor community. Toward these ends, IGADD has coordinated numerous foreign missions to donor countries and international organizations, hosted a relatively successful donor's conference in 1987, and concluded three summits of heads-of-state, the most recent taking place in January 1990. Among the regional development projects undertaken under the auspices of IGADD and of direct benefit to Djibouti are the construction of a road linking Djibouti with Berbera, a northern port town of Somalia, and the rehabilitation of the Djibouti–Addis Ababa railway, most notably with funds provided by the European Economic Community (EEC). Both projects embody the IGADD ideal of regional cooperation by fostering greater regional trade.

Equally important to the ideal of regional economic cooperation, IGADD and President Gouled have played seemingly substantial roles in contributing to the brokering of regional peace initiatives, most notably between Ethiopia and Somalia. As Hubert Edongo, former high commissioner of the United Nations High Commission for Refugees (UNHCR) in Djibouti, once noted: 'When there is a conflict between nations, a neutral ground is very important, and a leader willing to pursue opportunities is especially important'.[20] Indeed, using the IGADD heads-of-state summits as a neutral meeting ground for Ethiopian President Mengistu and Somalia's President Siyaad, President Gouled was able to contribute to the brokering of the April 1988 Ethiopian–Somali peace accord which included an exchange of prisoners of war, a withdrawal of military forces away from their common border, and a resumption of diplomatic relations. This does not mean, however, that IGADD as a component of Djibouti's foreign policy is destined for greatness in the Horn of Africa. Rather, numerous obstacles, including continuing conflicts in the region, economic nationalism, opposing national ideologies, lukewarm financial support from international donor agencies, the inability of some member countries to pay their allotted budgetary commitments, and preferences for national, as opposed to regional, projects (to name just a few), ensures that genuine success and, thus, alleviation of regional development problems will be at best difficult and at worst impossible.

Economy

Almost completely lacking in natural resources and any meaningful agricultural or industrial capacity, Djibouti suffers from economic problems indicative of most African countries, including rising budget deficits, increasing foreign debt and high unemployment. Yet, Djibouti is unique among African countries in that the 'services' sector has constituted the mainstay of the economy since independence in 1977. Djibouti's leaders have sought to capitalize on the country's unique geographical location by strengthening and expanding its role as a financial, telecommunications and trade hub for the Horn of Africa. Indeed, the Gouled régime would like to maᴋe Djibouti the 'Switzerland' or 'Hong Kong' of Africa.

Due to Djibouti's harsh landscape and limited levels of arable land, the country produces less than five per cent of its food requirements. As a result, almost all agricultural products must be imported at great cost to the local economy. The government has attempted to overcome this external dependency by sponsoring experimental agricultural projects and the development of fisheries projects in conjunction with the International Fund for Agricultural Development (IFAD). In the case of agricultural development, advances in sedentary agriculture have led to a growth in the number of small-scale farms producing vegetables and fruit from 180 in 1980 to 930 in 1985. As far as the fishing industry is concerned, Djibouti's Livestock and Fisheries Service (SEP) and the Marine Fisheries Cooperative Association (ACPM) have succeeded in producing marketable yields exceeding 400 metric tons. However, the rejection of fish as food by the cushitic peoples of the Horn of Africa constitutes a major constraint on fisheries development. For example, the extent of disdain for fish among the Somali peoples of the region is noted by the following traditional Somali proverb: 'Speak not to me with that mouth that eats fish'.[21]

Djibouti is also heavily reliant on the import of consumer products due to the rather limited development of its manufacturing and industrial sectors. Despite liberal investment laws and Djibouti's status as an economic free zone, high labour and energy costs, a small domestic market and regional instability have hindered the attraction of foreign investors. The government has sought to overcome this handicap by sponsoring the creation of state-owned companies (parastatals) in specifically targeted industries. Among these are the construction of a mineral-water bottling plant at Tadjoura, a dairy plant outside Djibouti City and the exploitation of significant geothermal activity in the hopes of making the country energy self-sufficient. As in many African countries, however, the parastatal sector has been plagued by inefficiency and, thus, the need for significant budget subsidies. For example, political motivations have led to the doubling of the number of parastatal employees almost every three years since independence despite the lack of commensurate growth in revenues from these same companies.[22] As a result, the Djiboutian government since the mid-1980s has initiated a privatization campaign in order to make these companies more profitable and productive.

Problems in the agricultural and industrial sectors are compounded by high unemployment and recurring budget deficits. Estimates of Djibouti's unemployment rate range from forty to seventy per cent of the national work force, an alarming statistic that is compounded by thousands of illegal economic migrants willing to work for less than the minimum wage. As concerns the budget, recurring deficits have been recorded since 1982. These deficits have only been brought into balance by generous gifts from France and other international donors, as well as greater reliance on international loans. As a result, Djibouti's external debt nearly tripled from $US 106 million in 1982 to approximately $US 300 million in 1988, with debt service payments constituting nearly ten per cent of government revenues in 1987. Attempting to rein in the budget – one of the key demands of foreign and, particularly, French donors – is a very delicate issue. Public spending not only provides the government with political patronage to reward political supporters and reduce unemployment, it also constitutes one of the largest mainstays of the economy (roughly thirty-five per cent of GDP).

The services sector, which contributes to an estimated forty per cent of Djibouti's GDP, is the most crucial element of the economy and the basis of plans for future development. In the financial realm, Djibouti boasts a currency (the Djiboutian franc) that is pegged to the US dollar at a fixed parity and is freely convertible into any currency. Moreover, liberal investment and banking laws allow businesspersons free movement of capital. Subsequently, foreign and, particularly, Somali and Ethiopian businesspersons have utilized Djiboutian banks as financial havens for investment capital and as centres for generating import transactions in order to avoid the more regulated banking systems of their respective countries. The downside of Djibouti's liberal financial system, however, has been the depreciation of the Djiboutian franc during the 1980s in conjunction with the decline of the US dollar.

The second component of Djibouti's services sector is an increasingly sophisticated telecommunications system designed to facilitate the country's role as a financial and business hub. In addition to the 1985 upgrading of an international telephone exchange, a new 'earth station' was built in 1980 linking Djibouti to the Arab Satellite (Arabsat) Communication Organisation. Finally, the connection in 1986 of a new undersea cable with Saudi Arabia made Djibouti the African landlink of the Western Europe–Middle East–Southeast Asia telecommunications system.

The most vital aspect of Djibouti's service economy and the key to its continued economic prosperity is its role as a regional trading centre, built upon its modern international port and the Djibouti–Addis Ababa railway. Djibouti's international free port provides capabilities for bunkering, transit of goods to Ethiopia and Somalia and trans-shipment of goods to other countries in the region. Although proceeds from the port account for over fifty per cent of the government's service earnings, revenues dropped off in the early 1980s as the number of ships calling at Djibouti dropped from 1,474 in 1977 to 955 in 1986. According to Djibouti's Port Authority, this drop-off in revenue is due to the worldwide collapse of refuelling and oil traffic as ships have become bigger and more technologically advanced. Recent attempts at diversification, most noted by the construction of a new 'roll-on, roll-off' container terminal in 1985 and the refurbishment of two berths in 1988, have centred on capturing a larger share of the worldwide trans-shipment of goods along the Red Sea and Gulf of Aden. Although the port still operates well under its maximum capacity, attempts at diversification have borne fruit as the volume of container traffic increased to over 200 ships in 1986.

The 778 kilometre Djibouti–Addis Ababa railway constitutes another important source of financial revenue for the Djiboutian service economy. Upgraded with the financial support from the EEC, the railway transported over 199,000 tons of transit goods in 1986 to Ethiopia, the majority of which constituted the importation of food staples and agricultural products. Also important from a revenue standpoint are the nearly 1.13 million passengers transported yearly by the rail system. Sadly, although revenues from rail traffic gradually increased during the 1980s after closure of the line in 1977-78, the railway does its best business when famine conditions affect Ethiopia and Ethiopian ports (such as Assab) cannot handle the enormous traffic of food aid. Such was the case during the 1983-85 drought, which accounted for increased Djiboutian revenues during 1984 and 1985. A Djiboutian–Ethiopian trade agreement signed in 1985 was designed to stabilize trade between these two countries and reduce Djibouti's significant trade deficit with Ethiopia.

Since 1982, however, Djibouti has suffered from an overall trade deficit. The country imports almost all goods for final consumption and almost all goods listed as 'exports' are either re-exports for neighbouring countries or for the nearly 10,000 expatriate personnel living within the country. Due to its former colonial links with France, it is not surprising that roughly twenty-nine per cent of Djibouti's imports come from France, with nearly fifty per cent coming from the European Community in general. Similar to most other African countries, its regional trade is minimal, with its dominant regional trading partner being Ethiopia. Indeed, the darker side of Djibouti's trade habits concerns its daily importation from Ethiopia by air and, to a lesser degree, by rail of eight to ten tons of khat. This item of trade, which is managed by a government-sanctioned private syndicate, is said to constitute nearly one-quarter of Djibouti's total imports and represents a financial drain of roughly $US 20 million. The Djiboutian government continues to support the khat trade, however, because it employs nearly eight per cent of the working population and contributes to a windfall in government revenue through taxes.

Social conditions and welfare

Although Djiboutians are on average better off than the populations of their immediate neighbours, several facets of Djibouti's social fabric require the ongoing attention of the Gouled régime. First, the combination of Djibouti's high unemployment rate and the growing numbers of high school and college graduates unable to find jobs within the economy constitutes a structural problem that will be difficult to resolve. One small step in seeking a solution was the creation in 1987 of the Association Nationale pour le Développement Économique et Sociale (ANDES; National Association for Economic and Social Development), an organization specifically targetted towards Djibouti's unemployed youth and designed to support private sector initiatives, especially the creation of small and medium enterprises.

A second social problem concerns the issue of infant mortality. In

Introduction

one attempt to gather data such that the problem could be addressed properly, the Djiboutian Ministry of Health, in conjunction with the World Health Organisation (WHO) and the United Nations Children's Fund, interviewed a total of 5,526 households in Djibouti City from 27 April to 16 May 1985. The results of the survey are rather alarming: the mortality rate in 1984 was 200 per 1,000 births (twenty per cent) meaning that two out of every ten infants born did not survive past their first birthday. Of the twenty per cent that die in their first year, 4.6 per cent die within the first ten days, 1.7 per cent between eleven and twenty-eight days, 45.2 per cent between one and six months, and 48.5 per cent between seven and eleven months. The most frequent causes of death are diarrhoea (forty-nine per cent), respiratory illness (seventeen per cent) and measles (nine per cent). Not surprisingly, the higher the education level of the parents, the lower the rate of infant mortality.[23]

A third social problem centres on the widespread chewing of khat throughout Djiboutian society, the usage of which is at least partially the result of the high unemployment rate within the country. In an attempt to gather data on the problem prior to the convening of a conference in Djibouti from 17-20 December 1984, the Djiboutian Ministry of Health and WHO carried out a survey of 500 households in Djibouti City. Similar to the above-mentioned report on infant mortality, the results of this report were again rather alarming: seventy-five per cent of all households chew khat; 86.4 per cent of the chewers are men; seventy-two per cent chew daily (sixteen per cent two to three times weekly); seventy-five per cent chew at home; and the average time spent chewing is 5.5 hours daily.[24] In addition to the obvious negative physical side effects associated with prolonged use, an important economic dimension of this drug's widespread usage is its effect on that portion of the Djiboutian work force which is gainfully employed. Indeed, it is widely recognized that the drug has a severe impact on labour productivity.

The issues of 'legitimate' refugees (who face a well-grounded fear of political persecution should they return home) and 'illegitimate' economic migrants (who migrate simply to improve their economic condition) constitute the final social problems which, perhaps, have generated the largest amounts of international criticism of the Gouled régime. In addition to thousands (who some say number as high as 20,000 at any given time) of illegitimate economic migrants who, on an ongoing basis, clandestinely enter Djibouti and illegally assume a variety of jobs, usually in Djibouti City, the country has been periodically inundated with waves of legitimate refugees fleeing political persecution in neighbouring Ethiopia and Somalia. At the end of the 1970s, for example, Djibouti was host to over 40,000

Ethiopian refugees who had fled their country due to a combination of drought and famine and the political excesses of the Mengistu régime. At the end of the 1980s, the intensification of the Somali civil war led to the arrival of an estimated 30,000-40,000 Somali refugees. In both cases, the Gouled government's handling of the refugees caused international outcries. As concerned the Ethiopian refugees, a 'voluntary repatriation' programme overseen by the UNHCR (which eventually repatriated over 25,000 refugees) included several cases of mistreatment of refugees. Among these were an incident on 20 December 1986 in which five Ethiopians being returned by rail to the border suffocated to death in a closed box-car, as well as a hunger strike-turned-riot at a Dikhil-based refugee camp that led to the involuntary return to Ethiopia of three UN-recognized refugees. In the case of the Somali refugees, the Djiboutian government has refused to recognize their status as legitimate refugees and, therefore, their right to international protection. As a result, the UNHCR has been unable to provide either legal or practical assistance, except in a few cases. This most recent action has been resoundingly denounced by Africa Watch, a non-governmental organization that monitors human rights practices in Africa.[25]

Toward the future

Despite its artificial creation as a multi-ethnic country under the tutelage of French colonial rule, Djibouti has managed to steer clear of the domestic upheavals that continue to plague its immediate neighbours of Ethiopia and Somalia. Despite the existence of inter-ethnic conflict and a host of other problems, such as the social ills associated with the chewing of khat and the presence of large numbers of refugees on Djiboutian soil, Djiboutians for the most part correctly believe that they are better off than their compatriots in neighbouring countries. In this regard, President Gouled and his relatively even-handed domestic and international policies deserve a significant amount of credit. However, the keys to Djibouti's future stability and prosperity will ultimately rest on two major factors. First, a smooth presidential succession in 1993 that maintains an ethnic balance within the government and, perhaps, gives greater credence to Afar demands for increased political power and spoils, will ensure domestic tranquillity for many years to come. Second, Djibouti's future economic viability is inevitably tied to the economic situations of Ethiopia and Somalia. In this regard, Djibouti must continue to press for further regional co-operation and economic agreements designed especially to enhance regional trade. Unfor-

Introduction

tunately, the still unsettled political situations in both Ethiopia and Somalia make this objective much more difficult to achieve.

References

1 The majority of this section was derived from *Informations de Voyage sur Djibouti – Djibouti travel facts* (q.v.), pp. 6-9.
2 The lower figure is derived from *Djibouti: les institutions politiques et militaires* (q.v.), whereas the higher figure is derived from a Djiboutian government-sponsored travel brochure, *Republic of Djibouti* (no date). The population figures discussed in this section are derived from the first source.
3 See I. M. Lewis, 'Physical and social geography', in *Africa South of the Sahara* (q.v.), p. 430.
4 These examples are drawn from Philippe Oberlé and Pierre Hugo, *Histoire de Djibouti: des origines à la république* (q.v.), p. 23.
5 For an excellent brief discussion of this period from which much of this section is drawn, see Virginia Thompson and Richard Adloff, *Djibouti and the Horn of Africa* (q.v.), pp. 3-22.
6 See Richard Pankhurst, 'Fire-arms in Ethiopian history (1800-1935)' (q.v.).
7 See Robert Tholomier, *Djibouti: pawn of the Horn of Africa* (q.v.), p. viii.
8 See Margaret Dolley, 'Recent History', in *Africa South of the Sahara* (q.v.), p. 430.
9 David Stoelting, 'The legal system of Djibouti', unpublished manuscript, August 1988.
10 *Ibid.*
11 See *Military powers: the League of Arab States: Djibouti, Somalia, Sudan, Egypt and Ethiopia* (q.v.), p. 11, 14.
12 'Djibouti: call for a multi-party system', *The Indian Ocean Newsletter* (28 April 1990): 4.
13 'Djibouti: opposition unite', *The Indian Ocean Newsletter* (24 February 1990): 4.
14 See, for example, the following articles carried in *The Indian Ocean Newsletter*: 'Djibouti: Issa-Issaq deal' (3 February 1990): 1, 4; 'Djibouti-Somalia: tension mounts' (12 May 1990): 1–2; 'Djibouti: Gadabursis – a target' (13 October 1990): 1, 3.
15 This was a common figure accepted by analysts at the US Embassy in Djibouti City, Djibouti.
16 See, for example, two reports in *The Indian Ocean Newsletter*: 'Djibouti: conditional French aid not to everyone's taste' (21 July 1990): 6; and 'Djibouti: France takes stock' (9 December 1989): 4.
17 'In brief: Djibouti', *The Indian Ocean Newsletter* (28 July 1990): 8.
18 For a good overview, see John Creed and Kenneth Menkhaus, 'The rise of Saudi regional power and the foreign policies of northeast African states' (q.v.).
19 See, for example, two articles in *The Indian Ocean Newsletter*: 'Djibouti–Somalia: a thin line' (10 November 1990): 1; and 'Djibouti: polemic over relations with Somalia' (6 January 1990): 2.
20 Personal interview, Djibouti City, 1987.
21 Quoted in J. F. Simmons, 'Rejection of fish as human food in Africa: a problem in history and ecology' (q.v.).
22 Interview with a French '*coopérant*' in Djibouti City during 1987.
23 Statistics are drawn from Mohamed Mahdi et al., *Résultats de l'enquête sur la mortalité infantine dans la ville de Djibouti* (q.v.).
24 Statistics are drawn from République de Djibouti: Ministère de la Santé Publique, Direction de la Santé Publique, *Résultats de l'enquête sur la consommation du 'khat'*

dans la ville de Djibouti (q.v.).
25 See Africa Watch, *Djibouti, ill treatment of Somali refugees: denial of refuge; deportations and harsh conditions of detention* (q.v.).

The Country and Its People

1 **Africa south of the Sahara.**
London: Europa Publications, 1971- . annual.
This massive volume continues to be one of the best introductions for individuals seeking a brief overview of a particular sub-Saharan African country. Whereas the first two sections offer up-to-date general essays by respected Africanists on numerous issues pertaining to the African continent, the majority of the volume is geared toward extensive country surveys which document recent economic, social and political trends, including a good section on Djibouti. In the volume published in 1988, I. M. Lewis, noted scholar of Somali studies, discusses Djibouti's physical and social geography. Margaret Dolley summarizes the country's recent history and economic trends. Each country survey is followed by relevant statistical data (e.g. trade and transport) and a very useful directory listing, grouped under the following headings (when applicable): constitution; government; legislature; political organizations; diplomatic representation; judicial system; religion; press; publishers; radio and television; finance; trade and industry; transport; tourism; atomic energy; power; defence; and education.

2 **Djibouti: the only stable state in the Horn of Africa?**
Osman Sultan Ali. *Horn of Africa*, vol. 5, no. 2 (1982), p. 48-55.
The former editor of *Horn of Africa*, the author paints an extremely positive portrait of Djibouti's first five years of independence. Djibouti is shown to have achieved a level of political stability unparalleled by the unsettled domestic politics of its Somali and Ethiopian neighbours. The author argues that this success is largely due to President Hassan Gouled Aptidon's 'statesman-like approach' to Djibouti's domestic, regional and international politics. A general survey is made of Djibouti's domestic political relations between Afar and Issa ethnic groups, foreign relations with France, the Arab states, and Ethiopia and Somalia, and the evolution of the country's service economy. Of particular interest is a discussion of refugees in Djibouti (which differentiates between urban and rural refugees), as well as that government's repatriation policy. The author concludes that President Gouled's policies 'will no doubt serve the long-term political and economic development and survival of the Republic of Djibouti'.

1

The Country and Its People

3 **Djibouti mer Rouge.** (Red Sea Djibouti.)
Geo, no. 94 (1986), p. 95-144.

An excellent pictorial and written presentation of all there is to experience in Djibouti. Essays explore Djibouti's peoples, religions, customs, French presence, history, geology, landscape, economy, maritime opportunities, aquatic life and strategic location. Especially interesting are three essays at the end of the article which comprise a general tourist guide. Among the topics discussed are the major tourist sites to visit in Djibouti City, restaurants, points of interest in the countryside, as well as a brief presentation of French literary figures who had spent time in Djibouti, such as Arthur Rimbaud. Especially striking are over fifty colour photographs outlining all major aspects of Djiboutian life, such as aerial views of the capital, national costumes of the major ethnic groups, Lake Assal, the birth of the Ardoukoba volcano on 7 November 1978, and aquatic life along Djibouti's shores. A must for individuals planning on visiting or living in Djibouti.

4 **Djibouti: crossroads of the world. (Djibouti: terre de rencontres et d'échanges.)**
Graham Hancock, Stephen Lloyd.   Nairobi: H & L Associates, 1982.
79p. map.

Geared primarily toward potential investors and travellers, this general introduction to Djibouti was simultaneously published in English, French and Arabic. Over seventy black-and-white and colour photographs document all aspects of life within the country. Chapter 1 examines the political history of the country, noting the independence period, foreign policy, and social programs undertaken. It is emphasized that Djibouti is a 'haven of peace and a refuge in a region of great strategic importance where great power rivalries clash'. Chapter 2 summarizes the nature of Djibouti's economy, including rail, air, maritime and road transportation, telecommunications, banking and monetary system, tourism, agriculture and fishing, industry, energy and natural resources, foreign assistance and private investment. Chapter 3 is devoted to topics of specific interest to the businessperson, such as the nature of selling and negotiating, cost of living, leisure activities, visas and availability of medical care. Finally, chapter 4 centres on travel within the country, describing possible trips to Lakes Assal and Abbé, the Bankoualé Oasis, the Day Forest, and the towns of Tadjoura and Obock. Three brief indexes contain useful addresses and telephone numbers, statistical tables, and a copy of Djibouti's investment code.

5 **Djibouti, tiny new nation on Africa's Horn.**
Marion Kaplan. *National Geographic*, vol. 154, no. 4 (Oct. 1978), p. 56-71.

A very optimistic article heralding Djibouti's independence in 1977. The easy-to-read text, geared toward giving the uninformed reader a glimpse of various aspects of life in Djibouti, is complemented by seventeen colour photographs. Emphasis is placed on discussing Djibouti's role as the 'eye of the storm' amid the region's 'swirling political turbulence', as well as providing a general description of local peoples, landscape, climate, agriculture, politics and other topics of interest. Although recognizing the existence of certain problems, such as the chewing of khat and the difficulty of finding jobs, the article ends on this optimistic note (as stated by a Djiboutian): 'Think of our country as a baby born with a large head on a frail body . . . we must cure this, then the baby takes its first steps, sometimes grabbing a hand to hold. But that child will walk on its own one day'.

2

6 **Djibouti: nation-carrefour.** (Djibouti: crossroads-nation.)
Andre Laudouze, preface by Haroun Tazieff. Paris: Karthala, 1982.
231p. map. bibliog.
Written in a journalistic style by a noted French spectator of Djiboutian life and
politics, this book offers an easy-to-read, enjoyable introduction to Djibouti. The title
encompasses the author's dominant theme: Djibouti's unique location at the crossroads
of Africa, Asia and the Middle East, and the problems and prospects that such a
location engenders. Brief chapters examine topics which range from the historical
influences on Djibouti's development and the continuing effects of French colonial rule
to the nature of the republic's political system, and major tourist attractions. Especially
interesting are the author's descriptions of development efforts prior to 1982 (chapter
7), daily life and customs (chapter 8), and the promise and problems of Djibouti's
foreign relations (chapter 9), including the refugee question, foreign aid and the
country's path of non-alignment in regional disputes. The text is peppered with
numerous brief descriptions of topics of interest in boxes set apart from the main text.

7 **Djibouti: pawn of the Horn of Africa.**
Robert Tholomier, translated from the French and abridged by Virginia
Thompson, Richard Adloff. Metuchen, New Jersey; London: Scarecrow
Press, 1981. 163p. map. bibliog.
Tholomier was a French civil servant who spent over fifteen years with Djibouti's
Public Works Service, including eleven years associated with the Djibouti-Addis
Ababa railway. Writing under the pseudonym of Robert Saint Véran, the author
penned the French translation of Virginia Thompson and Richard Adloff's book
Djibouti and the Horn of Africa (q.v.), as well as a volume of his own (*À Djibouti avec
les Afars et les Issas*) that carried their work forward by examining the 1967-77 period
of Djibouti's history. Thompson and Adloff have now returned the favour by penning
an abridged English translation of Tholomier's book (which won the prestigious Prix
Maréchal Lyautey from the French Académie des Sciences d'Outre-Mer). The book,
although now dated, constitutes the standard English-language introduction to
Djibouti. Six straightforward chapters centre on various general topics for the 1967-77
period, including ethnic relations (chapter 1), the government apparatus (chapter 2),
the internal policies of the territory (chapter 3), opposing viewpoints concerning how
and whether Djibouti should seek independence (chapter 4), the country's strategic
location and relations with regional neighbours (chapter 5), and the nature of the
economy (chapter 6). A brief conclusion (chapter 7) is followed by a postscript dealing
with the 1977-80 period (which was written by Thompson and Adloff).

8 **Djibouti and the Horn of Africa.**
Virginia Thompson, Richard Adloff. Stanford, California: Stanford
University Press, 1968. 246p. map. bibliog.
Although now dated, the book provides one of the few full-length English-language
studies of Djibouti. Obviously written before independence in 1977, the book offers a
useful summary of the French colonial period, especially the referenda of 1958 and
1967. The first section of the book describes the people and politics of Djibouti,
including the historical background and evolution of colonial penetration, the nomadic
and sedentary peoples who inhabit the territory, and the nature of the government
structure and politics. Especially interesting is chapter 5, which deals with Djibouti's
external relations with regional countries such as Ethiopia, Somalia and Egypt. The
second half of the book centres on the social and economic aspects of Djibouti.

3

The Country and Its People

Chapter 6 deals with the subjects of religion, education, cultural activities, communications media, and health and social welfare. Chapter 7 describes the 'traditional' economy, including electrical power, industries, finances and planning, trade, transportation and labour.

9 **Corne de l'Afrique.** (Horn of Africa.)
    Edited by Olivier Weber.   Paris: Autrement Revue, 1987. 249p. 4 maps.
    (La Série Monde, no. 21).

The book comprises forty-four brief chapters on the history, culture, cities, and politics of Ethiopia, Somalia, Djibouti, and North and South Yemen. Chapters dealing with Djibouti include the following: Alain Borer's 'Supplément au voyage en Rimbaldie' (Supplement to a trip in Rimbaldy) (p. 20-34); Ali Moussa Iyé's 'Le Djibouto-Ethiopien ou l'épopée du Far-East' (The Djibouto-Ethiopian or epic of the Far-East) (p. 48-53); 'Sa majesté le khat' (Her majesty the khat) (p. 64-67); and 'Bouh: un nomade urbain' (Bouh: an urban nomad) (p. 197-98); Jean-Claude Pomonti's 'L'oeil du cyclone' (Eye of the cyclone) (p. 141-48); Patrick Erouart Said's 'Adieu aux nostalgies coloniales' (Goodbye to colonial nostalgia) (p. 189-95); Philippe Soupault's 'Sous-prefecture' (Sub-prefecture) (p. 196); and Albert Londres's 'Djibouti, quelle oasis!' (Djibouti, what an oasis!) (p. 199-201).

Africa contemporary record: annual survey and documents.
See item no. 307.

The Horn of Africa: Ethiopia, Sudan, Somalia & Djibouti.
See item no. 347.

Tourist Guides

10 **Djibouti et la côte française des Somalis.** (Djibouti and the French Somali
    Coast.)
    Jean-Paul Poinsot. Paris: Librairie Hachette, 1964. 127p. map.

An excellent pictorial and written documentation of the French colony of Djibouti as it
existed in 1964. Fifty-five black-and-white photographs portray living conditions in
Djibouti and its smaller towns, as well as points of tourist interest, with numerous
photographs capturing the rich diversity of ethnic life within the territory. Especially
interesting for purposes of comparison with similar works published more recently are
aerial views of Djibouti City and various smaller towns. Three well-written sections
describe the geography of the territory, the customs and history of its ethnic groups,
and a pro-French, colonial interpretation of the history of the territory's external
relations and internal politics (entitled 'An extraordinary moral conquest'). The book
is full of interesting quotations from a vast array of French nationals who have visited
and lived in the territory.

11 **Djibouti.**
    République de Djibouti. Direction de l'Information et l'Office de
    Développement du Tourisme de Djibouti. Boulogne, France: Éditions
    Delroisse, 1977. 128p. map.

Originally published in 1973, this nicely done souvenir volume was updated and
republished in 1977 to coincide with Djibouti's newly acquired independence. Ninety-
two colour photographs, often covering an entire page and accompanied by brief texts,
document all there is to experience in the country. Included are both land and aerial
shots. Initial photographs centre on principle architectural sites and the peoples of the
country. Subsequent photographs detail the principal structures and activities
surrounding the airport, railroad and seaport, as well as the major tourist attractions
to be found outside Djibouti City. Special attention is paid to the diverse marine life
found along Djibouti's shores. Three final sections offer several excellent photographs
of tourist sites in Djibouti's neigbours, including the two Yemens and Ethiopia (this
latter country merits only one photograph); an interesting omission is any section
devoted to Somalia.

5

Tourist Guides

12 **République de Djibouti. Guide pratique de la République de Djibouti.**
(Republic of Djibouti. Practical guide to the Republic of Djibouti.)
République de Djibouti: Office de Développement du Tourisme.
Djibouti: The Author, 1982. 111p.

The primary attraction of this slightly dated tourist guide is its collection of fifty-seven colour photographs depicting relevant sites to see in Djibouti. After a brief introduction by Aden Robleh Awaleh, Minister of Commerce, Transports and Tourism, the photographs and accompanying text are divided into three major sections. The first section is devoted to the history, economy and general characteristics of the country, including geography, geology, climate, vegetation and population. Section two focuses on Djibouti's principal tourist sites. Separate sections centre on Djibouti City and surrounding areas, the countryside and 'pleasures' of the sea, as well as the regions of Ali Sabieh, Dikhil (and Lake Abbé), Lake Assal, Tadjoura (and the Day Forest) and Obock. A final section offers a variety of practical information on hotels, medical services, nightlife, day excursions and the various forms of transport available.

13 **République de Djibouti – Republic of Djibouti.**
République de Djibouti: Office National du Tourisme et de l'Artisanat (ONTA).
Djibouti: The Author, [n.d.]. 46p.

This handy little booklet produced by the Djiboutian National Office of Tourism and Art (ONTA) is an excellent travel and information guide for all wishing to visit Djibouti. Fifty-two colour photographs are complemented by forty-six pages of up-to-date text written in both English and French. A basic description of the country's geography and history is followed by a listing of popular excursions into various regions of the countryside (such as Dikhil, Ali Sabieh and Tadjoura), aquatic sports (especially scuba-diving), and the various means of transport available to the traveller. The remainder of the booklet summarizes a host of important data for any potential visitor, including information on hotels, medical services, consulates, leisure and sports clubs, cinemas, restaurants, crafts and shopping.

14 **Informations de voyage sur Djibouti.** (Djibouti travel facts.)
Sheraton Hotel, Djibouti.   Djibouti: The Author, [n.d.]. 27p.

This handy travel booklet, available through the Sheraton Hotel chain, matches French- and English-language texts on opposite pages. The first section, 'Getting to know Djibouti', offers general information on the country's climate, culture and history. Section two, 'Places to see', describes various tourist points of interest throughout the country. The final section, 'Useful tips and guidelines', gives general information on transport, telecommunications, doctors, money and other issues of importance to the businessperson and general traveller.

15 **Djibouti: énigmes et lumières.** (Djibouti: riddles and lights.)
Alain-Marie Thomas.   Vendée, France: Harfang Publications, 1984.
103p.

This is the first of a series of volumes to be published by Harfang Publications on little-known and -travelled countries of the world. Eighty-five colour photographs detail Djibouti's landscape, animals, flora and people in great detail and are accompanied by brief explanatory texts. Rather than the standard tourist fare of most books of this type (e.g. pictures of towns, classic points of interest), this pictorial essay captures unique topics of interest with original photographs. Especially interesting are panoramic shots of Djibouti's countryside. Yet there is too little accompanying text to satisfy the general traveller, and the photographs remain untitled.

16 **Traveller's guide to East Africa and the Indian Ocean.**
New York, London: IC Magazines Ltd., 1983. 232p. map.
This handy little booklet is an excellent travel guide to East Africa and includes information on the Comoros Islands, Ethiopia, Kenya, Madagascar, Mauritius, Reunion, Seychelles, Somalia, Sudan, Tanzania, Uganda and, most important, Djibouti. The publisher notes that 'our books are aimed at a wide variety of travellers – holiday-makers, businessmen, students, researchers and the independent traveller in search of adventure'. Initial information on Djibouti's temperature and rainfall, currency, 'Dos and Don'ts', document and medical requirements, and checklist of suggested items to pack is followed by four general essays: Roger Murray's 'East African holiday'; Colin Willock's, 'Wildlife of East Africa'; Jocelyn Murray's, 'Peoples of East Africa'; and Christopher Sheppard's, 'From Cairo to the Cape'. The majority of the booklet, however, is comprised of individual sections on each of the earlier mentioned countries, offering brief descriptions of the history, economy and culture of the country in question, as well as a wealth of practical up-to-date travel information.

Djibouti mer Rouge. (Red Sea Djibouti.)
See item no. 3.

Somalia: in word and image.
See item no. 333.

Manuel de conversation somali-français: suivi d'un guide de Djibouti.
(Somali-French conversation manual: followed by a guide of Djibouti.)
See item no. 355.

English-Somali phrase book of common and medical terms (for travellers, health field workers, etc.).
See item no. 374.

Geography and Earth Sciences

17   **The Afar November 1978 volcanic crisis and its relevance to the
      mechanics of accreting plate boundaries.**
      Anis Abdallah, Vincent Courtillot, Michel Kasser, Anne-Yvonne le
      Dain, Jean-Claude Lépine, Bernard Robineau, Jean-Claude Ruegg,
      Paul Tapponnier, Albert Tarantola.   *Nature*, vol. 282, no. 5734 (1979),
      p. 17-23.

This brief article offers the results of a seismic and tectonic study of the rift system that
links Djibouti's Ghoubbet with Lake Assal. The study constitutes an attempt to relate
the events of the November 1978 eruption of Djibouti's Ardoukoba volcano with the
geodynamical models of the Red Sea-Gulf of Aden plate boundary. Making use of a
network of twenty-two geodetic stations emplaced in the region prior to the 1978
eruption, measurements taken following the event revealed that 'at least 1.6 meters of
extension occurred perpendicular to the rift axis between 1973 and 1978'. Additional
technical findings include the following: 'Relevelling done in the Ardoukoba rift,
originally measured in 1972, indicated that the central portion of the inner floor had
subsided more than 70 cm. The subsidence decreased towards Lake Assal and the
Ardoukoba volcano, also, at a decreasing rate, towards the Ghoubbet. Tectonic
observations, made via aerial photographs and by direct land reconnaissance, revealed
that the recent structures (normal faults of 100 m to several kilometres and fissures of
various types) were associated with/followed older structures, with a north-west-south-
east trend'.

18   **Recherches préhistoriques dans le territoire des Afars (République de
      Djibouti).** (Prehistoric research in the Afars territory (Republic of
      Djibouti).)
      L. Balout, C. Roubet.   *L'Anthropologie*, vol. 82, no. 4 (1978),
      p. 503-38.

The authors note that well into the 1970s, prehistoric research in Djibouti was based
on the initial field research carried out in the late 1920s and early 1930s by a trio of
French archaeologists: Father Teilhard de Chardin, Abbé H. Breuil and Paul Wernert.

Based on more recent fieldwork in Djibouti during the 1970s and a re-examination of the trio's lithic collections in the Musée de l'Homme and Institut de Paléontologie Humaine, the authors conclude that the previously accepted hypothesis of quaternary terraces weathering classification may no longer be valid. The authors note that, since 1960, 'field investigation has led us to discover numerous other sites [in Djibouti] connected with middle and ancient Quaternary, either marine or continental. Stratigraphic and chronological informations enforce typological data'. The first half of the article, which summarizes the works and conclusions of Teilhard de Chardin, Breuil and Wernert, was written by Balout, while the second half of the article, which focuses on the results of more recent archaeololgical field research, was written by Roubet.

19 **Geologic and geochronologic constraints on the evolution of the Red Sea-Gulf of Aden and Afar depression.**
Seife M. Berhe. *Journal of African Earth Sciences*, vol. 5, no. 2 (1986), p. 101-17.
The technical results of this study of the Red Sea-Gulf of Aden and Afar depression in northeast Africa are as follows: 'New K-Ar age determinations show that the development of [the] Southern Afar since 14 Ma ago involved five stages of tectonism and volcanism at 14-11, 11-10, 9-7, 5-4 and post 1.6 Ma ago; while the major phases of rifting for the Red Sea-Gulf of Aden have been shown by geological and geophysical data to be 25, 14, 10 and 4 Ma ago. It is suggested that since 14 Ma ago, identical periods of volcanism preceded by rifting have affected both areas. Continental break-up in the Red Sea region was initiated along large transcurrent faults followed by extension manifested by normal faulting, block tilting in the brittle crustal region and repeated dyke injection. Two large scale transcurrent faults were identified, the Marda (NW-SE) and the Ambo (ENE-WSW) which, it is suggested, controlled the trends of rifting in the Red Sea and Gulf of Aden respectively. Structural and geological evidence indicate that these faults have had a relatively long history, since they were active in pre-Jurassic times. Because at least the Ambo fault cuts across the N-S trends of the late Proterozoic basement, its orientation must be primarily related to the Phanerozoic rift tectonics'.

20 **A stratigraphic scale of the volcanic and sedimentary formations of the Republic of Djibouti.**
M. Boucarut, R. Chessex, M. Clin, R. Dars, F. Debon, M. Delaloye, J. C. Fontes, J. P. Hauquin, H. R. Langguth, C. Moussie, J. Muller, P. Pouchan, P. Roger, M. Seyler, C. Thibault. In: *Geodynamic evolution of Afro-Arabian rift system: international meeting organized by the Accademia Nazionale dei Lincei and the Consiglio Nazionale delle Richerche, under the auspices of the Ministero degli Esteri, the Ministero per i Beni Cultiviali e Ambientali, and the Ente Nazionale Inocarburi (Rome, 18th-20th April 1979).* Edited by Accademia Nazionale dei Lincei. Rome: The Editor, 1980. p. 515-26.
The authors provide detailed stratigraphic data on the volcanic and sedimentary formations discovered in Djibouti as the result of a 1/100.000 mapping project. The technical conclusions of the authors are as follows: 'The oldest rocks form the Jurassic and Cretaceous sediments of the northern part of the Aisha uplift. The upper-Oligocene–Miocene volcanic formations are first acidic series: Golwa-Chinile forma-

Geography and Earth Sciences

tion (hypersilicic and potassic), Damerkadda'-Alayli Dadda' formation, then intermediate series: Maryan'Ad-Harsa formation, at last, flood basalts: Damayyi-Galemi
formation. During the Pliocene and Lower Pleistocene times, thin layered transitional
basaltic flows, with a few acidics, have spread according to a well defined
paleogeography. Abundant sediments are interbedded. During the middle and upper
Pleistocene and the Holocene, the basaltic and hyaloclastic volcanic formations are
distributed according to an obvious EW fracture pattern. During Pleistocene and
Holocene times, various stratigraphical and chronological data on sediments supply
additional indications which allow paleogeographical and structural interpretations'.

21 **Structural history of the Republic of Djibouti. a summary.**
    M. Boucarut, M. Clin.   In: *Geodynamic evolution of Afro-Arabian rift
    system: international meeting organized by the Accademia Nazionale dei
    Lincei and the Consiglio Nazionale delle Richerche, under the auspices of
    the Ministero degli Esteri, the Ministero per i Beni Cultiviali e Ambientali
    and the Ente Nazionale Inocarburi (Rome, 18th-20th April 1979).*
    Edited by Accademia Nazionale dei Lincei. Rome: The Editor, 1980.
    p. 541-54.

The authors note that various cenozoic and quaternary structures can be found in the
volcanic and sedimentary formations in Djibouti. The technical conclusions of the
authors are as follows: 'Three main stages of deformation occur as follows: a) upper-
Oligocene-Lower Miocene fracturing and rifting (Tadjoura uplift, 'Ali Sabieh uplift);
b) Pliocene to lower-Pleistocene NW-SE fracturing, with tilting and block uplift; c)
middle Pleistocene to present E-W fracturing with scissor-like opening of the Gulf of
Tadjoura. Kinematic interpretations are suggested for the quaternary deformations, to
account for the structural data, namely with respect of the possible drift with a
respective rotational motion and differential speed, of the Somali plate in one hand,
and the Danakil plate in the other hand'.

22 **Volcanic formations of the Republic of Djibouti: geochemical and
    petrological data.**
    M. Boucarut, M. Seyler.   In: *Geodynamic evolution of Afro-Arabian
    rift system: international meeting organized by the Accademia Nazionale
    dei Lincei and the Consiglio Nazionale delle Richerche, under the
    auspices of the Ministero degli Esteri, the Ministero per i Beni Cultiviali e
    Ambientali and the Ente Nazionale Inocarburi (Rome, 18th-20th April
    1979).*   Edited by Accademia Nazionale dei Lincei. Rome: The Editor,
    1980, p. 527-40.

The authors provide a wealth of geochemical and petrological data on the nature of
volcanic formations in Djibouti. Their technical conclusions are as follows: 'A detailed
1/100.000 geological mapping, petrological and geochemical studies on major elements,
some geochronological data and detailed studies on the quaternary formations allow to
demonstrate the existence of four magmatic cycles, every one is separated from the
others by one of the main geodynamic events which occurred in the Republic of
Djibouti. Moreover the three last magmatic cycles show an increasing alkalinity when
going up in the geological time; these three magmatic cycles are ended by some
differentiated series with fractional crystallization and gravity differentiation, the SI of
these series in higher and higher when going up in the geological time and reaches
some values higher than 30 at the end of each of these cycles. Finally, there are some

peculiar rhyolitic rocks (R, R_0) of lower Miocene age, which result of a crustal melting: they show a volume more than one hundred times higher than that of the contemporaneous basaltic rocks. These peculiar rhyolitic rocks are hypersilicic, and hypoaluminous and sodic; they are spreading before and after a rifting and crustal thinning occurrence'.

23 **Microbiological study of a hypersaline lake in French Somaliland.**
   J. Brisou, D. Courtois, F. Denis. *Applied Microbiology*, vol. 27, no. 5 (1974), p. 819-22.

This brief article offers the results of a study carried out in 1969 and 1970 to determine the nature and extent of bacterial populations in Djibouti's Lake Assal. Lake Assal is fed by hot springs with salinity similar to that of sea water, containing about 400 grams of mineral salts per litre. The lake waters are described as 'syrupy' due to the high mineral salt concentrations, with no obvious signs of life. However, a broad population of common bacteria were found in the waters of the lake. Interestingly, the common species of enterobacteria, *pseudomonas aeruginasa* and *streptoccus faecalis*, were not found in the bacteria present in the waters. However, 164 aerobic and partially anaerobic bacteria strains were found, isolated from some sixty-one species. While most of the bacterial cultures were halotolerant, they could normally be expected to survive and even thrive in saline conditions to some degree. Two strictly freshwater strains were also found in the waters of the lake. Only ten percent of the total strains encountered were strictly halophilic.

24 **K-Ar datations on volcanic rocks of the Republic of Djibouti.**
   R. Chessex, M. Delaloye, D. Fontignie. In: *Geodynamic evolution of Afro-Arabian rift system: international meeting organized by the Accademia Nazionale dei Lincei and the Consiglio Nazionale delle Richerche, under the auspices of the Ministero degli Esteri, the Ministero per i Beni Cultiviali e Ambientali and the Ente Nazionale Inocarburi (Rome, 18th-20th April 1979).* Edited by Accademia Nazionale dei Lincei. Rome: The Editor, 1980, p. 505-14.

This paper resulted from a mapping project carried out by Djibouti's Institut Supérieur des Études et des Recherches Scientifiques et Techniques (ISERST) in that portion of the Afar depression located in Djibouti. The authors discovered sixteen new 'K-Ar ages obtained on both acid and basic volcanic rocks' collected primarily in northern Djibouti. The authors conclude that these K-Ar ages, together with structural, stratigraphical and petrological data, allow a reconstruction of the volcanic evolution of the Djiboutian portion of the Afar depression. More technical findings, explained in the text, include the following: 'The acid products of the Damerkadda-Alayli Dadda formation (15-13 m.y.) are overlain by basaltic flows interbedded with intermediate and acid rocks of the Maryan Ad-Harsa and Galemi-Damayyi formations of Upper Miocene to Pliocene age (13-5 m.y.). Above these units, the Afar stratoid series has been divided into general formations; the Balho-Gamarri formation (4.5-2.5 m.y.) and the Oummouna formation (2.5-0.8 m.y.) represent the lowest members of the series'.

Geography and Earth Sciences

25 Evolution of the volcanic region of Ali Sabih (T.F.A.I.) in the light of
K/Ar age determinations.
R. Chessex, M. Delaloye, J. Muller, M. Weidmann. In: *Afar
depression of Ethiopia: proceedings of an international symposium on the
Afar region and related rift problems held in Bad Bergzabern, F.R.
Germany.* Edited by A. Pilger, A. Rösler. Stuttgart, GFR: Inter-
Union Commission on Geodynamics, 1976. 216p. (Scientific Report,
no. 16).

The authors present findings on the southeastern portion of what is commonly referred
to as the Afar triangle, which includes part of Djibouti. The technical findings of the
study are as follows: 'The substratum of the dated volcanic rocks is composed of a
precambrian basement overlain discordantly by Jurassic and Cretaceous formations.
The initiation of the Afar rift in the early Miocene (25 m.y.) is confirmed by the ages
obtained on the volcanic products (mainly basalts and rhyolites) of the Galile
formation. A second period of intense volcanic activity (mainly alkali rhyolites of the
Damerkadda Formation) occured between 15 and 10 m.y. ago. About 8 m.y. ago, a
basaltic volcanic activity of fissural type (flood basalts of stratoid series) took over in
the entire southern part of Afar and occurred further north also. The higher part of the
basaltic pile (about 5 m.y.) is made up of flows which form a thin crust on the other
formations'.

26 Colloque rift d'Asal: réunion extraordinaire de la Société Géologique de
France, Djibouti, 23-29 février 1980. (Assal rift colloquim: extraordinary
meeting of the Geological Society of France, Djibouti, 23-29 February
1980.)
Bulletin de la Société Géologique de France, vol. 22, no. 6 (1980),
p. 797-1013.

In November 1978, Djibouti's Ardoukoba volcano erupted, making this country the
focal point of geological and geophysical interest throughout the world. This resulted
in the convening of an international meeting of the Société Géologique de France
(SGF) in Djibouti during February 1980, the summary of which is contained in this
collection of papers. The papers were published in co-operation with the Centre
National de la Recherche Scientifique (CNRS), the Institut National d'Astronomie et
de Géophysique (INAG), the Programme Interdisciplinaire de Recherche sur la
Prévision et la Surveillance des Eruptions Volcaniques (PIRPSEV) and the Institut
Supérieur d'Études et Recherches Scientifiques et Techniques (ISERST). A total of
fifty-seven scholars took part in the conference which comprised twenty-seven papers,
all of which are reproduced in this special issue devoted to Djibouti. Each article is
accompanied by an English-language abstract.

27 Propagation of an accreting plate boundary: a discussion of new
aeromagnetic data in the Gulf of Tadjurah and Southern Afar.
V. Courtillot, A. Galdeano, J. L. Le Movel. *Earth and Planetary
Science Letters,* vol. 47 (1980), p. 144-66.

A detailed aeromagnetic survey of Djibouti and immediate surroundings was
performed in 1977. This paper summarizes the reduction techniques which are used in
order to produce a magnetic anomaly map and discusses the accuracy of this map,
which is presented as an insert at a scale of 1/250,000. Two distinct magnetic styles are
recognized: linear anomalies with both large amplitude and short wavelength,

considered to be typical of oceanic lithosphere, as well as areas of lower-amplitude longer-wavelength anomalies, which are found mostly in the northern part of the survey. This quiet zone of subdued magnetic style is thought to have undergone major tectonic deformation during the last several million years. The general morphology of magnetic anomalies is interpreted in terms of what is known as a 'propagating crack model'. The crack propagates westwards at approximately three centimetres per year and the crack tip is thought to lie close to Lake Assal, both on the basis of the magnetic data and other geographical evidence. The land section of the survey is a central topic of this paper and is interpreted in terms of the crack propagation model in light of other available geological, geochemical and geophysical data.

28 **Geology and petrology of Manda-Inakir range and Moussa Alli volcano, central eastern Afar (Ethiopia and T.F.A.I.).**
M. de Fino, L. la Volpe, L. Lirer, J. Varet. *Revue de Géographie Physique et de Géologie Dynamique*, vol. 15, no. 4 (1973), p. 373-86.

A summary of the geology and petrology of an area that straddles the border between Ethiopia and Djibouti. The technical conclusions of the study are as follows: 'Three volcanic units related to different tectonic controls have been distinguished in central-eastern Afar. Parallel open fissuring gives rise to a stratoid series. A continuous intensive distensive tectonics (WNW or NW) gives rise to elongated bulge shaped structure at Inakir and Manda. Crossing of various tectonic directions produces a magma chamber and the central volcano Moussa Ali. The first products of Moussa Ali are alkali olivine basalts and hawaiites. These have been covered by a great volume of mugearites-trachytes and ryolites showing a slight peralkaline tendency. The final activity is represented by alkali basaltic flows. Manda-Inakir may be considered as a unique axial range of oceanic affinity related to the megastructure Gulf of Aden-Red Sea. This range is made by a complete series of lavas ranging from mildly alkaline basalts to mugearites. All the basalts found in these three units are of a mildly alkaline to alkaline nature. Probably this suggests a similar nature of the underlying crust. The differences in the nature of processes of differentiation can be attributed to the tectonic control'.

29 **Late quaternary lake-level and environments of the Northern Rift Valley and Afar region (Ethiopia and Djibouti).**
F. Gasse, A. Street. *Palaeogeography, Palaeoclimatology, Palaeocology*, vol. 24 (1978), p. 279-325.

The authors compare the 'late Quaternary limnology' of lakes within the Northern Rift Valley and Djibouti's (and Ethiopia's) Afar region according to 'their record of lake-level fluctuations', and the 'evolution of their sedimentary facies and biocoenoses'. The similarities and divergences of the various lakes are examined in light of the 'volcano-tectonic' and 'hydrological setting' of the lake basins. The technical results of the study are as follows: 'Clear parallels exist between the main stages in the evolution of all the lakes. At least two distinct lacustral phases during the late Pleistocene were followed by a very arid period during which the lakes contracted to their present extent or less. An important early to mid-Holocene period of high lake levels, beginning ca. 10,000 B.P. in both regions, was followed by a clearly defined regression between 6,000 and 4,000 B.P.'.

Geography and Earth Sciences

30 **Earthquake history of Ethiopia and the Horn of Africa.**
Pierre Gouin. Ottawa: International Development Research Center, 1979. 258p.

The first portion of the book, which constitutes a general geological survey of Ethiopia and the Horn of Africa, includes a geological history of the region dating back 570 million years. Particular emphasis is placed on the junction of the southern Red Sea and Gulf of Aden due to the intensity of seismic and volcanic activity found there. The chronology of the seismic and volcanic related occurrences are also explained in terms of how they are determined (i.e. sources of information and selection of data) and their relationship to 'Ethiopian Eras'. The majority of the text, however, examines the earthquake histories of five separate regions of the Horn of Africa: (1) Ethiopian Western Plateau; (2) Southeastern Plateau; (3) Ethiopian Main Rift, Afar and Southern Red Sea; (4) Aden Western Sector; and (5) Gemu-Gofa and Turkana Rifts. Earthquakes within each of the five regions are discussed in chronological order, accompanied by historical accounts, and comments for each year mentioned. Eyewitnesses or meteorological station reports constitute the primary sources of the study. Comments provide bibliographic data from a wide range of secondary sources, such as newspapers. Also included are several geological and physical maps for each region, as well as selected photographs of faults and earthquake damage.

31 **Carte géologique de la République de Djibouti à 1:100,000.** (Geological map of the Republic of Djibouti at 1:100,000).
Institut Français de Recherche Scientifique pour le Développement en Coopération. Paris: Editions de l'ORSTOM. 12 vols. map. bibliog.

This twelve-volume set, each of which comprises a booklet and coloured fold-out map (1:100,000) of the region in question, is the result of co-operation between Djibouti's Institut Supérieur d'Études et de Recherches Scientifiques et Techniques (ISERT), the Ministère Français des Relations Extérieures and the Institut Français de Recherche Scientifique pour le Développement en Coopération. Having divided Djibouti into twelve geographical sections, the set, once fully completed, will constitute a separate volume for each region. The volumes already published to date are Ali Sabieh (1986, 104p.), Tadjoura (1985, 131p.), and Djibouti (1983, 70p.). Each booklet introduces geology as it exists in Djibouti today, summarizes the major aspects of an enclosed map, and describes volcanic and sedimentary formations and geophysical givens of the area in question. Finally, each volume contains a useful bibliography of major works on geology of the region in question (and Djibouti in general).

32 **Seismic profiles in the Djibouti area.**
J. C. Lépine, J. C. Ruegg, L. Steinmetz. *Tectonophysics*, vol. 15, no. 1/2 (1972), p. 59-64.

The authors provide the preliminary results obtained from the first 'seismic refraction profiles' of Djibouti. The authors note that these profiles 'can be summarized by a mean seismic section of the region centered on the Gulf of Tadjoura'. It is also noted 'that the part of the Gulf of Aden characterized by an anomalously low mantle velocity, extends towards the west. The shallowing of the sea seems to be accompanied by the thickening of the crust'.

33 **Gravity study of the Djibouti area.**
J. Makris, J. Zimmermann, A. Balan, A. Lebras. *Tectonophysics*,
vol. 27 (1975), p. 177-85.

In March and April 1972, 380 gravity stations were established in Djibouti to carry out a comprehensive gravity study of the region. Qualitative and quantitative results summarized in the article are based on the resulting gravity map, seismic data, and the magnetics and physiography of the area. The authors note that the crust of the Gulf of Tadjoura and the central part of Djibouti is 'strongly oceanized and is the direct continuation of the Sheba Ridge'. Furthermore, this 'oceanization is concentrated only in the area of deep injections, marked by gravity maxima, whereas the rest of the area is to be described as sub-continental'. Finally, the 'uppermost mantle' is described as having 'low velocity and density values due to thermal processes in the expanding zone. The state of the upper-mantle material must be that of partial melting due to high temperatures of the order of 800° to 1,000° C at about 15 km depth'.

34 **Proceedings of an international symposium on the Afar region and related rift problems, held in Bad Bergzabern, F.R. Germany, April 1-6, 1974. Volume 1: Afar depression of Ethiopia (1974); Volume 2: Afar between continental and oceanic rifting (1976).**
Edited by A. Pilger, A. Rösler. Stuttgart, GFR: E. Schweizerbart'sche Verlagsbuchhandlung, 1974/76. 2 vols. bibliog.

To geological enthusiasts, the Afar region is that area of northeast Africa, inclusive of Djibouti, which forms a triple junction of the Red Sea, Gulf of Aden and East African rift systems. The net result of this junction is a geological treasure trove of shifting rifts and volcanic and geothermal activity. The Inter-Union Commission on Geodynamics and the National Committee for Geodynamics of the Federal Republic of Germany hosted a symposium on the Afar region which was attended by 180 participants and resulted in the publication of this two-volume work. Certain articles contained in the first volume are especially useful to those interested in the geology of Djibouti: J. C. Ruegg's 'Main results about the crustal and upper mantle structure of the Djibouti region (T.F.A.I.)', p. 120-34; R. Chessex, M. Delaloye and M. Weidmann's 'Evolution of the volcanic region of Ali Sabieh (T.F.A.I.) in the light of K-Ar age determinations', p. 221-27; J. Muller and M. Boucarut, 'Evolution structurale de la region d'Arta-Ali Sabieh (T.F.A.I.), Afrique Orientale' (Structural evolution of the Arta-Ali Sabieh region (T.F.A.I.), East Africa) p. 228-31; P. Roger, C. Thibault and M. Weidmann's 'Sur la stratigraphie du pléistocene dans le centre et le sud du T.F.A.I.' (On the stratigraphy of the Pleistocene in the centre and the south of the T.F.A.I.), p. 232-38; J. N. Valette's 'Geochemical study of lac Assal and Ghoubet el Kharab (T.F.A.I.)', p. 239-49; and H. R. Langguth and P. Puchan's, 'Caractères physiques et conditions de stabilité du lac Assal (T.F.A.I.)' (Physical characteristics and conditions of stability of Lake Assal), p. 250-58.

35 **Study of the transition from deep oceanic to emerged rift zone: Gulf of Tadjura (Republic of Djibuti).**
O. Richard, J. Varet. In: *Geodynamic evolution of Afro-Arabian rift system: international meeting organized by the Accademia Nazionale dei Lincei and the Consiglio Nazionale delle Richerche, under the auspices of the Ministero degli Esteri, the Ministero per i Beni Cultiviali e Ambientali, and the Ente Nazionale Inocarburi (Rome, 18th-20th April 1979).*
Edited by Accademia Nazionale dei Lincei. Rome: The Editor, 1980, p. 569-82.

The authors note that Djibouti's Gulf of Tadjoura 'is an exceptional zone of the world rift system where an oceanic rift becomes visible at the surface'. In order to gain a fuller understanding of this rift system, the authors undertook a detailed geological study of the Gulf of Tadjoura using bathymetry, as well as geological methods. Emphasis was placed on tectonic structure, as well as the age determinations and petrology of volcanic rocks. The technical conclusions of the study are as follows: 'The age of opening ranges from 3.5 to 1 m.y. and one [must] consider a west progression of the Gulf of Tadjoura ridge including complex ridge jumpings between Red Sea-Afar and Aden rifts. Petrology of the basalts emitted from [the] Gulf of Tadjoura rift varies both in time and space. Along the same transect, magma evolves from more fractionated and transitional on the margins to more undifferentiated and tholeitic in the axis. Similar variations occur along the Gulf of Tadjoura axis from low K tholeitic in the Gulf of Aden to transitional in Asla'.

36 **A bathymetric and magnetic survey of the Gulf of Tadjura, western Gulf of Aden.**
D. G. Roberts, R. B. Whitmarsh. *Earth and Planetary Science Letters*, vol. 5 (1969), p. 253-58.

This brief article summarizes the results of two bathymetric and magnetic surveys in Djibouti's Gulf of Tadjoura. The technical conclusions of the study are as follows: 'The westward continuation into the Gulf of the axial trough and linear magnetic anomalies of the Sheba Ridge (which represents the continuation of the Carlsberg Ridge into the Gulf of Aden) is demonstrated. The axial trough and magnetic anomalies are offset north of Djibouti by a fault. It seems most likely that west of the fault the axial zone continues westwards toward Lake Abbé and not northwest into eastern Afar'.

37 **Present limitations of accurate satellite Doppler positioning for tectonics – an example: Djibouti.**
Annie Sourian, Alfred Piuzzi, Micheline Etchegorry, Philippe Machetel. *Bulletin Géodésique* (Paris), vol. 58, no. 1 (1984), p. 53-72.

The conclusions of an experiment using the case study of Djibouti to underscore problems associated with utilizing the 'doppler shift' of a radio signal broadcast by a satellite for the study of tectonic movements caused by seismic activity. Currently, the doppler shift of a satellite's radio signal as received by a worldwide web of earth stations is used to determine the parameters of satellite orbits and the calculation of the Earth's position. Djibouti was chosen for the experiment because it is host to a doppler receiver in an area (Ghoubbet-Assal) which was also the site of considerable seismic-volcanic activity in November 1978 that resulted in tectonic movement. However, the authors demonstrate how the doppler data falsely portrayed a two metre shift in tectonics *prior to* the 1978 seismic activity, a shift discounted by field observations and data supplied by other doppler stations. Various explanations for the incorrect results of the doppler data are examined at length, with the authors concluding that 'wave propagation effects in the ionosphere' (i.e. rapid solar activity) are to blame.

38   The Afar triangle.

Haroun Tazieff.   In: *Continents adrift: readings from Scientific American*.   San Francisco: W. Freeman, 1970. p. 133-41.

Documents a 1967 expedition by international specialists in the Afar triangle located in the northeastern part of Ethiopia at the juncture of the Red Sea and Gulf of Aden. The region is particularly famous for its display of plate tectonic movement on land, a process which usually occurs in the depths of the ocean. The author briefly discusses this geological process, which produces continental separation, and the similarities of oceanic ridges to those found in the Afar triangle. Through examining these ridges, composed of hardened magma, the expedition concluded that, from the indications of the crust being repeatedly fissured along the axis of the ridges, the continental blocks were moving further and further apart. The overall conclusion is that the continents have been moving apart at an average rate of a few centimetres per year. The Gulf of Aden and Red Sea rifts, which meet in the Afar triangle, are believed not only to contribute to the widening of the Ethiopian rift but the triangle is also believed to be an extension of the Red Sea floor. This argument is based on numerous topographical surveys which yielded evidence such as volcano peaks eroded by waves. Also, many of the rock formations parallel those found on the ocean floors today. A conclusion offers a brief economic proposal concerning the Afar region. Specifically, the author focuses on the subterranean fields of superheated water and steam which, if tapped, could possibly yield millions of kilowatt-hours of cheap electricity per year to service large mineral industries, such as aluminium and other metallurgies, canneries, petro-chemistry and fertilizer production centres.

39   Dating of quaternary tectonic movements in the Republic of Djibouti.

C. Thibault.   In: *Geodynamic evolution of Afro-Arabian rift system: international meeting organized by the Accademia Nazionale dei Lincei and the Consiglio Nazionale delle Richerche, under the auspices of the Ministero degli Esteri, the Ministero per i Beni Cultiviali e Ambientali, and the Ente Nazionale Inocarburi (Rome, 18th-20th April 1979)*.   Edited by Accademia Nazionale dei Lincei. Rome: The Editor, 1980, p. 555-68.

The article extensively examines the dating of the tectonic and volcanic movements in Djibouti. The technical results of the study are as follows: 'The major tectonic accidents of the Lower Pleistocene are oriented N 120° E and N 130° E to N 150° E. Only slightly marked at the Lower Pleistocene, the E-W direction influences, at the beginning of the Middle Pleistocene, a morphogenetic evolution which will orient the valleys basaltic flows. At the Upper Pleistocene, the same E-W tectonic activity, in connection with the extension of the Aden Rift toward the W, becomes preponderant and makes the ancient faults work again, especially the N 135° E direction which favours the most recent volcanism. In the same way, as after-effects, the N 30° E and N 50° E directions of the Ethiopian Rift are active once again at the Upper Holocene'.

40   **Geology of central and southern Afar (Ethiopia and Djibouti Republic).**
      (Géologie de l'Afar central et méridional (Éthiopie et République de
      Djibouti)).
      J. Varet.   Paris: Centre National de la Recherche Scientifique (CNRS),
      1978. 124p. map. bibliog.
      Incorporating both English- and French-language texts, the book offers a large fold-out
      map and accompanying analysis of the geology of the southern and central portions of
      what is known as the 'Afar triangle', an area encompassing both Djibouti and
      Ethiopia. The study of this portion of the Afar triangle was undertaken by a field
      group of approximately ten scientists, with chapter 5 being written by F. Gasse. The
      author notes that the scientific study of the Afar triangle provides a 'unique chance to
      observe the geology, tectonics, volcanology and petrology of an accessible accreting
      plate margin of the Earth'. Other than a site in Iceland, all other such formations are
      found under the oceans of the Earth. The book, which contains a wealth of geological
      data, is divided into the following chapters: 'Introduction' (chapter 1); 'Physiography
      and general geological framework' (chapter 2); 'Crystalline rocks: stratigraphy'
      (chapter 3); 'Sedimentary formations in northern and southern Afar' (chapter 4);
      'Recent volcanic units' (chapter 5); 'Summary of central southern Afar volcanic
      features' (chapter 6); 'Tectonics' (chapter 7); 'Geophysics' (chapter 8); 'Confronting
      Afar geology and plate tectonics theory' (chapter 9); and 'Conclusions' (chapter 10).

L'odeur du soufre: expeditions en Afar. (The odour of sulphur: expeditions in
Afar territory.)
See item no. 61.

Géographie médicale. Djibouti. (Medical geography. Djibouti.)
See item no. 109.

Technical-economic studies of geothermal projects: the Djibouti case.
See item no. 271.

Djibouti water resources and soils analysis: final report.
See item no. 289.

The use of Somali in mathematics and sciences.
See item no. 348.

An annotated bibliography on the climate of French Somaliland.
See item no. 408.

Travellers' Accounts

41 **The Somali coasts: an account of the T. A. Glover Senegal-Somali expedition in the Somalilands and Eritrea.**
R. B. W. G. Andrew. *Geographical Journal*, vol. 83, no. 2 (Feb. 1934), p. 81-99.

The primary purpose of the nearly 15,000 mile Senegal-Somali expedition organized by T. A. Glover was 'the collection and photography of animals together with scenic and human records of interest'. 'Geographical and geological work was to be attempted where possible', adds the author, 'though such eminently desirable objects must be restricted necessarily by the limitations of time and the method of travel by motor lorries'. The subject of this paper is that portion of the trip which traversed the various Somaliland colonial territories including Djibouti. Interesting descriptions are offered of Djibouti's Gulf of Tadjoura and town of Obock.

42 **Djibouti l'ignoré: récits de voyages.** (Djibouti the unknown: travel stories.)
Marie-Christine Aubry. Paris: Éditions l'Harmattan, 1988. 248p. bibliog.

This volume constitutes one of the best summaries and analyses of the large body of French-language works written by French nationals who have either worked or travelled through Djibouti. Extremely well documented and relying upon numerous revealing extracts, the volume is divided into three major sections: 'Trips and travellers'; 'Things seen'; and 'Myth and reality'. In short, one is provided with impressions of the origins and development of Djibouti as seen through foreign eyes. For a strong critique of this work from a Djiboutian standpoint, see '"Djibouti l'ignoré" ou l'ignorance qui s'ignore' ('"Djibouti the unknown" or an unconscious ignorance') as published in *La Nation* (q.v.) (30 March 1989, p. 5), the weekly Djiboutian newspaper.

Travellers' Accounts

43 A journey through Abyssinia to the Nile.
Herbert Weld Blundell. *Geographical Journal*, no. 2 (1900), p. 97-121.
This article documents the author's journey in 1898 from Zeila to Addis Ababa via Harar one year after the establishment of a British mission. Included is a detailed account of a reception at the palace of King Menelik in honour of Blundell's travelling companion and envoy, Captain J. L. Harrington, and Sir Rennell Rodd, in charge of the British mission. Blundell details his personal travelling experiences, perceptions of people and places, and an interesting account of Ethiopian life, court and military ceremony. Of particular interest is the author's comparison of the port cities of Zeila and Djibouti City, including the elaborate French administration in the latter. The author also comments on the initial stages of construction of the Djibouti-Addis Ababa railway, including attacks by local peoples opposed to the line. The author also presciently warned that, although the railway had only reached its twentieth kilometre, if completed it would severely disrupt the trade of Zeila. Historical information is also offered on the Afar peoples inhabiting the northeastern plains of Ethiopia, particularly local military conflicts based on religion and ethnicity.

44 The Horn of Africa.
John Buchholzer, translated by Maurice Michael. London: Angus & Robertson, 1959. 199p.
As with many a traveller seeking to explore the Ethiopian hinterland and the Somali coast, this account begins in Djibouti City. Although Djibouti merits only a few pages of discussion, the overall description is generally negative. After noting Djibouti's high summer temperatures (the day prior to arriving the author notes that the temperature topped 120° F 'in the shade') he quotes his companion's warning against trusting the Somalis living within the territory: 'Amongst other things he warned me against the Somalis, saying that they were born thieves and robbers – especially in Djibouti, where one always ought to keep one's hands in one's pockets, if one wanted to prevent Somali hands getting there instead'. Brief mention is also made of the French military presence within the country. The remainder of the book charts the author's travels through the former British and Italian-ruled Somaliland territories just prior to independence.

45 First footsteps in East Africa.
Richard Burton, edited with an introduction and additional chapters by Gordon Waterfield. London: Routledge & Kegan Paul, 1966. 320p.
This book is a re-issue of the author's famous 1856 account (under the same title) of his travels through Somali territories whilst impersonating a Muslim. Burton, who trekked to Harar and successfully made the pilgrimage to Mecca, was nearly killed when his ruse was discovered by Somalis upon a subsequent visit to Berbera. As Gordon Waterfield notes in the introduction, this book is 'one of the most exciting and entertaining' of Burton's over forty books based upon his numerous travels. 'It contains vivid descriptions of the Somalis and their country, and it is also a story of adventure, humour, philosophic and religious speculations, acid and amusing comments, and pungent attacks on those in authority. Burton bubbles over with so much strange information that his books are sometimes confusing; in *First Footsteps*, he jumps from personal narrative to history and speculation and is sometimes prolix, but he is a natural wit and conveys his own zest and enjoyment in travel'.

46 **Le regard colonial ou 'il y a peu de coloniaux qui n'aient fait escale à Djibouti au moins une fois dans leur vie'.** (The colonial glance or 'there are few colonials who did not stop over at Djibouti at least once in their life'.)
Jean-Pierre Diehl.   Paris: Éditions Régine Deforges, 1986. 284p. bibliog.

The purpose of this volume is to bring to light the most important aspects of France's colonial relationship with Djibouti (from the founding of the Third French Republic to Djibouti's independence in 1977) as seen through a host of French nationals who spent some time in this colony. The author chose thirteen texts which he felt were most representative and reproduced them in part to bring particular themes to light. Each text is followed by a discussion of that theme through a mixture of Diehl's thoughts with excerpts from other significant French nationals. Diehl notes that he summoned the thoughts of forty-eight French writers and two British writers. The thirteen major authors chosen (and their listed profession) are as follows: Arthur Rimbaud (merchant, 1854-91); Pierre Loti (naval officer and voyager, 1850-1923); Paul Soleillet (voyager-economist, 1842-86); Henri de Monfreid (entrepreneur, writer, 1879-1974); Roland Dorgeles (writer, 1886-1973); Hugues le Roux (explorer, writer, 1860-1925); Edgar Aubert de la Rue (geographer, 1901-); Jean d'Esme (writer, 1893-1966); Michel Leiris (ethnographer, writer, 1901-); Joseph Kessel (journalist, writer, 1898-1979); Paul Nizan (philosopher, 1905-40); Albert Londres (journalist, 1884-1932); and Romain Gary (aviator, diplomat, writer, 1914-80).

47 **Lone dhow.**
Adrian Conan Doyle.   London: John Murray, 1963. 174p. map.

A shark hunter describes his various adventures in hunting these creatures in the waters off the coast of Djibouti and the Gulf of Aden. 'I had come to Somaliland for a specific purpose. The Natural History Museum of Geneva was anxious to obtain an adult tiger shark and, as my interest in shark fishing was known to the Museum Director, Monsieur Dottrens, he had asked me to undertake the quest'. Although some mention is made of Djiboutian lifestyles and culture, this book is clearly intended for those who share the author's enthusiasm for the trials and tribulations of the hunt for these fierce creatures. Avid description is made of pursuing and killing hammerhead sharks, sawfish, alligator sharks, tiger sharks and the Great White. However, the author's enthusiasm for the hunt is matched by a distaste for Djibouti City: 'My first and last impression of Djibouti remained unchanged for though, as a general rule, one learns to know a town, in Djibouti there is nothing to know. The sprawling wharves with their tank farms, a square, the Governor's palace, a tree-shaded European quarter and a native shanty town, all linked together by, surprisingly enough, excellent roads, the capital of French Somaliland has very much the same personality as a sun-dried jelly-fish. It exists, and there it is to prove it'.

48 **Au pays des Somalis et des Comoriens.** (In the countries of the Somalis and the Comorians.)
Lucien Heudebert.   Paris: Librairie Orientale et Américaine, 1901. 281p.

This account is the result of the author's travels at the end of the 19th century in the French colonies of Djibouti and the Comoros Islands. Sympathy for the colonial effort – pervasive throughout the text – is captured by the last line of the book: 'We hope

Travellers' Accounts

that these day-to-day notes taken far from the Mother Country contribute to the grand and fertile idea of French expansion among our compatriots'. Chapter 1 describes the author's trip to Djibouti via the Suez Canal, while chapter 2 provides a general overview of the country's politics, economics and foreign relations. Chapters 3 and 4 describe the interior and outlying areas of the colony, including the Gulf of Tadjoura, Lake Assal and the Ghoubbet. Chapter 5, the last to deal with Djibouti, focuses on Obock and the efforts of the first governor of the territory, Léonce Lagarde.

49   **Sport and travel: Abyssinia and East Africa.**
   C. Allsop Hindlip.   London: T. Fisher Unwin, 1906. 332p.
The author describes his hunting forays – complete with hunting dogs – in British East Africa and Ethiopia. He was, however, extremely unhappy with the game to be found in northeast Africa: 'When in 1901 I made up my mind to travel and shoot in Africa early in the following year as circumstances would permit, I had no intention of entering Abyssinia, and I will at once say that from a sporting point of view I am sorry that I wasted my time for Abyssinia proper is but a poor game country'. Of interest to scholars of Djibouti is the author's description of various aspects of that country en route to Ethiopia. Especially useful are the author's remarks concerning the Djibouti-Addis Ababa railway and its effect on the traditional Zeila trade route.

50   **A leaf in the wind: travels in Africa.**
   Peter Hudson.   New York: Walker & Company, 1988. 267p.
'I approached Djibouti with a certain amount of apprehension. It is the smallest country in Africa and very little known. Whenever you mention that you happen to be going there, you are warned not to'. So begins a chapter on Djibouti of a well-written and enjoyable traveller's account of the author's 1985 trek across Africa that included journeys throughout Mali, Zaire, Somalia and Djibouti. Among the vivid descriptions in the chapter on Djibouti are the author's trip into town on a mini-bus, the daily ritual of those who chew khat (*catha edulis*), the clash of French and local customs, and the prevalence of prostitution. Of particular interest is the author's reminiscence of being befriended by a Somali named Ali and a description of the daily living habits of the local populations.

51   **Travels in southern Abyssinia, through the country of Adal to the kingdom of Shoa.**
   Charles Johnston.   Freefort, New York: Books for Libraries Press, 1972. 2 vols.
The author, a British naval surgeon, resigned his medical appointment to explore northeastern Africa while en route to India in 1842. 'I had long entertained the idea of travelling in Africa, and determined to carry this into effect by resigning at the end of the voyage out, and returning to England by a road across that continent'. In very readable and colourful text, the author describes his travels beginning with an initial disembarking at Tadjoura and then among the Afar peoples which inhabit current-day Djibouti and Ethiopia. The author describes the economic and social conditions of Tadjoura (including customs of the townspeople, public buildings, religious ceremonies, and law and justice) as they existed in the 1840s, but offers the most detail concerning the life and customs of the Afar peoples inhabiting the region. Topics discussed include the mode of warfare and compensation for wounds and injured property, relations with the Somali Issas, religious beliefs and marriage customs. The book is a reprint of the original *Travels in southern Abyssinia through the country of Adal to the the kingdom of Shoa during the years 1842-43* (London: J. Madden, 1844).

52   **Adventures in Africa with a motor cycle and on foot.**
Antoine Konstant.   *Blackwood's Magazine*, vol. 235 (Jan. 1934),
p. 120-36.

This article details the author's 1934 journey to Africa, including time spent in the French colony of Djibouti. The first half of the article describes his southward journey from Algiers to the Saharan Oasis of Ghardaia. This section discusses the desert terrain, the author's numerous motorcycle accidents, as well as advice concerning food rationing, weather conditions and transport breakdown. Reaching Cairo and leaving Egypt from Alexandria, the author arrived in Djibouti with the intention of travelling to Ethiopia by way of British Somaliland. The author describes the Somali people of the region as 'moderately intelligent, slim, tall and does not disfigure himself as so many other black Africans do'. Particular attention is paid to describing the Issa Somalis (who inhabit Djibouti), particularly in terms of their spartan lifestyles. The author claims that the Issa are the most 'savage' of all the Somali peoples. Their 'favorite pastime', according to Konstant, being mutilation of strangers (particularly Ethiopian Afars). European troops are described as unable to prevent this feuding. The author also describes an interesting encounter with an Issa war party which almost killed him, had his companions not intervened with rifle fire. The author claims that, had it not been for one of his French companions shooting down an eagle over the Issas, who regarded it as an evil omen, the author's party would not have been able to continue on its journey.

53   **Across widest Africa: an account of the country and people of eastern, central and western Africa as seen during a twelve months' journey from Djibuti to Cape Verde.**
A. Henry Savage Landor.   New York: Charles Scribner's Sons, 1907.
2 vols.

An account of an Italian traveller's 8,500 mile and 364 day journey across Africa. The importance of the account for those interested in Djibouti is that the trip began in this country where the author disembarked on 5 January 1906. Interesting notations are made concerning the nature of French influence, the local population and the Djibouti-Addis Ababa railway. Djibouti, however, was the source of much displeasure for the author: 'Those who have visited Djibuti remember and speak of it as the most odious place they have ever been. For my part, I have seen places as odious as Djibuti, but never one more odious'. Special respect is paid to the Somali populations who, although considered to be 'cruel by nature . . . can endure hardships silently and stand impassive in case of danger'. The author concludes at the end of the first chapter that 'of the great number of men I employed during my journey across Africa, it was only a Somali – a French Somali – who remained faithful to the very end, notwithstanding the severe hardships and sufferings which he had to endure'. For a shorter account with pictures by the same author, see 'Across widest Africa', *National Geographic*, vol. 19 (Oct. 1908), p. 694-737.

54   **1,200 km à vélo, en plein été, à la découverte du T.F.A.I..** (1,200 km by bicycle, in full summer, in the discovery of the T.F.A.I.)
J. M. Lavanceau.   Djibouti: [no publisher], 1973. 163p. map.

A hard-to-find, yet fascinating account of the author's trip, comprising over 1,200 kilometres through the southern and western portions of Djibouti. What makes this traveller's account unique is that it took place on bicycle during the hottest months of the year. In essence what one reads is a collated collection of the author's daily diary from the day he left Djibouti City on 18 June 1973, returning on 17 September of that same year. Thirty-six black-and-white photographs accompany the text. The booklet, which was published in Djibouti, was made possible partially through the sale of private advertisements which one finds scattered throughout the text.

55 **Les voyageurs français et les relations entre la France et l'Abyssinie de 1835 à 1870.** (French travellers and the relations between France and Abyssinia from 1835 to 1870.)
Georges Malécot.   Paris: Société Française d'Histoire d'Outre-Mer, 1972. 134p. map. bibliog.

The author explores the evolution of Franco-Ethiopian relations through an examination of various French luminaries who visited Ethiopia from 1835 to 1870. The first French attempts at establishing closer links with Ethiopia – the subject of chapter 1 – are said to have been initiated by private French citizens, such as Maurice Tamisier and Edmond Combes, two Saint-Simonists who visited Ethiopia in 1835. Chapter 2 is devoted to describing official initiatives of the French government, including the establishment of a French consulate in Massawa in 1840. Whereas chapter 3 focuses on the exploits of Charles Rochet d'Héricourt, most notably his conclusion of economic and political treaties with the King of Shoa in 1844, chapter 4 is devoted to exploring largely unsuccessful French efforts at recruiting Ethiopian workers during the 1840s and 1850s. Finally, chapter 5 centres on the period ranging from the efforts of Guillaume Lejean, French Consul at Massawa, to establish a new commercial mission in 1862 (which ultimately failed) to the death of Emperor Theodoros in 1868. The author concludes that the most tangible results of French travellers to Ethiopia during the 1835-70 period were achieved in the scientific realm. It would not be until the founding of the French colony at Obock and the accession to the Ethiopian throne of Emperor Menelik, that French economic and political influence in Ethiopia would become stronger.

56 **Narrative of a journey from Zeila and Tadjourra on the coast of Abyssinia to Ferri, on the frontier of Efat; in April and May 1839.**
Transactions of the Bombay Geographical Society, vol. 12 (1839), p. 31-34.

Although very brief, the article provides a unique, early glimpse of the Afar territory of Djibouti as recounted by an unknown European traveller prior to the onset of French colonial rule. Among the topics discussed are local customs, Afar relations with neighbouring peoples and the salt trade. Control of the salt trade, according to the author, was the key to possible subjugation of the region: 'These salt grounds supply the country of the Danakil [Afar] and Efat with salt; therefore if any foreign power should ever be involved in a war with the Danakil, it would be an easy matter to take their country, by vessels proceeding up the Gulf of Tadjourra, and taking possession of the salt lands; which are situated close to it'.

57 **Dead men do tell tales.**
Byrun Khun de Prorok.   New York: Creative Age Press, 1942. 328p.

As the author poignantly notes at the end of the book, 'In archaeological research it is necessary to locate and excavate the burial sites and tombs, for "dead men do tell tales". Earthquakes, sandstorms, tidal waves, cloud bursts, and warfare destroy everything above ground. Only in the deeply buried tombs can one find the true historical details intact; and only the dead can tell you many truths'. In this book, the author describes his archaeological forays in northeast Africa, including Djibouti, just prior to the onset of the Second World War and the declaration of a state of emergency by the French colonial authorities. The purpose of his trip to Djibouti was to trace the ancient caravan trails, many of the oldest of which used to end in the port city of Tadjoura. The author notes that Tadjoura 'may even have been the port the Queen of Sheba used. I could hope to find traces of the far past there'. Of particular interest in this account, aside from the ruminations concerning the Afar and Somali peoples inhabiting the territory, is chapter 21 which is devoted to describing the author's attendance at an Afar wedding in Tadjoura. Also of interest are the author's accounts of the various colonial rivalries prior to the onset of the Second World War.

58   **La Somalie française.** (French Somaliland.)
Edgar Aubert de la Rue.   Paris: Librairie Gallimard, 1939. 162p. map.
bibliog.
An interesting account of the author's travels, accompanied by his wife, in Djibouti from November 1937 to May 1938. A total of twelve chapters describe various points of interest such as Tadjoura, Dikhil, Obock and Lake Assal. Although an interesting account of the territory from the vantage point of the late 1930s, of particular interest are sixty-one excellent black-and-white photographs that appear throughout the text and which were taken by the author himself. The pictures document all aspects of life within Djibouti.

59   **A voyage to Abyssinia and travels into the interior of that country,**
executed under the orders of the British government in the years 1809 and
1810.
Henry Salt.   London: Frank Cass & Co., 1967. 506p.
'On Friday the 20th of January 1809, having taken charge of some presents prepared for the occasion, and a letter from his Majesty the King of Great Britain addressed to the Emperor of Abyssinia, I embarked at Portsmouth on board the Marian, a merchant vessel commanded by Captain Thomas Weatherhead, and on the 23rd we set sail on our destination, in company with an East Indian fleet, under convoy of his Majesty's ship Clorinde'. Thus begins a classic account of British exploration and travel in Africa, most notably in the Horn of Africa, during the years 1809 and 1810. The author offers interesting accounts and recollections of the Horn and, particularly, the customs and lifestyles of the Afar peoples. The book is a reprint of an original issued under the same title and published by F. C. & J. Rivington (London, 1814).

60   **Abyssinia of to-day: an account of the first mission sent by the American**
government to the court of the king of kings (1903-1904).
Robert P. Skinner.   London: Edward Arnold; New York: Longmans,
Green & Co., 1906. 227p. map.
After reportedly seeking the approval of President Theodore Roosevelt, the author in 1903 led the first US diplomatic mission to Ethiopia to sign a commercial treaty with the government of Emperor Menelik. The book constitutes an account of that diplomatic mission. Of particular interest to scholars interested in Djibouti are the author's descriptions of the Djibouti-Addis Ababa railway and living conditions within the French-ruled territory. The account is clearly sympathetic to the colonial presence within the region: 'These colonies are all administered with reference to the needs and feelings of the original inhabitants, and although occasionally critical remarks may emanate from countries without Red Sea colonies, it is just as well to recall that prior to the present status of affairs the native tribes were constantly warring with each other,

and knew no higher law than that of force'. Explaining that Djibouti 'is a monument to French persistence and creative skill', the author is clearly favourably disposed toward French colonial rule.

61 **L'odeur du soufre: expeditions en Afar.** (The odour of sulphur: expeditions in Afar territory.)
Haroun Tazieff. Paris: Le Livre de Poche, 1976. 250p. map.

The author, a famous volcanologist, has written extensively about volcanic events in Djibouti and what is called the 'Afar triangle'. In this reprint of a 1975 edition published by Stock (Paris), the author weaves a tale of his scientific expeditions among the Afar people in both Djibouti and Ethiopia. As Jean-Claude Barreau notes in a brief preface to the book, 'Haroun Tazieff is not only a scientist, he's also a wonderful storyteller'. After briefly describing his original, and what turned out to be a lifelong, interest in all things having to do with volcanoes, the reader is offered a unique mixture of scientific explanation and interesting discussion of the trials and tribulations of travel among the Afar in northeast Africa.

62 **The Awash river and the Aussa sultanate.**
Wilfred Thesiger. *Geographical Journal*, vol. 85, no. 1 (Jan. 1935), p. 1-23.

The article presents the text of a paper read to the Royal British Geographical Society on 12 November 1934 depicting the author's six-month journey, beginning in August 1933, from the Awash station of the Djibouti-Addis Ababa railway to the port city of Tadjoura (the exact path followed by the expedition is charted in two maps). The expedition was led by the author (whose father was part of the British legation to Ethiopia) and accompanied by David Haig-Thomas who 'fell ill towards the end of a two months' preliminary trek'. The purpose of the quest – to find the end of the Aussa river – leads the author through Afar country and the Aussa sultanate, both of which are described in detail throughout the text. Especially interesting is the author's description of the various stone cairns in which the Afar entomb their dead, and the continuing salt trade centred around Lake Assal. The author seems especially intrigued by the rule established in the Aussa sultanate: 'The Sultan rules Aussa with an iron hand, and here, in consequence, alone in Danakil, are peace and security to be found. I was astonished by the orderly conditions which prevail throughout the greater part of his land'.

63 **Sailing forbidden coasts.**
Ida Treat. *National Geographic*, vol. 60, no. 3 (Sept. 1931), p. 357-86.

The author offers a fascinating account complemented by over thirty photographs of a sailing expedition along Djibouti's coastline during the late 1920s. Accompanied by a crew of one Frenchman, one Somali, one Sudanese and seven Afars, vivid observations are made of life in Djibouti, Obock and Tadjoura. Among the various stories recounted are getting stuck in the desert and rescue by thirty wood-gatherers, the painting of the author's toe and fingernails in traditional Afar fashion with henna-coloured dyes, fishing for porpoises and the threat of shark attack, a trip to Lake Assal, and the 'zar', a traditional annual ritual among married Afar women. Focusing primarily on the Afar portion of Djibouti's multi-ethnic population, the author compares this people to the 'noble redskins' of the United States as described by the noted novelist James Fenimore Cooper.

64   **Under the flag and Somali coast stories.**
Langton Prendergast Walsh.   London: Andrew Melrose, 1925. 384p.

The book is an autobiography of a British colonial officer's birth and development
'under the flag' in India, with the entire second half being devoted to his exploits in
northeast Africa along the Somali coasts. Walsh's accounts offer an interesting insight
into British colonial attitudes as to why securing the Somali coast was important, as
well as to the nature of great power rivalry in the Horn during the 19th century. Stories
of intrigue include the infamous and shortlived Russian landing at Sagallo, the drawing
up of protocols with the Egyptian Khedive as a tool for protecting British interests, and
the British occupation of the Somaliland coast. Especially interesting is Walsh's
description of British rivalry with the French and his personal feelings on the subject.
Such stories include: 'The French score the first trick' (p. 204-19); 'Shipping camels
under difficulties, and a trick against the French' (p. 297-305); 'Combatting French
influence at Zeila' (p. 324-28); and 'My unpopularity with the French and with the
slave-traders well-sinking near Zeila' (p. 338-44).

**The periplus of the Erythraean sea: travel and trade in the Indian Ocean by a
merchant of the first century.**
See item no. 107.

The Danakil: nomads of Ethiopia's wasteland.
See item no. 151.

**The modern history of Ethiopia and the Horn of Africa: a select and annotated
bibliography.**
See item no. 405.

Flora and Fauna

65   **Birds of Africa.**
London: Academic Press, 1982-88. 3 vols. maps. bibliog.

This three-volume set, which awaits the fourth and final volume, constitutes one of the most comprehensive indexes to birds in Africa, including Djibouti. Over 1,800 different species of birds will eventually be described once the set is complete. Each species, after establishing its scientific, English and French names (as well as original name and citation) is described within the following categories: range and status, description, field characters, voice, general habits, food, breeding habits, and references. Especially useful is a map included in each range and status section that is shaded according to where that bird can be found, thus facilitating the determination of whether that particular species can be found in Djibouti. Numerous maps are complemented by hundreds of painted colour plates of each described species. Extensive bibliographies are divided into three major sections: general and regional references; references for each family; and acoustic references. Handy indexes, divided by a bird's scientific French and English names, facilitate easy access to a bird or species of particular interest.

66   **La végétation du territoire français des Afars et des Issas.** (Vegetation of the French territory of the Afars and Issas.)
Edouard Chedeville.   *Webbia*, vol. 28, no. 2 (1972), p. 243-66.

This brief article offers a good description and listing of the various types of vegetation found in Djibouti. A useful introductory section on the climatology of the territory includes statistics on rainfall and seasonal changes. For purposes of description, the territory is divided into eastern (maritime) and western (continental) zones. The author notes that Djibouti's rocky, volcanic soil and harsh climate ensure that its vegetation is similar to other arid regions. Yet the varying relief of the territory (between 150 and 2,020 metres in altitude), as well as its maritime coastline, contributes to a limited diversity in plant life. Of particular interest is the description of the vegetation found in the Goda region, which ranges from 800 and 1,700 metres in altitude. An appendix lists the 205 types and page numbers of vegetation cited in the text.

67 **Tropical East Africa (Ethiopia, Somalia, Kenya and Tanganyika).**
R. E. G. Pichi-Sermolli. In: *Plant ecology: reviews of research*. Edited
by the United Nations Educational, Scientific and Cultural Organization
(UNESCO). Paris: UNESCO, 1955, p.302-60.

Indicative of English-language studies of the flora of northeast Africa, the authors have
neglected the French-speaking Republic of Djibouti. Nonetheless, the excellent review
of research (although now dated) is of use to the study of the flora of Djibouti as it
deals with the neighbouring countries of Ethiopia and Somalia (as well as Kenya and
Tanzania). A brief overview of the soils and climates of the region is followed by an
extensive analysis of existing vegetation patterns. Of particular usefulness to the
scholar is an extensive bibliography of over 200 references that details earlier, more
narrowly-defined publications. Further English-language works detailing the flora of
adjacent areas to Djibouti include: 'The plant formations of Western British
Somaliland and the Harar Province of Abyssinia', by J. B. Gillett, *Kew Bulletin*, no. 2
(1941), p. 37-75; 'The vegetation of Eastern British Somaliland', by H. B. Gilliland,
Journal of Ecology, vol. 40 (1952), p.91-124; and *A provisional check-list of British and
Italian Somaliland trees, shrubs and herbs, including the reserved areas adjacent to
Abyssinia*, by Philip E. Glover (London: Crown Agents for the Colonies on Behalf of
the Government of Somaliland, 1947).

68 **Les animaux du territoire français des Afars et des Issas.** (Animals of the
French territory of the Afars and Issas.)
Edmond-Louis Simoneau. Djibouti: The Author, c.1973. 153p.
bibliog.

This is the only book uniquely examining the animals of Djibouti. Four major chapters
provide information on 61 mammals, 100 birds, 13 reptiles and 21 butterflies found in
Djibouti. Each animal is described in relatively detailed summaries which include a
black-and-white drawing and reproduction of a Djiboutian stamp issued in its honour.
Three shorter sections describe the imprints of the various animals mentioned, advice
on taking pictures, and a list of the 116 pictures and photographs throughout the book.
The author cautions, however, that the present volume should not be perceived as a
full scientific grouping of all the animals to be found in Djibouti. Rather, it is indicative
of the 'principal' types living in the territory, or those which are the most
'characteristic'. Unfortunately, as the book was published by the author himself,
accessibility to the general enthusiast is limited.

69 **Birds seen on an expedition to Djibouti.**
Geoff R. Welch, Hilary J. Welch. *Sandgrouse*, vol. 6 (1984), p. 1-23.

The authors offer a precise summary of the results of their three-week bird-watching
expedition to Djibouti during March and April 1984. The primary purposes of the trip
were to conclude a preliminary survey of raptor and seabird migration across the
Straits of Bab-el-Mandeb and to document the status of the indigenous Djibouti
francolin (*francolinus ochropectus*). Among the sites visited were Arta, Ambouli,
Dorale, Djibouti City, Obock, Godoria & Ras Siyan, Tadjoura, the Straits of Bab-el-
Mandeb and the Day Forest. Altogether they claim to have sighted 160 species of
birds, 60 of which had previously never been documented. A short summary is made of
the date, number of sightings and brief description of each species recorded, including
a more extensive summary of the Djibouti francolin. The authors warn that although
the francolin is 'found to be present in good numbers', its habitat, the Day Forest, 'is
disappearing, so its future survival is far from assured'. Ten plates illustrate several of
the francolin's principal habitats.

70 **Djibouti expedition, March 1984: a preliminary survey of francolinus ochropectus and the birdlife of the country.**

Geoff R. Welch, Hilary J. Welch. Whittlesey, England: The Authors, 1984. 60p. bibliog.

The authors published this report themselves as the result of an expedition carried out in Djibouti in 1984 (for an account of a later expedition by the same authors, see *Djibouti: II, Autumn '85* (q.v.). The purposes of this trip were threefold: to determine if the Djibouti francolin (formerly called Tadjoura francolin) *francolinus ochropectus* still survived in Djibouti's Day Forest National Park and, if so, document its population and habitat; discover migration routes, especially of raptors and seabirds, through the Bab-el-Mandeb straits; and establish a link between the International Council for Bird Preservation (ICBP) and relevant Djiboutian authorities. Among several appendices are a list and description of 160 birds seen on the trip, daily log, mammal observations and sites visited.

71 **Djibouti II, Autumn '85.**

Geoff R. Welch, Hilary J. Welch. Whittlesey, England: The Authors, 1986. 197p. bibliog.

The authors published this report themselves as the result of an eight-week expedition carried out in 1986 to document various aspects of ornithological inquiry in Djibouti. (For an account of a preliminary investigation carried out by the same authors in 1984 see *Djibouti expedition March 1984: a preliminary survey of francolinus ochropectus and the birdlife of the cou..'ry* (q.v.).) The authors' intents were fivefold: (1) Search for raptor migration across the Bab-el-Mandeb straits; (2) survey the Mabla mountains for the presence of the endemic Djibouti francolin (*francolinus ochropectus*); (3) research the state of the near-endemic Bankoualé palm (*livistona carinensis*); (4) describe variations in ground cover from their 1984 expedition; and (5) carry out a survey of the endangered Arabian bustard (*ardeotis arabs*). Each phase of the expedition is preceded by a French-language summary and the work contains twenty photographs of Djibouti bird life.

72 **A field guide to the birds of East Africa.**

John G. Williams. London: Collins, 1981. 415p. map.

An expanded version of the author's *A field guide to the birds of East and Central Africa* (London: Collins, 1963), the newer version constitutes a handy field guide to the birds of East Africa, including Djibouti. An initial section on how to use the book is followed by succinct coverage of 665 species divided into 50 categories. A further 633 species are noted in accompanying sections entitled 'allied species'. Very brief descriptions of each bird are grouped under the following headings: identification, voice, distribution and habitat, and allied species. The text is complemented by 48 coloured plates of over 660 species of birds. An index facilitates quick reference to a particular bird or species.

73 **Birds of eastern and north eastern Africa.**

Cyril Winthrop, Mackworth-Praed, Claude Henry Baxter Grant. London; New York: Longman, 1980. 2 vols. 2 maps. (African Handbook of Birds, Series One).

A slightly revised version of the authors' original work first published in 1951, the volume remains of much use to ornithologists travelling to northeast Africa, including

Djibouti. As the authors explain, 'This book is not meant for the library shelf; it is emphatically intended for use and reference in the field'. The range of coverage is fifty-five groups of birds found in eastern and northeastern Africa, including Djibouti. A total of 646 birds are described in brief passages under the following subheadings: distinguishing characteristics, general distribution, range, habits, nest and eggs, recorded breeding, food and call. The text is complemented by the illustration of over 1,027 species by coloured plates. An index facilitates easy reference.

Microbiological study of a hypersaline lake in French Somaliland.
See item no. 23.

Lone dhow.
See item no. 47.

Sport and travel: Abyssinia and East Africa.
See item no. 49.

L'agriculture maraichère et fruitière traditionnelle en République de Djibouti.
(Traditional market and fruit agriculture in the Republic of Djibouti.)
See item no. 280.

Development of fishing and fisheries in Djibouti – phase I.
See item no. 287.

Development of fishing and fisheries in Djibouti.
See item no. 288.

A glossary of botanical terms: explanations in English and Somali.
See item no. 364.

History

74 **The mini-republic of Djibouti: problems and prospects.**
Said Yusuf Abdi. *Horn of Africa*, vol. 1, no. 2 (April/June 1978),
p. 35-40.
Published approximately one year after Djibouti's independence on 27 June 1977, this
article nicely summarizes concerns of the period over the enormous internal and
external problems that could potentially threaten Djibouti's viability as an independent
mini-state. The author discusses the economic and political realities of independence,
the ideological effect on internal politics and possible scenarios for Djibouti's political
evolution. The second half of the article is devoted to analysing the linkages of
Djibouti's internal problems to external factors, most notably the impact of Djibouti's
regional neighbours (Ethiopia and Somalia) and the superpowers. The author notes
that the wisest path that Djibouti could chart – and one that President Hassan Gouled
Aptidon, indeed, did follow – was to steer a domestic and international course both
independent and neutral as concerns Ethiopian and Somali dictates. See also the
author's 'Independence for the Afars and Issas: complex background; uncertain
future', *Africa Today* (Jan. 1977), p. 35-40.

75 **Historical dictionary of Somalia.**
Margaret Castagno. Metuchen, New Jersey: Scarecrow Press, 1975.
213p. map. bibliog. (African Historical Dictionaries, no. 6).
Djibouti's common cultural, ethnic, religious, political and language ties with Somalia
make this historical dictionary an obvious starting point for scholars interested in the
Horn of Africa and, particularly, Djibouti. A brief introduction to various aspects of
life in Somalia is followed by a chronology of major political events dating from the 1st
century AD to 1972. The bulk of the book is devoted to the definition of hundreds of
terms which denote places, individuals, and social, political and economic concepts of
past and present significance in Somalia. Also included is an extensive forty-nine page
bibliography. Unfortunately, unlike later volumes in the same series, no index was
compiled to facilitate greater access to the wealth of data contained inside. See also
volume 32 of the series, *Historical dictionary of Ethiopia*, by Chris Prouty and Eugene
Rosenfeld (q.v.).

76 **The Cambridge history of Africa.**
Edited by J. Desmond Clark et al.   London, New York: Cambridge
University Press, 1975-86. 8 vols.

This eight-volume set provides an excellent introduction and comprehensive overview
of African history. The titles and editors of the set are as follows: volume 1, *From the
earliest times to c.500 BC* (J. Desmond Clark); volume 2, *From c.500 BC to AD 1050*
(J. D. Fage); volume 3, *From c.1050 to c.1600* (Roland Oliver); volume 4, *From c.1600
to c.1790* (Richard Gray); volume 5, *From c.1790 to c.1870* (John Flint); volume 6,
From c.1870 to c.1905 (G. N. Sanderson); volume 7, *From c.1905 to 1940* (A. D.
Roberts); and volume 8, *From c.1940 to 1975* (Michael Crowder).

77 **Obock to Djibouti: French imperialism on the Horn of Africa, 1835-1899.**
Michael S. Clinansmith.   In: *Graduate student conference on the history
of the African continent.*   Syracuse, New York: Syracuse University,
Program of Eastern African Studies, 1970, p. 1-17.

Written while a graduate student at Michigan State University, the author argues that
an understanding of the events leading to the founding of the French colony of
Djibouti provide unique insights into French imperialist thought and its development
throughout the 19th century. The author concludes that the French mercantile and
banking schemes, as well as the military enlargement of the colony of Obock after
1862, are very similar to the British experience in Africa. The paper is divided into the
following brief and historically-based sections: 'The French explorers and Ethiopia,
1835-1855'; 'The British challenge: Aden to Perim Island, 1839-1857'; 'Fleuriot de
Langle and the Lambert inquest, 1859-1862'; 'The Obock cession, March 11, 1862';
'Obock: the useless colony, 1862-1880'; 'The government reacts, 1874-1881'; 'The first
concessions: Soleillet and Arnoux, 1881-1882'; 'Soleillet and Denis de Rivoyre, 1881-
1884'; 'British and Italian encroachments, 1884-1885'; 'Léonce Lagarde and the
consolidation and expansion, 1884-1888'; and 'The establishment of French Somaliland, 1888-1899'.

78 **Factors of intermediacy in nineteenth-century Africa: the case of the Issa
in the Horn.**
Peter D. Coats.   In: *Proceedings of the second international congress of
Somali studies, University of Hamburg, August 1-6, 1983: vol. 2,
archaeology and history.*   Edited by Thomas Labahn.   Hamburg,
GFR: Helmut Buske Verlag, 1984, p. 175-200.

The author argues that a major impact of western imperialism throughout Africa
during the 19th and early 20th centuries was the rise (and ultimate marginalization) of
intermediary groups within the world capitalist system. The Issa, for example, served
and prospered as intermediaries in a steadily expanding import-export trade between
the highlands of Harar (and Ethiopia and beyond) and the Somali coast at the port city
of Zeila. This article demonstrates how the French construction and operation of the
Djibouti-Addis Ababa railway approximately 100 kilometres northwest of Zeila
disrupted traditional trading patterns, transforming the intermediate role of the Issa
'toward more marginalized functions within the evolving rail-based export and import
economy of the Horn'. Especially interesting is the author's discussion of how elements
of Issa social life and structure varied as their intermediate role within regional trading
patterns was slowly transformed.

History

79 **Histoire sommaire de la corne orientale de l'Afrique.** (Summary history of the eastern Horn of Africa.)
Jean Doresse. Paris: Librairie Orientaliste Paul Geuthner, 1983. 389p. 9 maps. bibliog.

Although somewhat dated, this reprint of the 1971 first edition constitutes one of the classic French-language histories of the Horn of Africa. The majority of the volume is devoted to historical developments in the region prior to the beginning of the Second World War. Early chapters, for example, discuss the region's prehistory (chapter 1) and maritime relations with foreign powers (chapter 5). Subsequent chapters follow a chronological approach as they describe Ethiopia's impact on regional politics from the 7th to the 15th centuries (chapter 7), the arrival of Portuguese influence within the region during the 15th and 16th centuries (chapter 8), the commercial precursors of European colonialism from the 17th to the 19th centuries (chapter 10), and the colonial partition of the region during the 19th and 20th centuries (chapters 11-14).

80 **The problem of French Somaliland.**
John Drysdale. *Africa Report*, vol. 11, no. 8 (Nov. 1966), p. 10-17.

A former adviser to the Somali government during the early 1960s, the author describes the events and repercussions of French President Charles de Gaulle's visit to Djibouti during August 1966. French authorities were taken by surprise as popular dissatisfaction over French administration turned into violent pre-independence demonstrations at Djibouti's Lagarde Square. 'Four demonstrators were killed in clashes with the police and military, who restored order but could not guarantee De Gaulle's safety for a public speech in the square'. The article centres on French efforts to maintain stability and, after several days of rioting, the public announcement that France would accept Djibouti's independence if desired by the majority of Djiboutians. Several short sections note Anglo-Franco competition in the Horn, the growing network of Franco-Ethiopian interests, and local political attitudes as obstacles to a political consensus prior to the 1967 referendum. Especially interesting is a brief question-and-answer section in which Ethiopia's Emperor Haile Selassie and Somalia's Prime Minister Abdirazak Haji Hussein offer their views concerning various future scenarios for the French enclave, such as partition, association with either Ethiopia or Somalia, or continued association with France.

81 **La République de Djibouti: naissance d'un état, chronologie.** (The Republic of Djibouti: birth of a state, chronology.)
Gaouad Farah. Tunis: Imprimerie Officielle de la République Tunisienne, 1982. 203p. map.

A Djiboutian national, the author prepared the chronology while working for Djibouti's Ministry of Foreign Affairs at its embassy in Tunis, Tunisia. The chronology comprises the 'important events' in Djibouti's political, economic and social realms from independence on 27 June 1977 to the end of 1981. Three major sections describe Djibouti's national politics, regional relations and international relations, with each section being subdivided chronologically into five sections (1977, 1978, 1979, 1980 and 1981). Although valuable in providing the general contours of Djibouti's first five years of independence, the chronology is far from being exhaustive, especially avoiding topics of political sensitivity. For example, under the section entitled 'Regional relations for the years 1977-1978' little mention is made of the Somali-Ethiopian war over the Ogaden region. Similarly, in a section devoted to domestic politics, little mention is made of the convulsive nature of ethnic politics, especially in Djibouti's first two years of independence. A brief index aids the reader in finding specific topics of interest.

82 Bloodless victory in French Somaliland.
Charles Fenn. *Travel*, vol. 81, no. 5 (Sept. 1943), p. 16-19, 31.

The French colonial territory of Djibouti, similar to other French territories in Africa, maintained its allegiance to the German-dominated Vichy government of Maréchal Pétain. The article is a brief, journalistic account of the events of 25-28 December 1942 which resulted in a bloodless transfer of power from the pro-Vichy forces to the 'Free French' forces in Djibouti. The Allied command is described as having hesitated to force a showdown earlier because 'they feared a strongly pro-Axis group inside the port [of Djibouti] would blow the docks sky-high rather than let them fall into the hands of the Free French'. Especially interesting is the author's description of the leader of the pro-Vichy forces in Djibouti, Major Antoine, and the policies he pursued vis-à-vis Germany, Britain, Italy and Vichy France during 1940-42. For example, the author attributes the following quote concerning Britain's blockade of Djibouti to Antoine: 'The British are starving you; let's seek our friends in the other camp'.

83 The East African coast: select documents from the first to the earlier nineteenth century.
G. S. P. Freeman-Grenville. London: Rex Collings, 1975. 314p.

The author has assembled forty-eight principal writings which offer important insights into East African history spanning the 1st to early 19th centuries. English translations are offered for Greek, Latin, Arabic, Portuguese, French, Italian and Swahili writings. 'The earliest, the Greek and Arab writers, illustrate the ignorance of the ancients and of the Middle Ages . . . If at first sight there may seem a concentration of sixteenth century documents, it is because many of these illuminate the centuries which preceded. We know little at present of the seventeenth and eighteenth centuries, and thus I have included some of the earlier European visitors and also translations of Swahili traditional histories. Some of these continue up to the time of the coming of the European powers at the end of the nineteenth century . . . While some of what these histories say is myth and some tedious genealogy, they include invaluable information on the life of the coast and its commerce'.

84 French Somaliland attains independence as Republic of Djibouti: report of the United Nations mission to observe the referendum and election in French Somaliland (Djibouti).
Objective: Justice, vol. 9, no. 2 (1977), p. 38-48.

This article contains an excerpted version of a United Nations (UN) Mission's report concerning a referendum on the question of independence for French-ruled Djibouti and elections for a Djiboutian Chamber of Deputies. The mission was in Djibouti 5-10 May 1977, and consisted of individuals from the UN member states of Norway, Sri Lanka and Venezuela. After briefly summarizing the history of Franco-Djiboutian relations, subsequent sections of the report deal with: constitutional development in the territory from 1945 to 1977 (including the nature of political parties and liberation movements); Djiboutian demands for independence and significant political developments in 1976 and 1977; international concern for the future of the territory (including the positions of the UN, Ethiopia, Somalia and the Organisation of African Unity); and the organisation of the referendum and elections. Especially interesting is a section

History

entitled 'Observation of the referendum and elections', in which the UN observer team notes the actual mechanics of and problems associated with the voting process. The UN Mission concluded that 'the referendum and elections were carried out without intervention by the French authorities, the local government or the political parties'. The official result of the referendum showed that 98.7 percent of the people who voted were in favour of independence and 92.4 percent were in favour of the list of candidates to the new Chamber of Deputies.

85 **The war dead of the commonwealth: the register of the names of those who fell in the 1935-1945 war and are buried in cemeteries in Ethiopia, the French Territory of the Afars and the Issas, the Somali Republic and Sudan.**
Great Britain: Commonwealth War Graves Commission.
London: Commonwealth War Graves Commission, 1974. 61p. map.

Lists those British servicemen who were killed and subsequently buried in Ethiopia, Sudan, Somalia and Djibouti during the Second World War. The first section offers an account of the various military campaigns that took place in the Horn of Africa, centring specifically on the role played by British forces. The majority of the book, however, offers a description of the cemeteries in which Commonwealth soldiers were interred, including a brief section on Djibouti's 'New European Cemetery'. The cemetery, located three miles (5 km) south of Djibouti City on the road leading to the airport contains the remains of thirteen Commonwealth servicemen. 'They comprise one sailor of the Royal Navy, four soldiers from the United Kingdom, six airmen of the Royal Air Force, one airman of the Royal Canadian Air Force, and one airman of the Royal Australian Air Force'. Five of the airmen were killed when their aircraft crashed on 15 July 1942.

86 **French Somaliland.**
Great Britain: Historical Section of the Foreign Office. In: *French African Possessions.* London: HMSO, 1920. 28p. (Peace Handbooks, vol. 17).

In preparation for the 1917 Paris Peace Conference, Great Britain's Foreign Office 'established a special section whose duty it should be to provide the British Delegates to the Peace Conference with information in the most convenient forms . . . respecting the different countries, districts, islands . . . with which they might have to deal'. These volumes, the seventeenth of which centred on French West Africa (inclusive of a section on the French colony of Djibouti), were subsequently made available to the public in published form in 1920. The section on Djibouti offers a unique insight as to British perceptions (and misperceptions) of the colony's worth in strategic, political and economic terms between the First and Second World Wars. Four major sections discuss the territory's physical and political geography, political history, social and political conditions, and economic conditions. It is Djibouti's economic role, most notably its rail link with Ethiopia, that is seen as the territory's greatest asset. An appendix reproduces the following three agreements: 'Agreement between the British and French governments with regard to the Gulf of Tajura and the Somali coast, February 2-9, 1888'; 'Convention between France and Abyssinia relative to the frontier of the French coastal zone, March 29, 1897'; and 'Protocol for the delimitation of the French and Italian possessions in the coastal region of the Red Sea and the Gulf of Aden, July 10, 1901'.

36

87 **The Arab factor in Somali history: the origins and the development of Arab enterprise and cultural influences in the Somali peninsula.**
Ali Abdirahman Hersi. PhD dissertation, University of California, Los Angeles, 1977. 310p. 3 maps. bibliog.

A welcome addition to the historiography of the Horn of Africa, the primary purpose of this PhD dissertation is to examine the historical impact of Arab culture and economics upon the Somali peoples inhabiting the Horn of Africa, including those found in present-day Djibouti. Based primarily upon the writings of medieval Arab geographers and historians as collected through extensive field research in Yemen, Oman, Egypt, Iran and Somalia, this work nicely complements the work of Kassim Shehim, *The influence of Islam on the Afar* (q.v.), which specifically focuses on Djibouti. The work is divided into the following, self-explanatory chapters: 'The land, the people, and their culture' (chapter 1); 'The Horn of Africa in ancient and classical times' (chapter 2); 'Arab and other west Asian settlements on the Somali coast, 7th-15th centuries' (chapter 3); 'Islamization of the Somalis' (chapter 4); 'The Horn of Africa in the commerce of the Indian Ocean, 900-1500 AD' (chapter 5); 'Southwest Asians and state formation on the Horn of Africa, 900-1560s AD' (chapter 6); 'The Arabs and Somaliland: from c. 1500 to c. 1800' (chapter 7); and 'Religious revivalism, imperialism, and the deepening of Arab-Somali connections during the 19th and 20th centuries' (chapter 8). A final chapter summarizes several of the central arguments made throughout the work.

88 **Italian colonialism in Somalia.**
Robert L. Hess. Chicago: University of Chicago Press, 1966. 234p. 3 maps. bibliog.

Although including only a few references to the French colony of Djibouti, the study is an important contribution to the study of the competition of the colonial countries for power and influence in the Horn of Africa. In this historical sketch, the author argues that, although in many respects Italian colonialism paralleled that of other countries, 'the Italian case also reveals a curious ambivalence toward colonialism and a counter tendency of minimalism that thwarted the expansionists'. The documentation rests heavily upon the Rome archives of the Comitato per la Documentazione dell'Opera dell'Italia in Africa, or the successor to Italy's Colonial Office of the Ministry of Foreign Affairs (1882-1912), the Ministry of Colonies (1912-37) and the Ministry of Italian Africa (1937-43). After a brief introduction and the description of early Italian efforts in East Africa (1885-93), chapters 2-3 examine the impact of two Italian government-chartered companies in Somalia, the Filonardi Company (1893-96) and the Benadir Company (1898-1905). Subsequent chapters discuss the Italian debate over the issue of slavery in the occupied territories of southern Somalia (chapter 4), the attempts at creating a colony (1905-23) in the aftermath of the Italian government's assumption of direct administration of southern Somalia in 1905 (chapter 5), and the administration of the newly created 'northern protectorates' from 1889-1923 (chapter 6). Of special interest to the student of Djibouti is the Fascist era of Italian control in the Horn (1923-41) and the creation of the so-called *Grande Somalia* (chapter 7). A final chapter offers some concluding remarks on the nature of Italian colonialism (chapter 8), while an epilogue focuses on the impact of Italian trusteeship in Somalia just prior to independence in 1960. Also included are useful appendices and an annotated bibliography of literature and primary sources dealing with the topic of Italian colonialism in Africa.

History

89 **General history of Africa.**
Edited by J. Ki-Zerbo et al. Paris: United Nations Educational,
Scientific and Cultural Organization (UNESCO); London: Heinemann
Educational Books; Berkeley, California: University of California Press,
1981-85. 8 vols.
Coordinated by the International Scientific Committee for the drafting of a General
History of Africa, an arm of the United Nations Educational, Scientific and Cultural
Organization (UNESCO), this massive, multi-volume work is an important contribu-
tion to the history of Africa, including the Horn of Africa. The committee was
composed of thirty-nine members (two-thirds of whom were African and one-third
non-African) and purposely solicited African scholars to edit the individual volumes.
Each volume represents an edited collection of papers which, for the most part, are
also written by African scholars. In this regard, the series provides an important
Africa-based interpretation of African history. Each volume contains biographies of
the individual authors, an extensive bibliography and indexes separated according to
subject, name and places. The titles and editors of the individual volumes are as
follows: volume 1, *Methodology and African prehistory* (J. Ki-Zerbo); volume 2,
Ancient civilizations in Africa (G. Mokhtar); volume 3, *Africa from the seventh to
eleventh century* (M. El Fasi); volume 4, *Africa from the twelfth to sixteenth century* (D.
T. Niane); volume 5, *Africa from the sixteenth to eighteenth century* (B. A. Ogot);
volume 6, *The nineteenth century until 1880* (J. F. A. Ajayi); volume 7, *Africa under
foreign domination, 1880-1935* (A. A. Boachen); and volume 8, *Africa since 1935* (Ali
A. Mazrui).

90 **France and the Italo-Ethiopian crisis 1935-1936.**
Franklin D. Laurens. The Hague: Mouton, 1967. 432p. bibliog.
This book documents French involvement in the 1935-36 conflict between Italy and
Ethiopia and, thus, is important for a complete understanding of the diplomatic history
of the Horn of Africa. French involvement is discussed in sixteen chapters which are
arranged chronologically: 'Background' (chapter 1); 'The Rome Agreement: January
1935' (chapter 2); 'The beginning of the crisis: December 1934-May 1935 (chapter 3);
'Further development of the crisis: June-July 1935' (chapter 4); 'Hopes for peace fade:
August 1935' (chapter 5); 'On the brink of war: September 1935' (chapter 6); 'The
outbreak of war: October 1935' (chapter 7); 'Mutual support: September-December
1935' (chapter 8); 'Sanctions and conciliation (I): October 1935' (chapter 9); 'Sanctions
and conciliation (II): November 1935' (chapter 10); 'The Hoare-Laval plan and its
aftermath: December 1935-January 1936' (chapter 11); 'The beginning of the end:
January-March 1936' (chapter 12) 'Mussolini victorious: March-May 1936' (chapter
13); 'Liquidation of the affair: June-July 1936 and after' (chapter 14); 'Economic
aspects of the crisis' (chapter 15); and 'Conclusions' (chapter 16).

91 **A modern history of Somalia: nation and state in the Horn of Africa.**
I. M. Lewis. Boulder, Colorado; London: Westview, 1988. 297p.
3 maps.
Originally published in 1980 (the first eight chapters appeared even earlier in 1965),
this is important reading for a full understanding of the history of the Horn of Africa
and Djibouti's place therein. After briefly tracing the history of the Somali nation in
the pre-colonial period (chapters 1-2), the bulk of the book is devoted to exploring the
impact of colonialism and the struggle for independence (chapters 3-7) and the
evolution of the Somali state during the post-1960 independence period (chapters 8-

10). Djibouti is discussed at several points throughout the text when relevant to the history of current-day Somalia. Of special interest are extended discussions concerning: French colonial rule in Djibouti at the end of the 1940s (p. 136-38); the 1958 referendum in Djibouti and that territory's place in the wider vision of a pan-Somali state (p. 179-81); the politics accompanying the end of French colonial rule in 1977 (p. 228-31); and Djibouti's place in the 1977-78 Ogaden War (p. 231-48). Of special general interest is the concluding chapter entitled 'Nationalism, ethnicity and revolution in the Horn of Africa'.

92 The referendum in French Somaliland: aftermath and prospects in the Somali dispute.
I. M. Lewis. *World Today*, vol. 23, no. 7 (July 1967), p. 308-14.

This brief article analyses the French-sponsored referendum in Djibouti in 1967 – the results of which ensured continued French colonial rule over the territory – against the backdrop of Ethiopian-Somali competition and conflict. 'The referendum', the author notes, 'has again brought world attention to bear on the problem posed by the continued dismemberment of the Somali nation, an issue which has now become perhaps the most intractable of all international disputes in Africa'. The competing interests of both Somalia and Ethiopia, as well as those of Djibouti's Afar and Issa populations, is set against France's wilful manipulation of ethnic cleavages to ensure Afar dominance and, therefore, a 'yes' vote for continued French rule. However, time has overruled the author's comment that the French may have been preparing the territory for eventual union with Ethiopia. The author concludes that resolution of the region's border conflicts ultimately will depend on a joint American-Soviet initiative with French participation. See also the author's 'Prospects in the Horn: after the referendum', *Africa Report* (April 1967), p. 37-40.

93 A 'Danzig solution'?
Harold G. Marcus. *Africa Report* (April 1967), p. 40-41.

Written by a noted historian of Ethiopian studies, this brief article examines a unique solution to the growing dispute between Ethiopia and Somalia over the future of French-ruled Djibouti. The point of discussion is the so-called 'Danzig solution' of Poland's conflict with Germany over achieving free and sovereign communication with the Baltic sea (which, by necessity, would have to cross a German ethnic zone). The solution was to provide Poland with free access to the sea through a land corridor that divided German Pomerania from East Prussia. The port city of Danzig became a 'free city' in which Poland 'was given extensive powers in foreign relations, customs, transportation, communications and harbor administration'. Applying this analogy to French-ruled Djibouti, Djibouti City would become a 'free city' in which Ethiopia would be guaranteed access to the sea. The author examines various dilemmas associated with such a solution. Among these are the expansionist visions of Somalia, the question of who would act as an 'honest broker' between the free city, Ethiopia and Somalia, and the nature of French interests and intentions.

94 Côte française des Somalis. (French Somali Coast.)
Alfred Martineau. Paris: Société d'Éditions Géographiques, Maritimes et Coloniales, 1931. 66p.

The author was a former governor of the French colony in Djibouti, and paints a sympathetic picture of colonial efforts in the territory until the 1930s. Chapter 1 outlines the origins of the colony, including a French treaty with the King of Choa in

1843, the acquisition of Obock in 1862, and various treaties with sovereigns of the Gulf of Tadjoura in the 1880s. Chapter 2 briefly discusses the traditions and repartition of Somalis and Afars (referred to as Danakils) in the territory, while chapter 3 describes the nature of France's relationship with Ethiopia. The creation and history of the Djibouti–Addis Ababa railway, which assured the economic growth of Djibouti and even closer relations with Ethiopia, are extensively described in chapter 4. Chapter 5 describes all aspects of French colonial administration in Djibouti. Topics broached include colonial security forces, finances, justice, population, religion, public works, agriculture and many more topics. The monograph is especially valuable for its reproduction of numerous treaties signed between France and various local leaders of what is currently known as Djibouti.

95   **The 1977 elections in Djibouti: a tragi/comic end to French colonial rule.**
     Edward Morgan.   *Horn of Africa*, vol. 1, no. 3 (July-Sept. 1978), p. 47-49.
The author presents a scathing attack on French colonialism in Djibouti as culminating in the 1977 independence elections. The tone of the article is set by the following opening statement: 'Pre-independence visions of large-scale infusions of Saudi Arabian dollars combining with French technical know-how and commercial activity to create an East African Hong Kong, have served to underline the note of absurdity inevitably present in the sad circumstances characterizing this last colony's arrival at political independence'. Special reference is made to successful French efforts at manipulating the independence process to decrease the power of Ali Aref's Afar ethnic group in favour of the Issa Somalis in the territory. An overview is offered of French manipulation of competing ethnic groups from the creation of Djibouti's Representative Council in 1946 onward, with a final section concentrating on the 'tragi-comic' outcomes associated with these actions.

96   **Arthur Rimbaud: trade and politics in northeast Africa 1880-1891.**
     Theodore Natsoulas.   *Northeast African Studies*, vol. 3, no. 2 (1981),
     p. 49-68; vol. 3, no. 3 (1981-82), p. 43-60.
Arthur Rimbaud is best known for his contribution to French literature as an avant-garde poet. Yet Rimbaud was also one of several French merchants who lived in Djibouti during the 1880s and was extensively involved in the arms trade of northeast Africa. The author argues that Rimbaud, first as an employee of a French firm and then on his own, contributed to the establishment of French influence and the opening of the interior to European mercantile activity. As one of the first permanent merchants in Harar he explored the Ogaden desert and the surrounding area. He foresaw the economic and strategic value of Djibouti and explored and recommended the route that the Djibouti–Addis Ababa railway was to take. His presence was so pervasive that a report sent to the British Foreign Office identified him as the 'cleverest French agent in that part of Africa'. Extensive use of Rimbaud's personal correspondence provides much of the basis for what is written in this two-part article.

97   **Histoire de Djibouti: des origines à la république.** (History of Djibouti:
     from its origins to republic.)
     Philippe Oberlé, Pierre Hugot.   Paris: Éditions Présence Africaine,
     1985. 339p. bibliog.
An updated version of Oberlé's *Afars et Somalis: le dossier de Djibouti* (Paris: Éditions Présence Africaine, 1971) constitutes the most comprehensive and readable French-language history of Djibouti. Chapter 1 sets the stage for the book by discussing the

traditional lifestyles and habits of the peoples indigenous to the region prior to the 'games of the colonial powers' (the subject of chapter 2). Included in this discussion are the primary roles played by the French and the British, as well as two regional powers: Egypt and Ethiopia. Chapter 3 centres on Djibouti's role as a prosperous and coveted colony (between 1900 and 1945), including discussions concerning its role in the arms and slave trades. Chapters 4-7 examine the political evolution of Djibouti under French tutelage from 1945 to 1967, with chapter 6 focusing on various problems – economic, social, political and intellectual – afflicting the territory in 1966. Chapter 8 centres on growing political unrest in Djibouti from 1968 to 1976, with chapter 9 describing the colony's attainment of independence in 1977. Finally, chapter 10 focuses on the successes obtained and the obstacles which remain into the 1980s.

98 **History of East Africa.**
Edited by Roland Oliver et al.   Oxford: Clarendon Press, 1963-76.
3 vols. bibliog.

This three-volume set provides a comprehensive history of the East African coast. Volume 1 (edited by Roland Oliver, Gervase Mathew) details the period beginning with the Stone Age and ending with colonial influence in 1898. Volume 2 (edited by Vincent Harbow, E. M. Chilver, Alison Smith) continues the historical overview up to 1950. Volume 3 (edited by D. A. Low, Alison Smith) details that period immediately preceding and following the independence of the East African countries. Five interesting chapters detail the impact of Christianity on East Africa, the role of immigrant communities (Europeans, Asians and Arabs) and changes in East African society.

99 **Economic history of Ethiopia, 1800-1935.**
Richard Pankhurst.   Addis Ababa: Haile Selassie I University Press, 1968. 772p. bibliog.

This economic history of Ethiopia is essential reading for a comprehensive understanding of the economic history of the Horn and Djibouti's place therein. The closing year of the work is 1935, or the occasion of the Italian invasion of Ethiopia. Among the numerous economic topics discussed are land tenure, agriculture, currency and banking, natural resources and their utilization, handicrafts, urban development, and taxation and government revenues. Other related topics include the army, health and education. Of special interest to the scholar of Djibouti are the chapters focusing on slavery and the slave trade (chapter 3), transport and communications (chapter 8) and trade (chapter 9).

100 **Fire-arms in Ethiopian history (1800-1935).**
Richard Pankhurst. *Ethiopia Observer*, vol. 6, no. 2 (1962), p. 135-80.

'The rulers of Ethiopia had for centuries been able to assemble huge armies, sometimes several hundred thousand strong, and could therefore be assured of out-numbering any potential invader', notes the author. 'After the advent of modern weapons, however, numbers became relatively unimportant, the decisive question becoming the ability to import arms from abroad'. In this article the author assesses Ethiopia's ability to import arms during both the 19th and 20th centuries, with the role of Djibouti and its port and railway figuring prominently in the discussion. For example, as early as April 1839, the Ethiopian emperor imported several 'small cannon' through Tadjoura, 'paying a female slave for each camel required for transportation'. This article, extensively documented (420 footnotes), is a must for

41

understanding the early history of arms trade in the Horn of Africa, of which Djibouti played an important role. For the author's analysis of the impact of fire-arms in Ethiopia prior to the 19th century, see 'The history of fire-arms in Ethiopia prior to the nineteenth century', *Ethiopia Observer*, vol. 11, no. 3 (1958), p. 202-25.

101   **Italian fascist claims to the Port of Jibuti, 1935-1941: an historical note.**
Richard Pankhurst.   *Ethiopia Observer*, vol. 14, no. 1 (1971), p. 26-30.
The author provides a brief, yet very important and interesting, historical overview of Italian fascist claims to the port of French-ruled Djibouti during the late 1930s. The historical starting point of the article is a Franco-Italian treaty signed on 7 January 1935 in which French Premier Pierre Laval ceded to Italy 1,800 square kilometres of Djiboutian territory bordering Eritrea and 2,000 shares in the Franco-Ethiopian railway company. The author demonstrates how Italian desires for full control of the port, which served as the 'only link' between Italian-controlled Addis Ababa and the 'outside world', contributed to growing conflict with France, especially in the aftermath of Laval's replacement as premier by the socialist Leon Blum in May 1936. Much of the source material is from newspaper articles of the period, most notably summaries of accounts carried by *Corriere dell' Impero*, a fascist newspaper published in Addis Ababa. The article also discusses French attempts at compromise in 1939 and preparations at fortifying the territory to stop an expected Italian invasion.

102   **La colonisation française au pays des Somalis.** (French colonization in Somali country.)
Henri le Pointe.   Paris: Librairie Jouve, 1914. 98p.
This highly sympathetic account of French colonialism in Djibouti offers a good overview of the French presence in that country during the first two decades of the 20th century. Whereas the first chapter focuses on the administrative side of French colonial rule, including the police, army, treasury, health service, public works, post and telecommunications, customs and education, chapter 2 describes the country itself. Topics include the climate, landscape, hygiene, flora and fauna, major customs, and the three major urban areas (Djibouti City, Obock and Tadjoura). Finally, chapter 3 highlights the commercial side of the colonial presence: caravan trading, the Djibouti-Addis Ababa railway, the port, agriculture, industry, handicrafts, population and budget. The author attributes the success of the colony to the hand-in-glove efforts of the colonial régime and private French entrepreneurs.

103   **Historical dictionary of Ethiopia.**
Chris Prouty, Eugene Rosenfeld.   Metuchen, New Jersey; London: Scarecrow Press, 1982. 436p. map. bibliog. (African Historical Dictionaries, no. 32).
Djibouti's common cultural, ethnic, religious, political, linguistic and economic ties with Ethiopia make this historical dictionary an obvious starting point for scholars interested in the Horn of Africa and, particularly, Djibouti. A preface regarding transliteration of terms into English from Ethiopic script is followed by a brief introduction. The bulk of the book is devoted to the definition of hundreds of terms which denote places, individuals, and social, political and economic concepts of past and present historical significance in Ethiopia. The text is complemented by a 216-page bibliography and a 28-page index. The bibliography is especially useful for historical works which are divided into three categories: 'Ancient and medieval'; 'c.1760-c.1930';

and 'c.1930-1974'. See also volume no. 6 of the series, *Historical dictionary of Somalia*, by Margaret Castagno (q.v.).

104 **British military administration of occupied territories in Africa during the years 1941-1947.**
Francis James Rennell.   Westport, Connecticut: Greenwood Press, 1970. 637p. 6 maps.

The author provides a comprehensive and (British military sanctioned) historical account of Great Britain's occupation of African territories during the Second World War, most notably in the Horn of Africa. A total of twenty chapters are arranged chronologically. Numerous references are made to Djibouti and the importance of its port and rail link with Ethiopia throughout the text. After briefly summarizing the nature of British military campaigns from 1940 to 1943, the first two chapters describe the general outlines of Britain's military administration of the occupied territories. Among those chapters of particular interest to scholars of the Horn are: 'The resurrection of Ethiopia' (chapter 3); 'The adolescence of the new Ethiopia' (chapter 4); 'The military government of Eritrea' (chapter 5); 'The development of Eritrea' (chapter 6); 'The pacification of Italian Somaliland' (chapter 7); 'The re-birth of British Somaliland' (chapter 8); 'The reserved areas of Ethiopia' (chapter 9); and 'Tripolitania and the end of Italy's African empire' (chapter 12). The author is unabashedly pro-British in outlook and offers excellent insights into the British colonial mind as concerns the Horn of Africa, inclusive of Djibouti. Other chapters of particular interest are those dealing with the relationship between 'internal' and 'international' law and British occupation (chapter 14), and the evacuation and repatriation of enemy property (chapter 17).

105 **Naissance d'une nation 'Djibouti'/ birth of a nation 'Djibouti'.**
République de Djibouti.   Boulogne, France: Presses des Éditions Delroisse, 1977. 81p. map.

This commemorative book of Djibouti's independence on 27 June 1977 contains both English and French texts, with a summary in Arabic at the end. Upon independence Djibouti became the 148th member of the United Nations, 49th member of the Organization of African Unity and 21st member of the Arab League. A simple history and geography of Djibouti is followed by the texts of speeches made by President Hassan Gouled Aptidon at the Presidential Palace on the morning of 27 June 1977 at the National Assembly and a celebration at the stadium. Fifty-seven colour photographs capture all aspects of the independence day celebrations, as well as points of interest throughout the country. The flag of Djibouti, comprised of a red star on a tri-coloured field of blue, white and green, is described by President Gouled as follows: 'These colours include the blue of the sea and the sky, the beneficent green of the earth, the white of peace and the star we shall follow in our hope and struggle'.

History

106   **Les Français à Obock.** (The French at Obock.)
      Denis de Rivoyre.   Paris: Librairie d' Éducation Nationale, 1889.
      237p.

An early and interesting summary of the establishment and evolution of the French
presence at Obock from the mid-to-late 19th century. The account begins in 1859 with
Henri Lambert, the French vice-consul at Aden, and his dream to gain a possession in
northeast Africa to guarantee France's maritime interests in the face of expanding
British influence in the region. Numerous topics are woven throughout the text,
including Anglo–French rivalry, the 'pretensions' of Egypt, the regional aspirations of
Ethiopia and the gradual growth of French commercial interests in the region. Of
special importance to the entrenchment of French interests, argues the author, were
the organization of the Franco–Ethiopian Company, the creation of the French Society
of Obock and the creation of a coaling station at Obock.

107   **The periplus of the Erythraean sea: travel and trade in the Indian Ocean
      by a merchant of the first century.**
      Translated from the Greek by Wilfred H. Schoff.   New Delhi:
      Devendra Jain (for Oriental Books Reprint Corporation), 1974. 323p.
      map. bibliog.

Originally published in 1912, this fully-annotated 1974 edition of *The periplus of the
Erythraean sea* is a must for scholars of the Horn of Africa. The *periplus* (which, in
loose translation, stands for a 'guide-book' dating back to Roman times) is the first
record of organized trading between the nations of the Indian Ocean and the Western
world as written by a Roman subject. The document itself, comprising a mere 28
pages, is complemented by nearly 300 pages of explanatory notes, including a brief
discussion of the date and authorship of the periplus, articles of trade and rulers
mentioned therein, articles subject to duty at Alexandria and a handy index. As the
translator notes in the introduction, 'The records of the pioneers . . . are of enduring
interest in the story of human endeavor . . . one of the most fascinating is this . . .
plain and painstaking log of a Greek in Egypt, a Roman subject, who steered his vessel
into the waters of the great ocean and brought back the first detailed record of the
imports and exports of its markets, and of the conditions and alliances of its peoples'!

**Recherches préhistoriques dans le territoire des Afars (République de
Djibouti).**
(Prehistoric research in the Afars Territory (Republic of Djibouti).)
See item no. 18.

Structural history of the Republic of Djibouti: a summary.
See item no. 21.

Earthquake history of Ethiopia and the Horn of Africa.
See item no. 30.

The ecology of survival: case studies from northeast African history.
See item no. 115.

**Addictives in northeast Africa: a brief survey of an aspect of 19th century
cultural history.**
See item no. 126.

The prehistoric cultures of the Horn of Africa: an analysis of the Stone Age cultural and climatic succession in the Somalilands and the eastern parts of Abyssinia.
See item no. 148.

Historical aspects of genealogies in northern Somali social structure.
See item no. 157.

Mahdism, Muslim clerics, and holy wars in Ethiopia, 1300-1600.
See item no. 198.

Caravan trade and history in the northern parts of East Africa.
See item no. 253.

History of the Franco–Ethiopian railway from Djibouti to Addis Ababa.
See item no. 255.

The Franco–Ethiopian railway and its history.
See item no. 261.

Origin and early development of food-producing cultures in north-eastern Africa.
See item no. 292.

Rejection of fish as human food in Africa: a problem in history and ecology.
See item no. 300.

The modern history of Ethiopia and the Horn of Africa: a select and annotated bibliography.
See item no. 405.

Social Conditions, Health and Welfare

108 **Amnesty International report.**
Amnesty International. London: Amnesty International Publications, 1975/76- . annual.

Amnesty International is an international organization which reports on human rights abuses through 3,400 local groups in 55 countries. Relying solely on donations from its worldwide membership, the purposes of the organization are threefold: 'It seeks the *release* of men and women detained anywhere for their beliefs, colour, sex, ethnic origin, language or religion, provided that they have not used or advocated violence. These are termed *"prisoners of conscience"*. It advocates *fair and early trials for all political prisoners* and works on behalf of such persons detained without charge or without trial. It opposes the *death penalty* and *torture* or other cruel, inhuman or degrading treatment or punishment of *all prisoners* without reservation'! Every country of the world, including Djibouti, is discussed according to its compliance with these three major areas of concern.

109 **Géographie médicale. Djibouti.** (Medical geography. Djibouti.)
Dr. Bouffard. *Annales d'Hygiène et de Médecine Coloniales*, vol. 8 (1905), p. 333-75.

The author served in Djibouti as a medical officer with the French Colonial Army at the turn of the 20th century. In this article he provides an interesting overview of medical conditions within the territory. The first section details 'local medicine' and includes a brief description of the Somali and Afar customs of circumcision and infibulation of the female sex. The second section offers a cursory overview of some of the medical problems which afflict the local residents such as dysentery and malaria. A final section details medical problems confronted by Europeans living in Djibouti, most notably sunstroke and heatstroke.

110 **Qat: changes in the production and consumption of a quasilegal commodity in northeast Africa.**
Lee V. Cassanelli. In: *The social life of things: commodities in cultural perspective.* Edited by Arjun Appadurai. Cambridge, England: Cambridge University Press, 1986, p. 236-57.

The chewing of khat (*catha edulis*) has a long and varied history in the Horn of Africa and, since 1921, has been banned by the region's governments numerous times with little permanent effect. This article, the best and most recent analysis available, discusses the production and consumption of khat during the last fifty years in the evolving society and political economy of northeast Africa, including the countries of Ethiopia, Somalia, Kenya, and Djibouti. The first section details 'popular ideas' about khat as described by the chewers themselves. For example, 'practicing Muslims say that chewing it in the evening enables them to work and pray without becoming drowsy, particularly during the month of Ramadan, when Muslims are obligated to fast from sunrise to sundown'. The next three sections detail the social and economic aspects of khat, including its production, distribution, and what the author describes as the 'culture of consumerism' (i.e. why demand has steadily increased). A final section explores the politics of prohibition. The author describes how this quasi-legal substance has 'always hovered on that distinct boundary between legality and illegality, and its official status at any one moment is the product more of political and economic calculations than of strictly medical or public health considerations'.

111 **The development of a middle class in British Somaliland, French Somaliland and in Somalia under trusteeship (with some references to Ethiopia and the Sudan).**
Guiseppe A. Costanzo. In: *Development of a middle class in tropical and sub-tropical countries, record of the XXIXth session held in London from 13th to 16th September 1955.* Brussels: International Institute of Differing Civilizations, 1956, p. 141-58.

The purpose of the conference convened by the International Institute of Differing Civilizations was to undertake a comparative analysis of the rise of urban and rural middle classes within Third World societies, with special focus on the rise of a middle class within the major ethnic group of each particular country. This 'social category' was perceived to be of special importance 'as it is the main source of supply of leaders in any democratic system of government'. In this article the researcher is provided with a unique comparative analysis of the rise of such classes in British Somaliland, the Italian trusteeship territory of Somalia and French colony of Djibouti. After briefly introducing the general economic conditions of each territory as of 1955, the author examines the impact of social conditions and the policies of the administering powers on the growth of middle classes. Two final sections critically assess why the growth of middle classes in all three territories had been slow and the impact that the presence of large numbers of Europeans had exerted on the process.

112 **Coutumes somalis.** (Somali customs.)
Djibouti: Libraire Goyon, 1975. 16p.

Simply noted as being written by a 'doctor from Djibouti', this short booklet offers a revealing presentation of the sexual custom of circumcising and infibulating young Somali girls in Djibouti. The author, who is clearly opposed to the practice, offers graphic detail of the various procedures involved in performing this ritual on

47

Social Conditions, Health and Welfare

Djiboutian girls, prior to puberty, usually between the ages of six to eight years old. The author then discusses the negative physical consequences of this 'sexual mutilation' should the girl ultimately decide to raise children. Important throughout are the doctor's personal observations concerning the negative effects of circumcision and infibulation: whereas numerous young girls die during the initial procedure or at the later childbirthing state, psychologically there is said to be an abnormal level of sadness and frigidity. A final section explores the origins of this custom.

113 **Low prevalence of infection by HTLV-1 in populations at risk in Djibouti.**
E. Fox, N. T. Constantine, E. A. Abatte, S. Salah, G. Rodier.
Annales de l'Institut Pasteur. Virologie, vol. 139, no. 4 (Oct.-Dec. 1988), p. 443-47.

A sad outcome of Djibouti's high unemployment rate, large numbers of refugees and the presence of a large contingent of French foreign legionnaires has been the rise of prostitution as a major business activity in Djibouti City. In this article, the authors report the findings of a medical survey carried out in June 1988 to determine the infection by HTLV-1 in high risk populations in Djibouti City. HTLV-1 is a recently-discovered retrovirus causing T-cell leukaemias and lymphomas, as well as tropical parparesis. The authors note that the study design consisted of a 'multi-high-risk-group screening survey' that included 576 individuals (the mean age of whom was twenty-six). Of this group, 240 were 'males who primarily had a sexually transmitted disease' and 336 'were females among whom 327 engaged in prostitution'. Of those tested, four were confirmed as postive for HTLV-1, by Western blotting, suggesting a seropositivity rate in the test population of 0.7 percent. All four of those testing positive were female prostitutes, suggesting a 1.2 percent seropositivity rate among prostitutes in Djibouti.

114 **The Hosken report: genital and sexual mutilation of females.**
Fran P. Hosken. Lexington, Massachusetts: Women's International Network News, 1979. rev. ed. 368p. bibliog.

The author has compiled an extensive volume on the circumcision of women, most notably in Africa, having revised and enlarged an earlier edition of the book after attending a World Health Organization (WHO) seminar on the same topic from February to March 1979 in Khartoum, Sudan. The first section of the book provides an overview of female circumcision, including medical facts, notes concerning the WHO seminar, its role vis-à-vis women and development, history of the practice and a geographical overview (map and rough estimates). The second section of the book analyses case histories. Although Djibouti is not explicitly examined, its cultural neighbours, Somalia and Ethiopia, are examined in great detail. Discussion is also made of other East African countries, West Africa, the Arabian peninsula, Asia (Indonesia/Malaysia) and the West. Section three discusses the reasons given for female circumcision, provides a comparison with male circumcision, and discusses the politics of female circumcision and the outlook for women's health. A useful five-page bibliography directs the reader to further reading on the topic.

115 **The ecology of survival: case studies from northeast African history.**
Edited by Douglas H. Johnson, David M. Anderson. London: Crook
Academic Publishers; Boulder, Colorado: Westview, 1988. 339p.
11 maps. bibliog.

In the aftermath of the 1984-86 drought and famine in northeast Africa, journalists and
scholars focused on the burgeoning ecological and environmental crises in this region
of the world. The purpose of this book is to go beyond this most recent crisis – and its
'crisis management' literature – by placing it in its proper historical context.
Specifically, this book 'examines the historical continuities of ecological change and
ecological stress' in northeast Africa through detailed case studies based on extensive
field research. Although not specifically focusing on Djibouti, twelve good chapters
serve as a useful beginning to understanding the historical nature of ecological change
in the Horn of Africa. Of particular general interest to the scholar of Djibouti are the
following chapters: 'Introduction: ecology and society in northeast African history' by
David M. Anderson and Douglas H. Johnson; 'The great drought and famine of 1888-
92 in northeast Africa' (chapter 2) by Richard Pankhurst and Douglas H. Johnson, and
'History, drought and reproduction: dynamics of society and ecology in northeast
Africa' (chapter 12) by James McCann.

116 **Étude sur la sous-alimentation en côte française des Somalis.** (Study of
malnutrition in the French Somali Coast.)
D. T. Leitner. *Bulletin de la Société de Pathologie Exotique*,
nos. 11-12 (1945), p. 344-56.

The article offers several interesting tables of statistics which document the diets of
Djiboutians during the 1940s. The purpose of the study was to examine the diets of the
indigenous populations to better comprehend and overcome the sicknesses associated
with malnutrition. Whereas the first half of the paper offers observations on the
differences in diet between Djiboutians living in the city and the countryside, the
second half documents the sicknesses associated with this condition. A final section
offers several means of disease prevention.

117 **Résultats de l'enquête sur la mortalité infantine dans la ville de Djibouti.**
(Results of the survey on infant mortality in Djibouti City.)
Mohamed Mahdi, M. P. Ramakavelo, G. Detre, B. Diawara, H. Maki,
A. Osman, M. A. Djama, A. Mahmoud. Djibouti: Ministère de la
Santé, Direction de la Santé Publique, Cellule des Statistiques
Sanitaires et de Surveillance Epidémologique, 1985. 53p.

The survey on infant mortality was carried out in Djibouti City from 27 April to 16
May 1985 in coordination with the World Health Organization and the United Nations
Children's Fund. Women were interviewed from a total of 5,526 households and a
copy of the questionnaire is reproduced within the report. The results of the survey are
rather alarming: the mortality rate in 1984 was 200 per 1,000 births (20 per cent)
meaning that two out of every ten infants born did not survive past their first birthday.
Of the 20 per cent that die in their first year, 4.6 per cent die within the first ten days,
1.7 per cent between eleven and twenty-eight days, 45.2 per cent between one and six
months, and 48.5 per cent between seven and twelve months. The most frequent
causes of death are diarrhoea (49 per cent), respiratory illness (17 per cent) and
measles (9 per cent). Not surprisingly, the higher the educational level of the parents,
the lower the rate of infant mortality. These and many other statistics are provided in
over thirty-five tables.

118   **The ecology of malnutrition in eastern Africa and from countries of western Africa; Equatorial Guinea, the Gambia, Liberia, Sierra Leone, Malawi, Rhodesia, Zambia, Kenya, Tanzania, Uganda, Ethiopia, the French Territory of the Afars and Issas, the Somali Republic and Sudan.**
Jacques M. May, Donna L. McLellan.   New York: Hafner Publishing, 1970. 675p. (Studies in Medical Geography, no. 9).
The purpose of this volume, commissioned by the US Army and which includes a chapter on the former French colony of Djibouti, is to present and analyse the various factors pertaining to the role of nutrition in social and economic development. The first section offers background information on Djibouti's physical setting, climate, population, history, government, agricultural policies and foreign aid. The second section describes food resources within the territory, such as the means of production (agricultural labour force, farms and fertilizers), production (food crops, animal husbandry and fisheries), food industries, trade, and food supply (storage and transportation). Subsequent sections centre on the diet of the local population, adequacy of food resources and nutritional disease patterns.

119   **The medical and social problems of khat in Djibouti.**
Bulletin on Narcotics, vol. 9, no. 4 (Oct.-Dec. 1957), p. 34-37.
French colonial authorities, alarmed at the rise in khat (*catha edulis*) use in its colonial territory of Djibouti, commissioned an analysis of its potentially deleterious effects on Djiboutian society. The result is this brief analysis submitted by the French colonial authorities to the United Nations Commission on Narcotic Drugs. Although emphasis is placed on summarizing the physiological and social effects of chewing khat, the researcher will also find useful references on rate of usage, levels of import and costs of purchase of the substance during the 1950s. The conclusion that khat represented a 'habit-forming substance' with negative effects resulted in the passing of an official decree (reproduced in full) on 2 April 1957 banning the 'importation, exportation, production, possession, trade in, and use of, khat and preparations containing khat or prepared with a khat base'. Although the decree obviously was unsuccessful (khat consumption continued to rise) and eventually was superceded by legalization, this article nicely summarizes French colonial attitudes concerning usage during the period and is, perhaps, the first detailing its usage in Djibouti.

120   **Public health, pastoralism, and politics in the Horn of Africa.**
R. Mansell Prothero.   Evanston, Illinois: Northwestern University Press, 1968. 26p. 3 maps. bibliog. (Sixth Melville J. Herskovits Memorial Lecture).
Solutions to the public health problems of the Horn of Africa are described as requiring an appreciation for the multidisciplinary and interdisciplinary aspects of the situation, including the epidemiology of disease (public health), population structure and mobility (pastoralism) and its interterritorial relationships (politics). The author demonstrates how both pastoralism and politics have impeded progress in eradicating various public health problems (e.g. tuberculosis). 'Here as elsewhere in Africa', the author notes, 'disease recognizes no boundaries'. He concludes that 'Interterritorial cooperation and coordination are essential measures to improve public health. Successful malaria eradication, for example, can be conceived of realistically only in terms of at least the whole of the Horn of Africa.

121 **Table ronde sur la création de petites entreprises 4 mai 1986, interventions et débat.** (Round table on the creation of small enterprises 4 May 1986, interventions and debate).
République de Djibouti. Ministère de l'Éducation Nationale, de la Jeunesse, des Sports et de la Culture. Djibouti: The Author, 1986. 52p.

Unemployment in Djibouti is very high (some say as high as seventy per cent) and weighs particularly heavily upon students graduating from the country's professionel lycées, such as the Lycée d'Enseignement Professionnel Djibouti (EPD). This booklet, which is the result of a conference convened by the Ministry of National Education, Youth, Sports and Culture and the EDP, focuses on how the employment market can be revitalized through small enterprises created by the lycée graduate. Specifically, the purpose of the round table was 'to bring together all useful information for the creation of a firm by students graduating from the EDP'. The booklet contains the texts of speeches by twelve participants on varied topics, as well as proceedings of the general debate that followed. A useful annex offers statistics concerning the nature and number of small businesses in Djibouti City.

122 **Résultats de l'enquête sur la consommation du 'khat' dans la ville de Djibouti.** (Results of the inquiry into the consumption of 'khat' in Djibouti City.)
République de Djibouti: Ministère de la Santé Publique, Direction de la Santé Publique. Djibouti: The Author, 1984. 52p.

The report was prepared for an international conference on the subject of khat (*catha edulis*) that was held in Djibouti from 17-20 December 1984. Seven to ten tons of khat are imported daily for domestic use in Djibouti, arriving via air and rail from Ethiopia. With the aid of the World Health Organization, 500 households in Djibouti City were interviewed to document the magnitude of khat consumption, its repercussions on public health and family budgets, the views of those who chewed the substance, and to gather suggestions as to how to establish a concrete program for controlling the drug's usage. Some of the results of the study were alarming: 75 per cent of all households chew khat; 86.4 per cent of the chewers are men; 72 per cent chew daily (16 per cent 2-3 times weekly); 75 per cent chew at home; and the average time spent chewing is 5.5 hours daily. The government at one point attempted to limit khat use, but quickly withdrew, noting its economic importance in the country.

123 **A negative human serosurvey of haemorrhagic fever viruses in Djibouti.**
S. Salah, E. Fox, E. A. Abatte, N. T. Constantine, P. Asselin, A. K. Soliman. *Annales de l'Institut Pasteur. Virologie*, vol. 139, no. 4 (Oct.-Dec. 1988), p. 439-42.

The authors report the results of a medical survey carried out in Djibouti during autumn 1987 to determine the prevalence of viral haemorrhagic fevers (VHFs) among the population. Of the thirteen VHFs known to medical practitioners worldwide, nine are said to be prevalent in the Horn of Africa and, therefore, were the object of the survey. Among these are yellow fever, dengue, Chikungunya and Rift Valley fever of the mosquito-borne VHF; Congo-Crimean of the tick-borne VHF; Hantaan and Lassa fever of the zoonotic VHF; and Ebola and Marburg of the VHF of 'unknown transmission code'. Of the 160 subjects sampled, 50 'were healthy soldiers from all parts of the country and presently enrolled in the National Djiboutian Army'; 69 'were healthy inhabitants of Randa, a small village in Northern Djibouti characterized by a rather stable population'; and 41 'were sick patients hospitalized in Djibouti City for an undiagnosed febrile illness'. Each individual underwent an epidemiological interview and had up to ten millilitres of venous blood drawn (which was then subjected to serological tests in Cairo, Egypt).

124 **French Somaliland.**
James S. Simmons, Tom F. Whayne, Gaylord W. Anderson, Harold M. Horack. In: *Global epidemiology: a geography of disease and sanitation* (vol. 2) *Africa and the adjacent islands*. Philadelphia; London; Montreal: J. P. Lippincott, p. 85-91.

A unique glimpse of health and medical conditions in Djibouti during the 1940s. An initial section on population and socio-economic conditions of the territory warns the reader about the unreliability of 'vital statistics' (e.g. infant mortality rate) published to date of population, and is followed by a brief discussion of sanitation conditions in the territory (water supplies, waste disposal and food sanitation). Of most interest is the description of health services and medical facilities offered by the French colonial administration through the Direction du Service de Santé and a larger section on the prevalence of various diseases in the territory. Separate sections detail the incidence of diseases spread or contracted chiefly through intestinal or urinary tracts (e.g. dysenteries and typhoid and paratyphoid fevers); the respiratory tract (e.g. tuberculosis and smallpox); personal contact (e.g. venereal diseases); or arthropods (e.g. malaria and filariasis). In many cases the authors offer interesting statistics concerning the history of health care. For example, it is noted that mass vaccination against smallpox by the government health services began in 1929 'when an epidemic of haemorrhagic smallpox was responsible for 119 cases and 111 deaths'.

125 **Special issue devoted to catha edulis (khat).**
Bulletin on Narcotics, vol. 32, no. 3 (1980).

Khat (*catha edulis*) grows in eastern Africa and southern Arabia and, more specifically, in Democratic Yemen, Ethiopia, Kenya, Madagascar, Somalia, the United Republic of Tanzania and the Yemen Arab Republic. The user chews the freshest plant material available (usually the leaves and young shoots). 'The pleasurable, stimulating and euphoric effects obtained following absorption of khat constituents are reported to be similar to the effects of amphetamine and its congeners and have been considered as a strong inducement for khat users to procure, by any means, the necessary supplies once a day or more frequently to prolong the periods of chewing'. In this issue of the *Bulletin on Narcotics* an analysis is made of the chemistry of khat and its behavioural effects upon users. Articles include 'Catha edulis (khat): some introductory remarks' (editors); 'The chemistry of khat' (K. Szendrei); 'The cathedulin alkaloids' (L. Crombie); 'Khat: pharmacognostical aspects' (A. Nordal); 'Conclusions and recommendations of the expert group on the botany and chemistry of khat'; 'Behavioral effects of cathinone, an amine obtained from catha edulis forsk: comparisons with amphetamine, norpseudoephedrine, apomorphine and nomifensine' (J. L. Zelger, Hji. X. Schorno, E. A. Carlini); 'Review of the pharmacology of khat' (report of a WHO advisory group); and 'Selected bibliography on khat'.

126 **Addictives in northeast Africa: a brief survey of an aspect of 19th century cultural history.**
Bairu Tafla. *Afrika und Übersee*, vol. 64, no. 2 (1981), p. 281-309.
The purpose of the essay is to survey the types, geographical distributions, uses and nomenclatures of various 'addictives' in northeast Africa, centring specifically on their 'historical significance in the nineteenth century, the period during which the use of known drugs was widely spread, new ones were introduced and attempts to stamp out some of them failed'. The primary addictives examined include alcohol (beer, mead, wine and liquor), khat (*catha edulis*), coffee and tobacco. Offering a brief comparative list of the various names for addictives in the Oromo, Amharic, Tigrean and Somali languages, the author notes that, in most cases, 'recently borrowed products or adopted habits are designated by loan words from the Arabic or some of the European languages'. A final section offers an interesting summary of the cultural role of addictives in northeast Africa (primarily focusing on Ethiopia) during the 19th century.

127 **Les femmes djiboutiennes dans le processus de développement; situation et besoins.** (Djiboutian women in the process of development: situation and needs.)
United Nations. Addis Ababa: African Center for the Research and Formation of Women, Economic Commission for Africa, 1984. 74p. bibliog.
This is but one of a general series put out by the United Nations Economic Commission for Africa on the role of women in development. The study is the summary of interviews with 149 Djiboutian women (56 from the capital and 93 from the rural areas). The first section of the study describes the education, work, health and social life of Djiboutian women. Several useful annexes describe the mechanics of the study, various jobs held by women, health statistics, social life, the self-image held by Djiboutian women, the nature of educated women living in the capital, responses of males concerning the role of women, refugee women, and a brief presentation of 'L'Union Nationale des Femmes Djibotiennes' (The National Union of Djiboutian Women).

128 **Country reports on human rights practices: report submitted to the Committee on Foreign Relations, U.S. Senate and Committee on Foreign Affairs, U.S. House of Representatives by the Department of State.**
United States. Department of State. Washington, DC: US Government Printing Office, 1979- . annual.
Although a publication of the United States government, a fairly even presentation of human rights practices on a country-by-country basis is provided on a yearly basis. Every country is evaluated according to the following topics: section (1) – respect for the integrity of the person, including freedom from (a) political and other extra judicial killing, (b) disappearance, (c) torture and other cruel, inhuman or degrading treatment or punishment, (d) arbitrary arrest, detention or exile, (e) denial of fair public trial, (f) arbitrary interference with privacy, family, home or correspondence; section (2) – respect for civil liberties, including: (a) freedom of speech and press, (b) freedom of peaceful assembly and association, (c) freedom of religion, (d) freedom of movement within the country, foreign travel, emigration and repatriation; section (3) – respect for political rights: the right of citizens to change their government; section (4) – governmental attitude regarding international and nongovernmental investigation

Social Conditions, Health and Welfare

of alleged violations of human rights; section (5) – discrimination based on race, sex, religion, language or social status; section (6) – worker rights: (a) the right of association, (b) the right to organize and bargain collectively, (c) prohibition of forced or compulsory labour, (d) minimum age for employment of children, (e) acceptable conditions of work. In the 1989 report published in February 1990, the human rights situation in Djibouti is described as remaining 'tightly circumscribed'. Areas of concern include 'the continued denial of political pluralism, in particular the domination of the government and single legal political party by the Issa tribe; restrictions on freedoms of speech, press, and assembly; refusal to recognize the refugee rights of Somali civil war; incidents of arbitrary arrest, detention, and deportation; and allegations of the use of torture by the security services'.

129 **Réunion consultative Djibouti/OMS sur l'usage et le contrôle du khat: Djibouti, 17-20 décembre 1984.** (Consultative meeting between Djibouti and WHO on the usage and control of khat: Djibouti, 17-20 December 1984.)
World Health Organization (WHO). Djibouti: The Author, 1985. 19p.

The purpose of a four-day meeting in Djibouti in 1984, as convened by that country's Ministry of Public Health and sponsored by the World Health Organization, was to discuss the nature and effects of khat (*catha edulis*) usage in Djibouti. One outcome of the meeting was the creation of a national committee (which seemingly had little effect) to elaborate a national plan of action to deal effectively with what is considered to be a major health problem. The majority of the report summarizes the various topics of discussion at the meeting including the epidemiology of khat usage, as well as its chemistry, pharmacology and medical effects. Other topics of discussion included the social, economic and legal aspects of khat, and the role of religious institutions and education in potentially curbing its usage.

Observation ethnopsychiatrique de l'infibulation des femmes en Somalie. (An ethno-psychiatric observation of the infibulation of women in Somalia.)
See item no. 152.

French Somaliland.
See item no. 167.

Demographic yearbook.
See item no. 387.

54

Migration and Refugees

130 Djibouti, ill treatment of Somali refugees: denial of refuge; deportations and harsh conditions of detention.
Africa Watch. *News from Africa Watch* (30 Oct. 1989), 12p.
Created in May 1988, Africa Watch is a non-governmental organization which monitors human rights practices in Africa. In this issue the organization focuses on the alleged ill-treatment of approximately 30,000-40,000 Somalis who sought refuge in Djibouti in the aftermath of the intensification of civil conflict in Somalia in May 1988. In particular, Africa Watch expresses concern over certain practices condoned by the Djiboutian government. Among these are denial of refuge, ill treatment and harsh conditions of detention, deportations and the expulsion of residents of Somali origin. Three major sections focus on the denial of refuge, arrests and deportations, and general political harassment of the Somali Isaak community in Djibouti. Especially useful are brief summaries of individual cases of refugees and a listing of political transgressions by the Djiboutian government during the 1980s. An argument is made for the strengthening of the activities in Djibouti of the United Nations High Commission for Refugees. Two final sections include 'What you can do to help' and 'Watch publications on Somalia'.

131 Djibouti's refugee hordes.
Claire Brisset. *Horn of Africa*, vol. 2, no. 2 (1979), p. 12-14.
This brief but informative article offers an overview of the refugee situation in Djibouti in 1979. Among the topics discussed are limited resettlement of refugees in third countries, the status and location of refugee camps, dilemmas over who constitute legal refugees (and, therefore, receive food, medical treatment and shelter), and disagreements over policy between the United Nations High Commission for Refugees and Djibouti's National Assistance Committee for Refugees and Disaster Victims. The author states that the Djiboutian government is doing 'its best' to deal with the refugee problem as 'objectively' as possible.

Migration and Refugees

132 **Country reports on five key asylum countries in eastern and southern Africa.**

Lance Clark. Washington, DC: Refugee Policy Group, 1987. 63p.

Good, concise summaries of the refugee populations maintained by five key asylum countries in Africa: Somalia, Tanzania, Zambia, Zimbabwe and, most relevant to this bibliography, Djibouti (p. 1-12). The first two sections provide a country profile and briefly discuss five main refugee movements in Djibouti from 1975 to 1985. The bulk of the section is devoted to analysing 'key issues' in long-term assistance to refugees in Djibouti. Among these are the search for durable solutions (voluntary repatriation, local integration and resettlement to a third country), problems associated with self-sufficiency programs, assessing the impact and needs of urban-based refugees, and the erosion of support for the provision of asylum. An appendix updates the refugee situation as of March 1987, including an English-language reproducton of a 29 July 1986 refugee circular distributed by the Djiboutian government.

133 **Key issues in post-emergency refugee assistance in eastern and southern Africa.**

Lance Clark. Washington, DC: Refugee Policy Group, 1987. 44p.

The booklet represents the culmination of a Ford Foundation-sponsored project to study the problems associated with post-emergency refugee assistance in eastern and southern Africa, including Djibouti. (See the other two articles written by the same author as contained in this section). Six sections describe and analyse the major issues associated with refugee populations and the provision of assistance. Among these are the burden which refugees create for the host country, refugee participation, rural refugee settlements, spontaneously settled refugees, the role of liberation fronts in refugee assistance and 'new approaches' to voluntary repatriation.

134 **Post-emergency assistance for refugees in eastern and southern Africa: an overview.**

Lance Clark. Washington, DC: Refugee Policy Group, 1987. 33p.

Prepared through a Ford Foundation field office grant (Nairobi), this report offers an overview of post-emergency assistance for refugees in eighteen African countries: Angola, Botswana, Burundi, Ethiopia, Kenya, Lesotho, Malawi, Mozambique, Namibia, Rwanda, Somalia, South Africa, Swaziland, Tanzania, Uganda, Zambia, Zimbabwe and Djibouti. Four brief sections operationalize terms and definitions, discuss phases of refugee assistance, and offer a statistical summary of refugees as well as prospects for durable solutions in the future. The brief section on Djibouti notes that, although the country's refugee population is not large in absolute terms, 'the situation has been one of the most difficult and controversial in Africa'.

135 **The politics of repatriation: Ethiopian refugees in Djibouti, 1977-83.**

Jeff Crisp. *Review of African Political Economy*, no. 30 (Sept. 1984), p. 73-82.

Djibouti's reputation as an island of political and economic stability amidst the internal and external turmoil of its two larger neighbours, Ethiopia and Somalia, has ensured that this small republic has become a haven for an increasing number of the Horn's refugees. In this brief article, the author, a former member of the Information Division of the British Refugee Council, discusses the political dilemmas faced by Djiboutian authorities in their attempts to resolve the refugee problem. The author discusses the evolution of Djibouti's policy of voluntary repatriation of refugees to their country of origin, centring specifically on Ethiopian refugees in Djibouti during the period 1977-83. Ethiopian refugees are said to have fled Ethiopia and settled into Djibouti because of the 1977 Ogaden War between Ethiopia and Somalia, periodic droughts, repressive government policies in Ethiopia (e.g. land reform) and the desire to find jobs. Discussion of the evolution of Djiboutian refugee policy as concerns voluntary repatriation also includes an analysis of the roles played by the US government (which ceased recruiting refugees for third country resettlement as of January 1982), the United Nations High Commission for Refugees and the Ethiopian government.

136   **Referendum and displacement of population in French Somaliland, 1967: political factors creating refugee situations in Africa.**
      Yassin El-Ayouty.   In: *Refugees south of the Sahara: an African dilemma.*   Edited by Hugh C. Brooks, Yassin El-Ayouty.   Westport, Connecticut: Negro Universities Press, 1970, p. 133-42.

A description of the interplay between politics and the creation of refugees in the French colonial possession of Djibouti. The analysis centres on the French referendum of 19 March 1967 in which the residents of Djibouti were to vote 'yes' or 'no' to the question of continued association with France. The refugee dimension of the vote revolves around a disputed number of ethnic Somalis expelled from the territory before the vote was taken (it was assumed they would vote for independence and subsequently seek Djibouti's unification with Somalia) so that the pro-French Afars (who were in favour of continued association with France) would dominate the vote and ensure continued French control. The author notes that, while the French estimated the number of expelled persons to total roughly 3,000 (and, therefore, not enough to have affected the vote), Somalia claimed that over 10,000 were indeed displaced (and thus ensured a 'no' vote which was won by 7,800 votes). The author lists nine political factors considered key to the 1967 refugee dilemma and pays particular attention to the roles played by the United Nations, Somalia and Ethiopia in the 1967 referendum.

137   **The peopling of the Horn of Africa.**
      Vinige L. Grottanelli.   In: *East Africa and the Orient: cultural syntheses in pre-colonial times.*   Edited by H. Neville Chittick, Robert I. Rotberg.   New York; London: Africana Publishing Company, 1975. 343p. 7 maps. bibliog.

This contribution to the debate over the origins and migratory patterns of the peoples of the Horn of Africa adopts a 'geo-ecological' approach in which four major groups are considered: (1) 'the hunters who first roamed through the arid mainland stalking game'; (2) 'the herdsmen who thousands of years later followed in the wake of the hunters and found that the thorn bush and steppe provided grazing for their cattle, sheep, and camels'; (3) 'the farmers who settled along the river banks to cultivate the narrow strips of rich black soil'; and (4) 'the sailors and merchants from faraway lands who, having found landing places to establish their trading posts, eventually became the founders of towns along the coast'. Despite the difference in approach, the author's argument substantiates that of Lewis (*The Somali conquest of the Horn of Africa* [q.v.]), in which Galla and, subsequently, Somali migrations occurred in basically a north-south pattern.

Migration and Refugees

138 **Involuntary migration and resettlement: the problems and responses of dislocated people.**
Edited by Art Hansen, Anthony Oliver-Smith.   Boulder, Colorado: Westview Press, 1982. 333p. 6 maps. bibliog.

Although not specifically focusing on Djibouti, this offers the best introduction and overview of the problems associated with involuntary migration and resettlement of refugees – an overwhelming problem in the Horn of Africa and, particularly, Djibouti. Unlike other, more limited surveys, the authors divide involuntary migration and resettlement according to three major causal agents: political upheaval (e.g. the 1977-78 Somali-Ethiopian war); natural disasters (e.g. drought); and planned government programs (e.g. government resettlement schemes). Central themes include: (1) characteristics of the stresses of dislocation and resettlement; (2) patterns of individual and group reactions and strategies; (3) similarities and differences among the cases of involuntary migration; and (4) similarities and differences between cases of involuntary migration and cases of voluntary migration and urbanization. Three chapters are of particular interest: 'Introduction: involuntary migration and resettlement: causes and contexts' by Anthony Oliver-Smith and Art Hansen (chapter 1); 'Pastoral nomad settlement in response to drought: the case of the Kenya Somali' by James L. Merryman (chapter 7); and 'From welfare to development: a conceptual framework for the analysis of dislocated people' by Thayer Scudder and Elizabeth Colson (chapter 15).

139 **The origins of the Galla and Somali.**
Herbert S. Lewis.   *Journal of African History*, vol. 7, no. 1 (1966), p. 27-46.

The author discounts the hypothesis that Somali migration began in the northeast of the Horn and pushed in southerly and southeasterly directions, forcing out previously established populations (most notably the Galla). Building on linguistic evidence, the author instead argues that the Saho, Galla, Somali and Afar ethnic groups originally belonged to a 'single speech community' located in southern Ethiopia. Gradually separating into three distinct groups, these peoples moved in easterly and northeasterly directions eventually populating this portion of the Horn. In evidence directly relevant to the current make-up of Djibouti, the author argues that the 'Afar and Saho were evidently the first to move north-east while the Somali moved into the Horn sometime later. It was not until the sixteenth century, however, that the Galla began their great expansion in all directions but West'. This theory possibly explains the origins and current status of Djibouti's Afar population which is pressured on both sides by the Somali and Galla peoples. After moving northward, the Afars were displaced by Somalis who moved onward to the coast of the Horn. Subsequent northward movements of the Gallas met resistance among the Somali and Afar populations with the Afars eventually being pressured on both sides.

140 **The Somali conquest of the Horn of Africa.**
I. M. Lewis.   *Journal of African History*, vol. 1, no. 2 (1960), p. 213-29.

The historical migrations of peoples in the Horn of Africa, which inevitably contributed to the multi-ethnic make-up of Djibouti, continues to be debated by scholars. In this early article, a noted anthropologist and scholar on Somalia argues that the Hamitic Somali peoples expanded southward from the shores of the Gulf of Aden to the plains of northern Kenya during the last ten centuries. As a result of this southward movement, heavily influenced by Arab migrations, the Somalis displaced the Galla peoples westward into present-day Ethiopia. Furthermore, Bantu populations, who occupied the river basin between the Juba and Shebelle rivers, were pressed further southward into Kenya. As concerns Djibouti, an accompanying westward movement of the Dir Somali grouping is said to have resulted in the establishment of that country's Somali Issa and Gadaboursi groupings. In a later article by the same author, however, the hypothesis of a north-south migration of Somalis is discounted. Rather, the author argues that both the Galla and the Somali peoples originated in southern Ethiopia, with the Somali expanding to the east and north long before the Galla. See I. M. Lewis's 'The Origins of the Galla and Somali' (*Journal of African History*, vol. 7, no. 1 (1966), p. 27-46).

141 **Beyond the headlines: refugees in the Horn of Africa.**
Hiram A. Ruiz.   Washington, DC: US Committee for Refugees, 1988.
44p. map. bibliog.

The US Committee for Refuges (USCR) is a public information and advocacy program of the American Council for Nationalities Service (ACNS) and, since 1958, has sought to encourage greater involvement of the US public in efforts to assist refugees throughout the world. This particular issue of the USCR's occasional paper series is an excellent summary and analysis of the refugee problem in the Horn of Africa and, particularly, Djibouti as of the beginning of 1988. The first portion of the essay summarizes the historical aspects of the refugee problem, centring specifically on the numerous conflicts both within and between the various states of the Horn. The second section documents the changing nature of refugee populations in individual countries in the Horn and how their governments have responded to the refugee challenge. Each particular refugee population is discussed separately at length, including Ethiopian refugees in Somalia, Ethiopian refugees in Djibouti (divided between urban and rural refugees), Ethiopian refugees in Sudan, Sudanese refugees in Ethiopia and Somali refugees in Ethiopia. In a concluding section, USCR makes seven recommendations for revising/changing several aspects of refugee policy in the Horn. Yearly updates of refugee populations and policies can be found in *World refugee survey* (q.v.), annually published by USCR.

142 **Bantu, Galla and Somali migrations in the Horn of Africa: a reassessment of the Juba/Tana area.**
E. R. Turton.   *Journal of African History*, vol. 16, no. 4 (1975),
p. 519-37.

The article presents a reinterpretation of population movements in the Horn of Africa, particularly the early Bantu, Galla, and Somali inhabitants of the region. The author argues that the Somali obtained control around the area of the Juba River in the 15th century by pushing out the Bantu-speaking peoples. At a later date the Galla from southern Ethiopia encroached upon the area causing further retreat of the Bantu-speaking peoples and also the migration of the Somalis northwards. The author concludes that the traditional view of Somali movement southward in the 19th century as a conquest of the Galla must be seen instead as the reconquest of the area long disputed.

143 **Horn of Africa: the eternal coming and going.**
United Nations High Commission for Refugees. *Refugees*, no. 72
(Feb. 1990), p. 19-38.

The most up-to-date summary (at the time of writing) of the refugee problem in the
Horn of Africa, including Djibouti. Written under the auspices of the United Nations
High Commission of Refugees (UNHCR), ten articles focus on the individual countries
of Somalia, Ethiopia, the Sudan and Djibouti. The two articles on Djibouti are written
by Tala Skari. The first article, entitled 'Reluctant asylum' (p. 24-26), describes the
dilemmas faced by Djiboutian authorities due to the influx of over 30,000 Somali
refugees since the intensification of the Somali civil war in mid-1988. The second
article, entitled 'No longer any reason to stay' (p. 26-27), describes how Dikhil, once
the home of approximately 20,000 Ethiopian refugees during the 1980s, is no longer a
home to refugees due to the success of a UNHCR-sponsored program of 'voluntary
repatriation'. The authors note that of approximately 40,000 Ethiopians who lived as
refugees throughout Djibouti, 25,000 took part in the UNHCR repatriation program,
9,000 emigrated to 'third' countries or resettlement (most notably the United States,
Australia, Sweden and Canada), and 1,450 remain in-country.

Profil d'une minorité: les Yéménites de Djibouti à la veille de l'indépendance.
(Profile of a minority: the Yemeni of Djibouti just prior to independence.)
See item no. 163.

World refugee survey.
See item no. 316.

Ethnicity and Population

144 Afar vs. Issa: looming conflict?
Bulletin of the Africa Institute of South Africa, vol. 15, no. 5 (1977),
p. 100-107.

Written just prior to Djibouti's independence on 27 June 1977, the article attempts to
present the obstacles to that country's internal stability by focusing on ethnic rivalry
between the Afars and Issas. The article attributes the stabilization of the situation to
the French military presence of 6,000 troops in Djibouti. The two primarily ethnically-
based political parties – the Afar-based National Union for Independence (UNI) and
Issa-dominated African Popular Independence League (LPAI) – are described as
mutually distrustful of the other's intentions. The article promotes the idea that the
Soviet Union is, perhaps, the best power to ensure stability between the two socialist
states of Ethiopia and Somalia. Indeed, a significant portion of the article is devoted to
discussing Ethiopian and Somali intervention in Djibouti's domestic politics.

145 Les Danakils du cercle de Tadjourah. (Afars of the Tadjoura circle.)
Max Albospeyre.   In: *Mer Rouge, Afrique orientale, études
sociologiques et linguistiques: préhistoire – explorations – perspectives
d'avenir.*   Edited by Max Albospeyre et al.   Paris: J. Peyronnet,
1959, p. 103-61. (Cahiers de l'Afrique et l'Asie, no. 5).

An excellent overview of the Afar peoples who inhabit the Tadjoura region of
Djibouti. The first half of the article focuses on the socio-political customs and beliefs
of Afar society, including concepts of justice and property. Especially useful is the
graphic representation of the markings utilized by different Afar groups to brand their
camels, a genealogical table of the Tadjoura region's pure Adali (reigning families),
and an eighteen-page table of the various heads of Afar sultanates. Specifically, the
table lists the historical names and various heads of numerous Afar groups, subgroups,
and factions and subfactions of the Tadjoura and Raheita sultanates. The second half
of the article describes Afar material life (e.g., food, clothing, habitat and
transhumance), family life (e.g. marriage, divorce, circumcision and funerals) and
folklore (e.g. dance, music, proverbs and sorcery). Also included is a listing of existing
mosques in the area as of the early 1950s.

146 **Notes sur les 'Afar de la région de Tadjoura: Tadjoura, Sismo, Djibouti, novembre 1935-septembre 1937.** (Notes on the Afar of the region of Tadjoura: Tadjoura, Sismo, Djibouti, November 1935-September 1937).
Marcel Chailley, reviewed and corrected by E. Chedeville, R. Ferry, preface by Robert Cornevin. Paris: Académie des Sciences d'Outre Mer, 1980. 124p. bibliog.

The author was a French officer stationed in Djibouti from 1935 to 1937 during which time he wrote this manuscript. The original manuscript was reviewed and corrected by E. Chedeville and R. Ferry and, subsequently, was published in 1980. The book is a very authoritative source on the ethnography and general customs of the Afar ethnic group of Djibouti, especially as pertains to those living in the Tadjoura region. Numerous short sections are devoted to the Afar legend concerning that people's origins; clothing, hair styles, jewellery and scars; living quarters; life in the rural areas; birthing customs; initiation ceremony for young men; circumcision; the rite of marriage; funeral customs; social societies and hierarchy; reunions; alliances; etiquette; ornaments of war; usage of tobacco and khat (*catha edulis*); literature; rural medicine; religion, superstition and sorcery; games; arms, forges and tools; usage of fire; fashioning and tanning of sandals, rope and skins; slave trade; and caravan trade with Ethiopia. The text is complemented by numerous hand drawings and twelve photographs of the various aspects of Afar ethnography described in the text.

147 **Comparaison anthropologique entre les Afars et les Issas de Djibouti.** (Anthropological comparison between the Afars and Issas of Djibouti.) M. Charpin, J.-P. Georget. *Mémoires de la Société d'Anthropologie de Paris*, vol. 13 (1977), p. 113-19.

The purpose of this study is to explore the morphological differences between the two major indigenous ethnic groups of Djibouti: the Afars and the Issas. Toward this end, the authors collected a host of data from a sample of 208 Afars and 180 Issas. Among the points of comparison were measurements of physical features (such as height), blood type and digital patterns of the hands of each individual. Two tables list the similarities and differences between the two groups. The authors conclude that some of the differences are due to cross-breeding between the Afars and members of the Arabian peninsula.

148 **The prehistoric cultures of the Horn of Africa; an analysis of the Stone Age cultural and climatic succession in the Somalilands and the eastern parts of Abyssinia.** John Desmond Clark. New York: Octagon Books, 1972. 386p. bibliog.

This book, the result of field research carried out between 1941 and 1946, serves as a useful introduction to the Stone Age archaeology or prehistory of the Horn of Africa, including the region currently known as Djibouti. The introductory portion of the book describes the physical geography (chapter 1), and work of previous investigators prior to the 1940s (chapter 2), including a special section entitled 'French Somaliland and the Southern Danakil [Afar] rift'. Part two, which comprises five chapters, accumulates geological and climatic evidence from six major (deemed 'special') areas of the Horn: western British Somaliland, the Nogal Valley, the Webi Shebelli Valley, the Afar rift, the north coast and the east coast. Part three, comprising six chapters, examines the cultural and derivative industrial prehistories of each of the special areas denoted above. Finally, in chapter 14, an attempt is made to correlate the findings of the relationship between the cultures and climates in the Horn with other areas of the African continent and southern Arabia. The author cautions, however, that his 'correlations must not be considered to be other than tentative until they have been confirmed by further research'.

149 **Étude odontologique comparative des Afars et des Somalis.** (A comparative odontological study of Afars and Somalis.)
C. Cluzel, H. Stalens, J. Dehedin. *Bulletins et Mémoires de la Société d'Anthropologie de Paris*, vol. 7 (8th series), no. 1 (Jan.-March 1980), p. 13-27.

In an unusual, but interesting, attempt to study the human geography of juxtaposed ethnic groups, the authors carried out a comparative odontological study of Afars and Somalis living in Djibouti. Specifically, the authors sought to determine what, if any, differences existed between metrical and morphological characters of the teeth of Afars and Somalis living in Djibouti City. One portion of the study consisted of making plaster moulds of the teeth of eighty-eight Djiboutians (eighteen Afars and seventy Somalis). The second portion of the study consisted of the creation of a master file through the direct examination of the teeth of 320 Djiboutians (72 Afars and 248 Somalis). Although minor differences were found between the various subgroupings of the Somali population (Issas, Isaaks, Gadaboursi and Daroud), as well as between the Afars and Somalis, the general conclusion is that 'no relevant differences' exist between the two groups. The data is also compared throughout the text with the results of similar studies carried out among bedouins in Israel, Jewish communities in Yemen and Indochina, and the Tesos of Uganda.

150 **Dermatoglyphes digitaux et palmaires d'Afar (Danakil) et d'Issa (Somali), et le problème du peuplement de la corne de l'Afrique.** (Finger and palmar dermatoglyphics of the Afar (Danakil) and Issa (Somali) and the problem of the peopling of the Horn of Africa.)
Jacqueline Ducros. *L'Anthropologie* (Paris), vol. 83, no. 1 (1979), p. 91-103.

In a unique approach to shedding some light on the debate concerning the origins of Djibouti's population, an analysis was made of the digital patterns (including digital ridge-count) of the hands of the two dominant ethnic groups in that country: the Afars and the Issa Somalis. The author finds that the 'Afar and Issa resemble each other more closely than neighbouring groups; their dermatoglyphics (especially those of the Issa) tie them more closely to Melano-African populations and separate them from leucoderms [such as the Yemenis or Egyptians] which could have contributed to their genesis'. In brief, the data does not support traditional anthropological theories which argue that the origins of the population in Djibouti can be found in a mixture between northern Saharan Arab and sub-Saharan African populations. The bibliography at the end of the article is especially useful.

Ethnicity and Population

151   The Danakil: nomads of Ethiopia's wasteland.
      Victor Englebert.   *National Geographic*, vol. 137, no. 2 (Feb. 1970),
      p. 186-211.
Twenty-one colour photographs and a journalistic text by a Belgian photographer (and
writer) provide an interesting introduction to the Afar peoples who inhabit Ethiopia
and Djibouti. Discussion centres on the author's initial nervousness in crossing the
paths of 'fierce' Afars unassociated with the trek, a meeting with scientist Haroun
Tazieff, the harsh landscape and climate of the Afar territory, and the hazards of
Ethiopia's ongoing guerrilla war for the traveller. A map charts the circular route of
the author's trek around the Afar region in Ethiopia. Discussion clearly focuses on the
sensationalist side of Afar life and customs.

152   Observation ethnopsychiatrique de l'infibulation des femmes en Somalie.
      (An ethno-psychiatric observation of the infibulation of women in
      Somalia.)
      Michel Erlich.   *Ethno-psychiatricia* (Paris), vol. 3 (1979), p. 15-37.
The title of the article is misleading in that the author's observations focus on Djibouti.
Specifically, the article is devoted to explaining the practice of circumcision and
infibulation of young girls among the Somali and Afar peoples who inhabit the
territory. The observations of the author are of special interest due to his unique
experience as having spent eleven years as a doctor in Djibouti. After detailing the
various types found worldwide of what the author calls 'genital mutilation', discussion
turns to the historical origins of the practice. A final section focuses on the functions of
the practice. Whereas one explicit function is described as the protection of the
'chastity of virgins', another explicit function is to 'socially master' the sexuality of the
woman.

153   Djibouti.
      Agnes Guillaume.   In: *L'évaluation des effectifs de la population des
      pays africains*, vol. 1.   Paris: Groupe de Démographie Africaine, 1982,
      p. 41-50.
A short but informative article which summarizes various demographic characteristics
of Djibouti's population as of September 1979. Of particular interest are four charts
and tables documenting the growth and repartition of the country's population. Based
on Djiboutian census statistics, the first table charts the growth of Djibouti's
indigenous and non-indigenous (e.g. French) populations from 1921 to 1961. The
second table (including citations for the sources of some figures) portrays the evolution
of the population living in Djibouti City, as well as the country as a whole, from 1885
to 1972. The two graphs portray the population's growth (1880-1970) and repartition
by age groups (1972). According to this latter graph, fifty-one per cent of Djibouti's
population in 1972 was less than fifteen years of age.

154   An analysis of Afar pastoralism in the northeastern rangelands of
      Ethiopia.
      Johan Helland.   Nairobi: International Livestock Centre for Africa,
      1980. 61p. bibliog. (Working Document, no. 19).
The result of field research among the Afar pastoralists in an area subsumed in 1980
under Ethiopia's Northeast Rangelands Development Project, much of the descriptive

content is directly relevant to the Afar peoples who inhabit neighbouring Djibouti – especially as concerns development among pastoral groups. After briefly introducing the situational aspects of the study, an examination is made of over-stocking and over-grazing among the Afar and the resilience and self-regulating processes of pastoral systems. Other brief sections describe herding and husbandry among the Afar, labour and livestock requirements, and methods of correcting food and labour deficiencies. Of particular interest is a short description of territorial and political organization among the Afar. Among these are distinctions between the Asaihimera and Adohimera Afar subgroupings and the Afarfima, or a code for the maintenance of peaceful relations and interaction among members of the Afar ethnic group. Final sections deal with the problems associated with the Northeast Rangelands Development Project and the place of pastoralists in development planning. The author also offers a schematic of the essential elements of Afar pastoralism.

155 **Dualism in Somali notions of power.**
I. M. Lewis. *Journal of the Royal Anthropological Institute*, vol. 93, part 1 (1963), p. 109-16.
An argument is made by the author that Somali pastoralists distinguish between two types of power, secular and nonsecular, and this distinction is directly related to the ecological and social environments in which they must operate. Secular power has its origins in the pastoralist's unending search to secure livestock and kin. The competitive nature of politics among Somali pastoralists requires that secular power be equated with numerical and physical strength. This point is well made given the primacy of the *dia* paying group and physical force in Somali politics and social interaction. There are no attempts to validate secular power in religious terms. Instead the author states that Somalis believe that 'might makes right'. He also points out that the 'politically' or 'numerically' weak members of society are attributed with mystical powers to assist them in their secular interactions with the 'numerically' powerful.

156 **Force and fission in northern Somali lineage structure.**
I. M. Lewis. *American Anthropologist*, vol. 63, part 1 (1961), p. 94-112.
The traditional view of politics in segmentary lineage systems is that relations among members is dependent upon genealogical position. The author states that consistent with this view is the belief that groups which are descended from a common ancestor are genealogical equivalents, political equals and often united political actors. However, the Somali segmentary lineage system does not fit this typical interpretation of politics. Rather, the author discusses those factors that cause the Somali system to differ from other such systems. Among these are the nature of pastoralism among the Somali and the dominance of a contractual alliance represented by the *dia* paying group. The author concludes with a discussion of how those factors influence the nature of conflict, conflict resolution and social relationships in Somali society.

157 **Historical aspects of genealogies in northern Somali social structure.**
I. M. Lewis. *Journal of African History*, vol. 3, no. 1 (1962), p. 35-48.
The author debates whether the often believed position that oral tradition, particularly genealogies, and legends of the past are used by segmentary societies to validate actions in the present. In other words anthropologists must use caution when using oral tradition as an historical source, since it is often manipulated to reflect the current balance of political power in a 'tribal' society. The author is of the opinion that

Ethnicity and Population

Somalia does not fit this model because the clan families of the north are too large to act as politically united and organized bodies. Instead it is the *dia* paying group and the contractual alliance developed on the basis of patrilineal affiliation that define political activity and form the basis of political unity. Somali genealogies do represent a certain amount of myth-making since they trace their descent from Arabia. However, this is an attempt to illustrate the historical links Somalia has had with Arabia and its commitment as a people to the religion of Islam.

158 **Peoples of the Horn of Africa: Somali, Afar and Saho.**

I. M. Lewis.   London: International African Institute, 1969. 204p. map. bibliog.

This volume, the first of a three-part series on northeastern Africa (which in turn is part of a comprehensive ethnographic survey of Africa), remains the standard ethnographic survey in the English language of the Somali, Afar and Saho peoples who inhabit the Horn of Africa. The majority of the volume is devoted to a discussion of the Somali and Afar peoples with analysis falling under the following broad categories: demography, physical environment, main features of the economy, social organization and political structure, main cultural features and religion.

159 **The so-called 'Galla graves' of northern Somaliland.**

I. M. Lewis.   *Man*, vol. 61 (June 1961), p. 103-06.

In this brief article the author examines the significance and purpose of stone burial cairns found throughout the Somali-inhabited territories, including Djibouti. The author notes that the cairns vary considerably in height from six to eighteen feet and in diameter from twelve to twenty feet. In contrast to conventional wisdom that these cairns constituted ancient graves of the Galla peoples of the region, the author argues that some are of fairly recent construction and contain Somali remains. These results are based on the excavation of three cairns in northern Somalia. Of particular interest is a table comparing the measurements of skeletal remains from the cairns with those of Somali and Galla skeletons.

160 **Spirit possession and deprivation cults.**

I. M. Lewis.   *Man*, vol. 1, no. 3 (1966), p. 307-29.

The author examines the existence of spirit possession among Somali nomadic pastoralists and discerns that there is a relationship between spirit possession and certain groups or classes in society that feel deprived in some absolute sense. For example, the author sees a relationship between Somali women who are afflicted by a *sar* (a malevolent spirit seeking luxurious things) and insecurity in their marriages. Spirit possession in this sense may be interpreted as an inhibitor of abuse and/or neglect of one's wife. The author describes the different contexts of spirit possession in Somalia and the groups or classes often afflicted by them.

161 **Guerriers et sorciers en Somalie.** (Warriors and sorcerers in Somalia.)

Alphonse Lippman.   Paris: Hachette, 1953. 256p.

The author, the son of a French colonial administrator, followed in his father's footsteps and served throughout the Red Sea region from 1921-37 and 1945-49. This book focuses on that portion of the author's career spent in Djibouti (1921-30). His job was to carry French colonial authority into the interior of the country and 'pacify' the often bloody conflicts between Afars and Issas. He offers an extremely well-written account of French colonial administration and, most important, the 'warriors' and

66

'sorcerers' of Somaliland, or those Issa and Afar populations inhabiting Djibouti. The account is especially intriguing as the author describes his conversion to Islam and how this aided him in seeking the respect of the Islamic Afar and Issa populations (chapter 2), resignation of his position because of serious differences with the local French governor (chapter 18), and his relationship with Henry de Monfreid, a famous French writer living in the territory (chapters 5 and 19).

162 **Les populations de la côte française des Somalis.** (The populations of the French Somali Coast.)
Robert Muller.   In: *Mer Rouge Afrique orientale, études sociologiques et linguistiques: préhistoire – explorations – perspectives d'avenir.*
Edited by Max Albospeyre et al.   Paris: J. Peyronnet, 1959, p. 45-102.
(Cahiers de l'Afrique et l'Asie, no. 5).

The author offers an interesting overview of the non-European populations inhabiting Djibouti as of the late 1950s. After briefly introducing the reader to the repartition of the various populations within the country, the bulk of the essay is devoted to describing various details of the nomadic Issa and Afar ethnic groups. Several characteristics of the two major groupings are compared and contrasted: social organization; family and the individual; livestock and the nomadic lifestyles; material life; justice, customary law and war; religion and beliefs; and languages and folklore. A final section examines those populations which are sedentary, including portions of the Issa and Afar peoples. The primary foci of this section, however, are various immigrant populations within the country: Arabs, Somalis (from other territories), Ethiopians, Indians and Sudanese (European populations are not discussed). Several observations are made concerning the differences between the urban and nomadic populations.

163 **Profil d'une minorité: les Yéménites de Djibouti à la veille de l'indépendance.** (Profile of a minority: the Yemeni of Djibouti just prior to independence.)
Alain Rouaud.   In: *Minorités et gens de mer en océan Indien, XIXe-XXe siècles: table ronde IHPOM, CHEAM, CERSOI, ACOI, Sénanque 1979, GRECO-océan Indien.*   Aix-en-Provence, France: Institut d'Histoire des Pays d'Outre-Mer, Université de Provence, 1979, p. 163-79.

This profile of the minority Yemeni population in Djibouti just prior to independence constitutes but one portion of a larger conference devoted to examining the role of minority populations within the Indian Ocean region as a whole. The organizations taking part in the conference include: Institut d'Histoire des Pays d'Outre-Mer (IHPOM); the Centre d'Études et de Recherches sur les Sociétés de l'Océan Indien (CERSOI); Association des Chercheurs de l'Océan Indien (ACOI); and the Centre de Hautes Études de l'Afrique Moderne (CHEAM). The author demonstrates how the Yemeni – primarily skilled construction workers – migrated to Djibouti City in the late 19th century as a result of French colonial needs. Underscoring the preliminary nature of his research, the author offers tables demonstrating the growth of the Yemeni population (both in total numbers and as a percentage of the non-European indigenous population). In 1906, for example, the Yemeni numbered 2,576 (49 per cent of the local population). By 1977, the Yemeni population had grown to roughly 18,000 but only constituted 15 per cent of the local population. Very informative brief sections

67

subsequently detail the evolution of the Yemeni population's importance within the local community; social, ethnic and geographical origins; professional activities; social cohesion; political representation within various colonial executive bodies; and relations with other ethnic groups. Two tables document the Yemeni percentage of Djiboutian boat traffic with neighbouring areas in 1947 (922 boats out of a total of 971) and the evolving political weight of Yemeni representatives (relative to other groups) within seven colonial executive bodies from 1946 to 1968.

164 **Cross cousin marriage among the patrilineal 'Afar.**
George Savard.   In: *Proceedings of the third international conference of Ethiopian studies, Addis Ababa (3-7 April) 1966.*   Addis Ababa: Institute of Ethiopian Studies, Haile Selassie I University, 1970, vol. 3, p. 89-98.

The Afar kinship system, like that of most African ethnic groups, is based on patrilineality. Yet the author demonstrates how the Afar are unique in their preference for cross-cousin marriages, which are said to be related to ecological and social factors. For example, a man can marry a woman born from another woman of his clan. Conversely, a woman can marry a man from her mother's clan (excluding the mother's brother, father and father's brother). Yet, the Afar usually marry only one cross-cousin with other wives belonging to different clans. Also discussed are the living arrangements that result from such marriages, inheritance rights and potential conflicts with both matrilateral and patrilateral clansmen, and the importance of the mother in Afar society. In the case of inheritance rights, for example, the author notes that paternal brothers, who have rights to the father's wealth, are potential enemies. 'On the other hand, one expects no trouble at all, but only help from his matrilateral relatives. They have no right to the paternal inheritance and will not compete for it'.

165 **Un example du pouvoir traditionnel Afar: le sultanat de Tadjoura.** (An example of traditional Afar power: the Tadjoura sultanate).
Aramis Houmed Soule.   *Pount*, no. 17 (May 1986), p. 3-11.

This article is a much-welcomed description of traditional power and organization among Djibouti's Afar population. The case study selected for description is the Tadjoura sultanate. The first section of the article details the political organization of the sultanate, including the alternating of power among two major families (to avoid the autocratic excesses that one family rule would portend) and the powers inherent in the office and figure of the sultan. The second section briefly describes the social organization of the Tadjoura sultanate, including the stratification, command and hierarchy of various Afar subgroups. The second half of the article focuses on the political process of designating a new sultan and the official ceremony that accompanies his enthronement, including the *kukta* or announcement/reading of the official proclamation. The last such ceremony took place on 8 April 1985 when Chehem Ahmed became the sultan. Especially useful is a full-page, hand-drawn map delimiting the areas inhabited by the Afar populations of the Horn, as well as the political boundaries and names of the various traditional Afar sultanates.

First footsteps in East Africa.
See item no. 45.

Travels in southern Abyssinia, through the country of Adal to the Kingdom of Shoa.
See item no. 51.

Coutumes somalis. (Somali customs.)
See item no. 112.

A pastoral democracy: a study of pastoralism and politics among the northern Somali of the Horn of Africa.
See item no. 177.

Ethiopia, revolution, and the question of nationalities: the case of the Afar.
See item no. 183.

Djibouti and the question of Afar nationalism.
See item no. 184.

Le xeer Issa: étude d'un contrat social. (The Issa xeer: study of a social contract.)
See item no. 192.

The influence of Islam on the Afar.
See item no. 200.

Afar pastoralists in transition and the Ethiopian revolution.
See item no. 283.

Politics and
Administration

166 **Djibouti's three-front struggle for independence: 1967-77.**
Fanter Agonafer.   PhD dissertation, Denver University, Denver,
Colorado, 1979. 204p. map. bibliog.

The 'three-front' struggle for independence noted in the title of this dissertation refers
to Djibouti's efforts toward independence vis-à-vis France, Ethiopia and Somalia.
Whereas in 1958 and 1967 Djiboutians voted in national referenda to preserve
continued association with France, the 1977 referendum resulted in a Djiboutian vote
for independence. This study examines Djiboutian politics from 1966 to 1977 to
determine the internal and external forces that resulted in the 1977 outcome. The first
two chapters serve as a brief introduction and historical background to Djibouti's
independence movement. The following three chapters examine the character of
Djibouti's economy and politics from 1957 to 1967, regional and international interests
in the territory, and internal political developments from 1967 to 1977. Especially
valuable are the author's discussions of competing Djiboutian political parties and
guerrilla movements.

167 **French Somaliland.**
Alphonso A. Castagno.   In: *The educated African: a country-by-
country survey of educational development in Africa.* Edited by Helen
A. Kitchen.   New York: Praeger, 1962, p. 108-13.

French-administered education in Djibouti was established by a decree of 12 April
1913, with the first school, the Djibouti public primary school, opening in 1923,
followed by the establishment of schools in Tadjoura (1932) and Dikhil (1940). This
article, though obviously dated, offers a good overview of French educational efforts in
Djibouti prior to and including the 1950s. Discussion includes indigenous opposition to
educational growth, the nature of the school system (i.e. programs offered, nomadic
education and teacher training), comparisons with educational development in the
Somali Republic, and comparisons of French efforts with those of the other colonial
and regional powers. Especially useful are various statistics noting the number of
schools and students in 1944 and 1956.

70

168 **Politics, security and development in small states.**
Edited by Colin Clarke, Tony Payne. London: Allen & Unwin, 1987.
238p.

Although this volume does not deal specifically with Djibouti, it provides an excellent
theoretical overview of the dilemmas facing so-called 'mini-states' within the
international system. The first four chapters examine in general fashion the political,
social, economic and security aspects of mini-states, while the following eight chapters
examine in detail the case studies of Grenada, Antigua and Barbuda, Fiji, Mauritius,
the Gambia, Swaziland, Malta and Cyprus. Especially interesting is chapter 13, by
Robin Cohen, entitled 'An academic perspective'. The major sections of this chapter
include 'The triumph of self-determination or the weakness of empire'; 'The collapse
of ideological legitimacy'; 'The rise of rival powers'; and 'From nations without states
to states without nations'. One of the primary conclusions of the book directly relevant
to Djibouti is that 'geopolitical location backed by skilful bargaining can be used to
extract financial support from a regional or superpower patron, especially now that
foreign bases have taken on renewed significance'. For another useful general overview
which, however, also ignores the case study of Djibouti, see Robin Cohen's (ed.)
African islands and enclaves (Beverly Hills, California: Sage Publications, 1983.)

169 **Encore la France coloniale: Djibouti, Antilles, Guyane, Mayotte,
Nouvelle-Calédonie, Réunion, Tahiti.** (Still colonial France: Djibouti,
Antilles, Guiana, Mayotte, New Caledonia, Reunion, Tahiti.)
Collectif des Chrétiens pour l'Autodétermination des Départements
d'Outre-Mer-Territoires d'Outre Mer (DOM-TOM). Paris:
L'Harmattan, 1976. 164p.

This book is the result of a colloquium held at the Sorbonne on 15 May 1976 and
sponsored by the Collective of Christians for Self-Determination of Overseas
Departments-Overseas Territories (DOM-TOM), an organization which opposes
continued French rule in what it terms the 'forgotten of decolonization'. Included in
the proceedings are two sections on Djibouti which, prior to 1977, remained an
overseas territory of France. The first section of the book describes France's approach
to maintaining continued control over the overseas lands. Sections two and three
examine the case studies which fall under the headings of either overseas departments
or territories, respectively. Finally, section four centres on what has been termed 'the
struggle for self-determination'.

170 **La brigade des missions impossibles.** (The brigade of impossible
missions.)
Gilbert Deflez. Paris: Jacques Granchier, Éditeur, 1979. 215p.

A documentary of the birth and evolution of France's Groupe d'Intervention de la
Gendarmerie Nationale (GIGN; Intervention Group of the National Police),
nicknamed in the title of the book as the 'Brigade of impossible missions'. Of
particular interest to the scholar of Djibouti is the chapter entitled 'Les 30 otages de
Djibouti' ('The thirty hostages of Djibouti', p. 39-50), which is the official and
colourful account of the GIGN's rescue operation at Loyoda, Djibouti in January
1975. The target of the operation was the rescue of thirty French school children who
had been taken hostage in their school bus by members of the Liberation Front of the
Somali Coast (FLCS). The net results of the operation, which also included the
exchange of fire with Somali Republic troops, were the deaths of one child and six of
the FLCS combatants.

Politics and Administration

171 **Djibouti: mini-state on the Horn of Africa.**
Alain Fenet. In: *Horn of Africa: from 'scramble for Africa' to East-West conflict. (Das Horn von Afrika, vom scramble for Africa zum ost-west konflikt).* Bonn, GFR: Forschungsinstitut der Friedrich-Ebert-Stiftung, 1983, p. 59-69. (Analysen aus der Abteilung Entwicklungsländerforschung; hr. 106/07).

This chapter emerged from a symposium on the Horn of Africa held in Bonn, West Germany, 28-29 June 1982. Although this chapter is written in English, several others in the volume are written in German. The author, a French scholar at the Université de Picardie, offers a cautious presentation of Djibouti's first five years of independence. It is noted that Djibouti as of 1982 had achieved superficial control over its political and economic destiny. Since President Hassan Gouled Aptidon is noted as successfully eliminating foreign threats to the established *status quo* of Djibouti independence, the author argues that 'only internal splits could endanger the balance . . . and provoke foreign intervention'. After summarizing efforts in the field of economic development – most notably the diversification of Djibouti's economic links with France – ethnic problems and the president's alleged favouritism toward his clan (Mamassan) are criticized. In this regard, the author argues that President Gouled has sought to 'preserve Issa positions' at the expense of 'national conciliation'. Cautious of what the future holds for Djibouti, the author concludes: 'Everything is still possible in Djibouti, nothing is irreversible yet'.

172 **The right of self-determination in very small places.**
Thomas M. Franck, Paul Hoffman. *Journal of International Law and Politics*, vol. 8, no. 3 (winter, 1976), p. 331-86.

Relying heavily on United Nations documents, this article centres on the evolution of the international legal dictum of self-determination and how it relates to smaller territories – 'the flotsam and jetsam of empire' – bypassed by the decolonization process of the post-Second World War period. The authors note that the 'importance of these seemingly unimportant imperial shavings lies not merely in their capacity for generating passionate and dangerous international disputes, not in the territories' very considerable strategic and economic value, but in the legal precedents being established in the troubled process of their decolonization'. The international legal precedents established by the decolonization of the Spanish Sahara and Portuguese Timor are applied to the case studies of Djibouti and Belize. In short, the authors argue that the crises engendered in both the Western Sahara and Timor cases have cracked the international 'normative structure' of 'democratic self determination within recognized boundaries', which bodes ill for orderly processes of decolonization in both Djibouti and Belize. Also discussed are the implications of the denial of self-determination in Gibraltar and the Falkland Islands.

173 **African liberation movements: contemporary struggles against white minority rule.**
Richard Gibson. London: Oxford University Press, 1972. 350p. bibliog.

Following the guidelines established by the Organization of African Unity's (OAU) African Liberation Committee, the author set out to establish a general survey of those national liberation movements seeking independence against colonial and other direct forms of white-minority rule. A brief but, informative, section is devoted to an examination of two Djiboutian liberation movements: the Front de Libération de la

Côte des Somalis (FLCS – Liberation Front of the Somali Coast) and the Mouvement de Libération de Djibouti (MLD – Liberation Movement of Djibouti). Whereas the FLCS was a Somali-supported guerrilla movement which sought Djibouti's inclusion in a pan-Somali state, the Afar-based MLD organization sought Djibouti's closer association and, perhaps, attachment to Ethiopia. Other sections examine the evolution of liberation movements in South Africa, Southwest Africa (Namibia), Rhodesia (Zimbabwe), and the former Portugese territories of Angola, Mozambique, Guinea-Bissau, Cape Verde, and Sao Tome and Principe.

174 **Workers, capital and the state in the Ethiopian region, 1919-1974.**
Thomas Charles Killion.   PhD dissertation, Stanford University, Stanford, California, 1985. 2 vols. bibliog.

Adopting a political-economy approach, the author argues that the historical development of workers' organizations in the Ethiopian region – culminating in the 'high water mark' of the 1974 Ethiopian revolution and the 1984 creation of the Workers' Party of Ethiopia – is the result of differing patterns of relations between capital, the Ethiopian state and precapitalist socioeconomic systems in the region. Included in the designation of an 'Ethiopian region' or 'Ethiopian political economy' is the Ethiopian empire and the former European political enclaves of Italian-ruled Eritrea, French Somaliland (Djibouti) and British Somaliland. These three political enclaves are said to have contained numerous distinct ethno-linguistic groups whose members maintained their own noncapitalist socioeconomic systems, becoming incorporated into the Ethiopian regional political economy during the 20th century due to combined Abyssinian and European imperialist expansion. A significant portion of the dissertation is devoted to Djibouti. Chapter 2 centres on the nature of French penetration into the Horn of Africa through the creation of Djibouti while chapter 5 offers a highly illuminating analysis of the evolution and development of workers' organizations (1919-38) in Djibouti connected with the Djibouti–Addis Ababa railway. Chapter 8 focuses on the relationship between the formation of workers' organizations and state intervention as concerns the railway during the 1946-62 period.

175 **Somalia: a nation in search of a state.**
David D. Laitin, Said S. Samatar.   Boulder, Colorado: Westview Press, 1987. 188p.

Written by two noted specialists on Somalia, this general volume is important reading for a full understanding of the politics of the Horn of Africa and Djibouti's place therein. Seven chapters offer succinct overviews on various aspects of Somali political-economy. Among those are: 'The peopling of the Somali peninsula' (chapter 1); 'Society and culture' (chapter 2); 'Colonialism and the struggle for national independence' (chapter 3); 'Government and politics' (chapter 4); 'The economy' (chapter 5); 'Foreign relations' (chapter 6); and 'Into the 1990s: problems and possibilities of social transformation' (chapter 7). Minor references to Djibouti are interspersed throughout the text.

176 **Nationalism and self-determination in the Horn of Africa.**
Edited by I. M. Lewis.   London: Ithaca Press, 1983. 226p. 2 maps.

This twelve-chapter volume, the result of an interdisciplinary workshop sponsored by the Ford Foundation in 1980, is an excellent general introduction to the ambiguous relationship between 'nation' and 'state' in the Horn of Africa. Eleven authors document and discuss competing claims of self-determination and centralization of

Politics and Administration

both national and subnational actors in the region. In chapter 1, I. M. Lewis nicely summarizes the numerous aspects of nationalism and self-determination in the Horn of Africa. Subsequent chapters include Joseph Tubiana's 'The linguistic approach to self-determination' (chapter 2); Hussein M. Adam's 'Language national-consciousness and identity – the Somali experience' (chapter 3); Hakan Wiberg's 'Self-determination as an international issue' (chapter 4); I. M. Lewis's 'Pre-and post-colonial forms of polity in Africa' (chapter 5); James Mayall's 'Self-determination and the OAU' (chapter 6); Sally Healy's 'The changing idiom of self-determination in the Horn of Africa' (chapter 7); A. Triulzi's 'Competing views of national identity in Ethiopia' (chapter 8); Paul Baxter's 'The problem of the Oromo' (chapter 9); Michael Reisman's 'Somali self-determination in the Horn' (chapter 10); David Pool's 'Eritrean nationalism (chapter 11); and Patrick Gilkes' 'Centralism and the Ethiopian PMAC' (chapter 12).

177   **A pastoral democracy: a study of pastoralism and politics among the northern Somali of the Horn of Africa.**
       I. M. Lewis.   New York: Africana Publishing, 1982.

Written by a noted British anthropologist in the early 1960s, as the result of twenty-two months of field research, this book constitutes one of the landmark works on Somali politics and pastoralism of direct relevance to the Somali populations found in Djibouti. Among the topics discussed are: the relationship between Somalia's ecological environment and clan divisions (chapter 2); pastoralism and the structure of grazing encampments (chapter 3); settlement and cultivation (chapter 4); clanship and the paradigm of the lineage system (chapter 5); clanship and contract (chapter 6); authority and sanctions (chapter 7); force and feud (chapter 8); and nationalism and party politics (chapter 9). A new preface briefly situates the book in relation to recent advances in the field of Somali studies. For a highly critical analysis, which takes Lewis to task for overemphasizing the importance of clan politics, see Ahmed I. Samatar's *Socialist Somalia: rhetoric and reality* (London; Atlantic Heights, New Jersey: Zed Books, 1988).

178   **National and class conflict in the Horn of Africa.**
       John Markakis.   Cambridge, England: Cambridge University Press, 1987. 314p. 11 maps. bibliog. (African Studies Series, no. 55).

The scope of this study of politics in the Horn of Africa covers Ethiopia, Somalia, Sudan, Djibouti and that portion of Kenya inhabited by Somali nomads, although discussion of Djibouti is very limited. The approach is unique, as discussion centres on dissident nationalist political movements whose goal is to change or completely transform the structure of existing states in the Horn. Emphasis is placed on the 'material' nature of conflict which is said to be inevitably directed against the state – 'the custodian of wealth and protector of privilege'. The author argues that the state 'is both the goal of the contest and the primary means through which the contest is waged. Consequently, it lies at the centre of this study, which focuses on the twin linkages between nationalism and the state on the one hand, nationalism and class on the other. The intention is to highlight the material dimension so crucial in forging these links, and it seeks to show that the initial force which binds a group to an emerging state or a nationalist movement is material in nature'. The first four chapters examine adaptation to the environment and the fashioning of social institutions and cultures by pre-colonial traditional societies of the Horn (chapter 1), the impact of imperialism by external powers (chapter 2), the rise of anti-colonial nationalism (chapter 3) and challenges to the post-colonial state (chapter 4). Subsequent chapters deal primarily with the Eritrean revolution (chapter 5), revolution in the southern

Sudan (chapter 6), the Somali unification struggle (chapter 7), and 'garrison socialism' and 'defending the state' in Sudan and Somalia (chapter 8) and Ethiopia (chapter 10). The final chapter draws general conclusions making reference to various theories of nationalism.

179 **Military powers: the League of Arab States: Djibouti, Somalia, Sudan, Egypt and Ethiopia.**
Paris: Société I3C, 1987. 182p.
This hard-to-locate volume offers a detailed comparative summary of the defence establishments within northeast Africa, including a lengthy section on Djibouti. A chronology of major post-independence events and a brief description of political and administrative structures in Djibouti is followed by a three-chart comparison of the economic and military regional balance of power between Djibouti, Ethiopia and Somalia, and a 'geostrategic evaluation' of the country. Of particular interest is an organizational chart of the Djiboutian Armed Forces, as well as a wealth of data on the country's army, air force, navy, gendarmerie and police force. A further five-page chart lists Djibouti's major arms suppliers and the dates and types of equipment bought and delivered during the 1980s. Individual sections also detail Djibouti's military and technical co-operation with France, the US and other foreign countries.

180 **New flags: Republic of Djibouti.**
The Flag Bulletin, vol. 16, no. 5 (Oct.-Nov. 1977), p. 135-37.
Describes the new national flag and coat of arms adopted by Djibouti upon independence in 1977. The flag 'consists of two equal horizontal stripes of light blue over light green, with a white triangle at the hoist bearing the red five-pointed star'. The coat of arms consists of 'a shield and spear flanked by fists brandishing short swords . . . framed by a wreath of leaves in shades of green'. The authors note that differing interpretations surround the choice of colours: 'While some sources have indicated that the green and blue are for the major population groups, the Afars and Issas, with the triangle indicating the unity between them in their struggle for independence as indicated by the red star, Djibouti's president explained the blue as a symbol of the sea and sky, green for the earth, and white for peace'. Afars are said to favour green as representative of their Muslim heritage, while the Issas are said to favour blue as it is the primary colour of the Somali flag. (The Somali flag also contains a star, one point of which is representative of Djibouti as one part of the still divided Somali nation.)

181 **Législature 1982-1987.** (Legislature 1982-1987.)
République de Djibouti. Djibouti: The Author, 1983. 52p.
Upon independence, Djibouti's National Assembly was enlarged from forty to sixty-five deputies. This government-produced publication provides a brief history of the National Assembly, outlines the constitutional bases of executive power, and the organizational structure and functions of the body. Especially useful is a brief description of the different commissions of the assembly. The majority of the booklet provides black-and-white photographs of all the elected deputies (although now somewhat dated), along with their full names, birth date and position within the National Assembly.

Politics and Administration

182 **The independence of Somalia.**
Talaat Saleh. [no place of publication known]: Middle East
Publications, 1959. 56p. map.

Although difficult to find, this booklet constitutes an interesting, but propagandistic, diatribe against Western imperialism in the five Somaliland territories including French-ruled Djibouti. It was published in the Middle East after the independence of Italian Somaliland but prior to the independence of British Somaliland. The author is very supportive of the creation of a 'Greater Somaliland' due to the expectation that such a country would pursue close ties with the Middle Eastern countries. The flavour of this anti-French booklet is portrayed by a section entitled, 'Persecution in the French Somaliland' in which the Somalis are described as fighting 'tooth and nail' against the 'ferocious French imperialists'. Various sections centre on the relationship between Western imperialism and the spread of Arabic, Arab blood relationships, Israeli intrigues, border disputes, and the 'anxieties' of the West as concerns the 'Greater Somaliland' issue.

183 **Ethiopia, revolution, and the question of nationalities: the case of the Afar.**
Kassim Shehim. *Journal of Modern African Studies*, vol. 23, no. 2
(1983), p. 331-48.

The writer notes that the Ethiopian government – both before and after the 1974 revolution – recognized the strategic and commercial importance of those regions inhabited by the Afar known as the 'Afar triangle'. The Afar triangle includes several provinces of Ethiopia and the three districts which comprise northern and eastern Djibouti. Although the article emphasizes the evolving historical relationshp between the Afar in Ethiopia and the central government in Addis Ababa, it has important implications for the Afar triangle as a whole. For example, it is noted that Afar elders unsuccessfully attempted to convince Ethiopian Emperor Haile Selassie of the benefits of creating an Afar state, a proposal that ultimately surfaced in the post-revolution years as a goal of the Afar National Liberation Movement (ANLM). It was argued that the 'creation of such a state would serve as a pole of attraction for the Afar of Djibouti, who would seriously consider joining the Ethiopian Empire as an alternative to absorption in a greater Somalia, and would also aid in the pacification of the Province of Eritrea by detaching the Afar areas and thus assuring access to the Red Sea port of Assab'.

184 **Djibouti and the question of Afar nationalism.**
Kassim Shehim, James Searing. *African Affairs*, vol. 19, no. 315
(April 1980), p. 209-26.

The authors paint a dismal picture of Djiboutian nationalism and the future viability of this nation-state two years after independence in 1977. This interpretation resulted from a perceived conflict between the politically dominant Issa (Somali) ethnic groups and growing Afar nationalist demands. Summarizing what they believe to be the historical factors which have determined the development of Afar political conscious-ness in both the pre- and post-independence periods (centring especially on the role of the French and the Somali–Ethiopian conflict), the authors suggest that ethnic conflict within Djibouti is irremediable and that a partition of the country between Ethiopia and Somalia is the best possible way to defuse 'a potential powder keg in the Horn of Africa'. The authors conclude that there is increasing evidence that the current breakdown of the political system of Djibouti has led to the *de facto* partition of the country into Afar and Issa districts, while the central government controls the capital city. 'Under these conditions it seems abusive to extend the principle of "sacred inviolability" to the borders of Djibouti: such a step would probably only perpetuate the existence of a neo-colonial outpost in the Horn of Africa'. Although twelve years of independence have fostered a unity within Djibouti that seemingly discounts the authors' initial conclusions, the article is an excellent preliminary look at an issue – Djiboutian nationalism – which requires much further analysis and exploration.

185 **Problems of political development in a ministate: the French Territory of the Afars and the Issas.**
Nancy A. Shilling. *Journal of the Developing Areas*, vol. 7 (July 1973), p. 613-34.
The author discusses the possible future viability of Djibouti as an independent 'ministate' or 'mini-territory' within the international political system. Comprising a mere 9,000 square miles, it is argued that Djibouti and other mini-states (such as Lesotho or Fiji) face unique political and economic difficulties which have led some commentators to question whether these states 'can long enjoy genuine independence' and 'fulfil the obligations of international sovereignty sufficiently to merit full, voting membership in international bodies'. The first half of the study centres on potential problems of nation-building within the territory in the context of the 1958 and 1967 referenda. Among these are the economy, cultural pluralism, élite formation, political consensus-building and institution formation. The second half of the study concentrates on the external factors – the interests of neighbouring states and major international powers – which will possibly affect the future political and economic viability of the country. The author concludes that only independence with international guarantees (as opposed to simple independence), continuation as a French colony, total annexation by either Ethiopia or Somalia, or partition and then annexation by Ethiopia and Somalia, can satisfy 'the conflicting demands of the various interested parties' and ensure Djibouti's future viability as an independent mini-state.

186 **Somali nationalism: international politics and the drive for unity in the Horn.**
Saadia Touval, foreword by Rupert Emerson. Cambridge, Massachusetts: Harvard University Press, 1963. 214p.
Originally the author's PhD dissertation, this constitutes a seminal work on Somali nationalism and the drive to unify the Somali 'nation' – including those members found in current-day Djibouti – within one 'state'. Reference to Djibouti is found throughout the text, including brief discussions of France's early explorations in the region and establishment of the French Territory of the Afars and Issas, constitutional progress within the territory, and the rising nationalism among the colony's Somali population. Especially important for the scholar of Djibouti is a brief section (chapter 10) entitled 'The politics of French Somaliland'. However, like many scholars at this time, Touval wrongly assumed that Djibouti could not withstand the competing pressures of two ethnic groups (the Issas and the Afars) within one state: 'Like any conflict between ethnic groups within the political boundaries of one territory, the issue is likely to be intractable'. Indeed, Touval believed that a 'more realistic expectation regarding the territory's future is that it will be annexed to Ethiopia, or conceivably, partitioned between Ethiopia and the Somali Republic'.

Politics and Administration

187 **Djibouti: the political stability of a Somali state in a troubled area.**
Ismail Wais. In: *Proceedings of the second international congress of Somali studies, University of Hamburg, August 1-6, 1983, vol. 2, archaeology and history* . Edited by Thomas Labahn. Hamburg, GFR: Helmut Buske Verlag, 1984, p. 405-24.

The author argues that Djibouti has become integrated into the capitalist world system as a periphery state and, therefore, is highly prone to economic and political instability at the hands of competing regional powers and the major world capitalist states. Its lack of strategic resources reduces its bargaining power and position in the international arena to a minimum but, at the same time, increases its dependency to a high degree. Djibouti's peripheral status within the world capitalist system is said to result from the following factors: (1) strong dependency on foreign physical and financial capital; (2) a high degree of foreign ownership in key economic sectors; (3) the insignificant nature of primary and manufacturing production which leads to dependency on foreign trade; (4) the strength of imported cultural values; (5) reliance on French military forces to defend Djibouti's territorial integrity and sovereignty; and (6) dependency on foreign organizational skills and institutional structures. The author concludes that decades of colonial exploitation of ethnic sentiment and uneven development within the country make ethnic rivalry and conflict (i.e. political instability) inevitable.

188 **Djibouti: les institutions politiques et militaires.** (Djibouti: political and military institutions.)
Absieh Omar Warsame, Maurice Botbol. Paris: Banque d'Information et de Documentation de l'Océan Indien, 1986. 200p.

Prepared under the auspices of the Documentary Studies Service of *La Lettre de l'Océan Indien* (q.v.), this publication spells out in a very precise manner the internal functioning of Djibouti's political and military institutions through 1986. The Djiboutian government reacted angrily to the book, apparently because it deals with the 'taboo' topic of political tensions which have resulted from the ethnic make-up of the government. The first chapter provides data on the population, including the census of 1983 (results were not made public) and ethnic politics. Chapter 2 analyses various Djiboutian laws and legal codes, followed by an extensive discussion of executive power (chapter 3). Chapter 4 outlines legislative power, including a description of the first general assembly (1977), second general assembly (1982), and budget and method of functioning. Chapter 5 discusses the organization of the country's sole legal party, Le Rassemblement Populaire pour le Progrès (RPP). Chapter 6 presents an outline of past and present opposition parties of the RPP. Among those discussed are the Front Populaire pour la Libération de Djibouti (FPLD), the Mouvement Populaire de Libération (MPL), the Front Démocratique pour la Libération de Djibouti (FDLD) and the Parti Populaire Djiboutien (PPD). Chapter 7 examines the structure of the national army and forces of order (national police and national security force). A final chapter analyses the 'grand stakes' of internal and external politics, most notably the future succession of President Hassan Gouled Aptidon. Most important, chapters 3-7 contain 103 extensive biographical sketches on the major political and military personalities within the Djiboutian government.

189   **The French Foreign Legion: the inside story of the world-famous fighting force.**
John Robert Young, with an introduction by Len Deighton.   London; New York: Thames & Hudson, 1984. 212p. bibliog.

Over 251 photographs (200 in colour) are accompanied by well-written descriptions and articles which provide an intriguing (and sympathetic) view of the history and continued presence of the French Foreign Legion throughout the world, including Djibouti. Created by a royal decree of King Louis-Philippe of France in 1831, the Legion has fought in Europe, Mexico, Africa and Southeast Asia. More than 600,000 men from over 100 different nationalities have served French interests, with over 35,000 losing their lives. A section of the book, entitled, 'Return to Africa: Djibouti and the desert' (p. 124-41), provides details on the Legion's 13th Half Brigade stationed in Djibouti. The force numbers 800-1,000 men, and has fought at Bir Hakeim, El Alamein, Dien Bien Phu and in Algeria. Several excellent photographs capture both the day-to-day living of the soldiers and interesting Djiboutian scenery.

Djibouti: pawn of the Horn of Africa.
See item no. 7.

The referendum in French Somaliland: aftermath and prospects in the Somali dispute.
See item no. 92.

The 1977 elections in Djibouti: a tragi/comic end to French colonial rule.
See item no. 95.

Arthur Rimbaud: trade and politics in northeast Africa 1880-1891.
See item no. 96.

Public health, pastoralism, and politics in the Horn of Africa.
See item no. 120.

The politics of repatriation: Ethiopian refugees in Djibouti, 1977-83.
See item no. 135.

Referendum and displacement of population in French Somaliland, 1967: political factors creating refugee situations in Africa.
See item no. 136.

Guerriers et sorciers en Somalie. (Warriors and sorcerers in Somalia.)
See item no. 161.

Un example du pouvoir traditionnel Afar: le sultanat de Tadjourah. (An example of traditional Afar power: the Tadjoura Sultanate.)
See item no. 165.

Le xeer Issa: étude d'un contrat social. (The Issa xeer: study of a social contract.)
See item no. 192.

Politics and Administration

The impact of the Ethiopian and the Somali Republic linkages on the domestic structure of the French Territory of the Afars and Issas; a study on transnational politics and economics.
See item no. 205.

Institution strengthening in rural development: the case of Djibouti.
See item no. 293.

Le Progrès. (Progress.)
See item no. 314.

Somali liberation songs.
See item no. 332.

Constitution and Legal System

190 **Code pénal (mis à jour au 31/1/1985) et textes complémentaires relatifs à la législation pénale et au droit pénal spécial djiboutiens (antérieurs et postérieurs au 27/06/1977 jusqu'au 31/01/1985).** (Penal code [in place as of 31 January 1985] and complementary texts relative to Djibouti's special penal legislation and penal law [prior to and later than 27 June 1977 up until 31 January 1985].)
Pierre Grapinet, preface by Charles Russier.   Djibouti: République de Djibouti, Ministère de la Justice et des Affaires Musulmanes, Bureau de la Formation et de la Documentation, 1985. 2 vols.

The author explains that the point of departure for this massive two-volume work (1,117p.) is the penal code promulgated in France on 22 February 1810, as well as in Obock, Djibouti in November 1887. Section 1 of the first volume reproduces the 486 articles of the Djiboutian penal code (as of 31 January 1985) and subsequent modifications of the code as culled from the *Journal Officiel de la République de Djibouti* (q.v.). Section 2 focuses on penal legislation which is complementary to the penal code. The second volume is devoted to examining the unique aspects of Djibouti's penal law. Unfortunately, not only is this massive volume difficult to obtain, it is also unavailable in the English language.

191 **Manuel pratique d'organisation judiciaire djiboutienne suivi du recueil général des textes concernant la procédure et l'organisation judiciaire moderne, coutumière et charienne publiés à Djibouti de 1887 à 1985.**
(Pratical manual of Djiboutian judiciary organization followed by a general collection of texts concerning the procedure and organization of modern, customary and shariah judiciary published in Djibouti from 1887 to 1985.)
Pierre Grapinet, preface by Farah Ali Waberi. Djibouti: République de Djibouti, Ministère de la Justice et des Affaires Musulmanes, Bureau de la Formation et de la Documentation, 1985. 3 vols.

This massive three-volume work offers the best summary of judicial organization in Djibouti. Unfortunately, the text is difficult to obtain and does not appear in English. The first volume constitutes an introduction to the study of customary, shariah, and 'modern' judicial practices in Djibouti. Volume 2 reproduces legal texts falling within these three categories both prior to and after independence in June 1977. Finally, the third volume offers an analytical and chronological summary of the reproduced legal texts.

192 **Le xeer Issa: étude d'un contrat social.** (The Issa xeer: study of a social contract.)
Ali Moussa Iyé. *Pount*, no. 17 (May 1986), p. 17-27.

The Issa 'xeer' constitutes the social, political and economic code which both organizes and polices the Issa subgrouping of the Somali peoples found in Djibouti. This code, according to the author, a renowned Djiboutian scholar, constitutes the base of Issa pastoral democracy and is best typified in Western thought by Jean-Jacques Rousseau's concept of the 'social contract'. This excellent article first recounts the *xeer* legend and the eight principles upon which the code is based. The author describes how the *xeer* regulates Issa social life in three major aspects: (1) as a penal code which protects an individual's person and material goods, subsequently defining appropriate sanctions for those who transgress the law; (2) as a political constitution governing the election and enthronement of the Ogas (spiritual leader of the Issas) and the relative power of various Issa subgroupings; and (3) as a means of regulating conflict with other ethnic groups. The majority of the article, however, concentrates on the *xeer's* role as a penal code. Special attention is paid to describing the two major groupings of punishments for those who transgress the law: 'bogol' or 'blood price', and 'buulo' or the caring for the needs of the victim. Five extremely detailed tables and charts concretely specify the punishments and payments which the perpetrator must submit to for various types of acts committed against another person.

193 **L'organisation judiciaire à Djibouti.** (Judicial organization in Djibouti.)
Henri Jacquemin. *Revue Juridique et Politique: Indépendence et Coopération*, vol. 39, nos. 3-4 (1985), p. 892-902.

At the time of publication, the author was the Adjunct Inspector General of Djibouti's Judiciary Services (Inspecteur Général Adjoint des Services Judiciaires). The author demonstrates how the organization of Djibouti's judiciary system is the result of that country's triple heritage as a crossroads of African, Arabic and French legal cultures. After briefly discussing two of these legal forums – the customary and Islamic (*Chaira*) courts – the majority of the article focuses on the 'modern' judicial system which is based on the French model. The author offers succinct summaries of the various organizational components of this system, such as the lower courts, the intermediate appellate court, the Supreme Court, as well as a variety of courts of specialized jurisdiction.

194 Djibouti.
Marie Meller. In: *Constitutions of the countries of the world.* Edited by Albert P. Blaustein, Gisbert H. Flanz. Dobbs Ferry, New York: Oceana Publications, 1979. [not paginated].

This series serves as a useful introduction to the nature and evolution of various constitutions throughout the world. This section of the series documents various legal promulgations leading to the independence of Djibouti as a sovereign state. The first portion serves as a brief chronology of events from Charles Rochet d'Héricourt's exploration of the coastline beginning in 1839 to independence in 1977. The second portion provides the original French texts (accompanied by English translations) of: Law no. 77-625 of 20 June 1977, which ended Djibouti's territorial status and made independence effective on 27 June; Law no. LR/77-001 of 27 June 1977 (known as Constitutional Law no. 1); and Law no. LR/77002 of 27 June 1977 (known as Constitutional Law no. 2), which declares Djibouti's independence and governmental organization.

195 Republic of Djibouti: code of international arbitration.
International Legal Materials (Washington, DC), vol 25, no. 1 (Jan. 1986), p. 1-16.

The translation of the text into English and the writing of an accompanying introductory note was carried out by Yves Derains, former Secretary General of the Court of Arbitration of the International Chamber of Commerce. The text comprises Djibouti's code of international arbitration which, officially adopted on 13 February 1984, was designed to facilitate Djibouti's use as an arena of international arbitration by the international business community. The code encompasses the 'principle of freedom' whereby the parties desiring arbitration may organize their arbitration as they see fit, including *ad hoc* arbitration, arbitration under the rules of an international institution (e.g. International Chamber of Commerce), or arbitration under the rules of the United Nations Commission for International Trade Law. The code also entails the creation of a special court – the 'Commission for Arbitration Appeals' – which acts as the authority of last resort. The author concludes that 'Djibouti's code offers arbitration users the possibility of organizing arbitration proceedings in a Third World country within a legal framework, which, although denationalized, provides indispensable legal security'.

196 Journal Officiel de la République de Djibouti. (Official Journal of the Republic of Djibouti.)
République de Djibouti: Présidence de la République. Djibouti: L'Imprimerie Nationale, Présidence de la République, 1900- . monthly.

This journal represents the official legal record of all Djiboutian public decrees and laws approved by the Council of Ministers for the presidency and various government ministries. The Council of Ministers (held every Tuesday) is presided over by Hassan Gouled Aptidon, President of the republic. Published solely in French, the journal began publication in 1900. Numeration of the journal was changed on 27 June 1977,

Constitution and Legal System

the date of Djibouti's independence from French colonial rule. The issue carrying this date started anew as no. 1). The first issue carries the constitutional laws officially changing the name of the country from the 'Territoire française des Afars et des Issas' to the 'République de Djibouti' and recognizing that all previous legislation maintained its binding nature.

Un example du pouvoir traditionnel Afar: le sultanat de Tadjourah. (An example of traditional Afar power: the Tadjoura sultanate.)
See item no. 165.

The right of self-determination in very small places.
See item no. 172.

The statesman's yearbook: statistical and historical annual of the states of the world.
See item no. 386.

Religion

197 Bible translation from SVO to SOV languages in Ethiopia.
Loren F. Bliese. *Folia Orientalia*, vol. 21 (1980), p. 163-69.
Bible translation of the New and Old Testaments into Ethiopia's numerous indigenous languages had expanded considerably during the late 1970s and early 1980s. This article summarizes twenty-three ongoing translation projects as of 1980 undertaken by The Bible Society of Ethiopia (and various other churches). These efforts are approved by the United Bible Societies. Translators are described as needing to pay special attention to subject (S), verb (V) and object (O) placement because the languages from which they are translating (e.g. English) follow an SVO (subject-verb-object) pattern, while the languages of translation generally fit the SOV (subject-object-verb) pattern. As of 1980, both the Old and New Testaments had been translated into the Somali language (using Roman script), whereas numerous portions of both books had been translated (or were in progress) into the Afar language. For lists of previous Ethiopian language translations, see Gustav Arén's *Evangelical pioneers in Ethiopia: origins of the Evangelical church Mekane Yesus* (Stockholm: no publisher, 1978).

198 Mahdism, Muslim clerics, and holy wars in Ethiopia, 1300-1600.
B. G. Martin. In: *Proceedings of the first United States conference of Ethiopian studies, Michigan State University, 2-5 May 1973.* Edited by Harold G. Marcus. East Lansing, Michigan: African Studies Center, Michigan State University, 1975, p. 91-100. (Occasional Papers Series, monograph no. 3).
'The first African region touched by Islam', begins the author, 'was the Eritrean and Somali coast on the Red Sea, directly opposite the shores of Yaman and Hijaz.' In this brief, but informative, article the reader is introduced to the rise of Islam and the impact of 'jihads' (holy wars) on the Ethiopian Empire and surrounding areas, which ultimately influenced the religious orientation of the peoples inhabiting Djibouti. Particular attention is paid to the religious exploits of Ahmed Gran, the famed Islamic conqueror in Somali folklore and political history. An interesting conclusion is that continual conflict between Muslims and Christians during the period made them 'easy prey' for the Galla.

Religion

199 **Status of Christianity profile, Djibouti.**
Open Doors East Africa. Nairobi: Daystar Communications, 1983.
20p. 2 maps. bibliog.

This unique publication, the third of a three-volume series, briefly describes the status of the Christian faith in the predominantly Muslim country of Djibouti (the other two volumes centre on Burundi and Chad). After summarizing the political, social and economic conditions in Djibouti, two brief sections document the history and current nature of the country's Roman Catholic, Prostestant and Orthodox Churches. The authors note, for example, that as of 1970 the Catholic Church was the most active of the four Christian denominations in the country. Moreover, it was the only Church that had made converts from the local population. (Of 11,000 members, 10,400 are said to be metropolitan French on temporary contracts and 600 are indigenous converts, 'mostly middle-class Somalis'.) Interesting statistics are offered on the spread of Christianity. Also included are recommendations for the creation of a potential ministry on Djibouti.

200 **The influence of Islam on the Afar.**
Kassim Shehim. PhD dissertation, University of Washington, Seattle, 1982. 230p. 4 maps. bibliog.

Utilizing Arabic-language sources and oral histories (in addition to substantial English-language materials), the author constructs the first significant study on the influence of Islam on the Afar pastoralists who inhabit the eastern part of Ethiopia and Djibouti. Chapter 1 describes the geographic, ethnographic and historical backgrounds of the Afar people. Chapter 2, centring on the Kingdom of al-Habasha (which included present-day Djibouti), explains the 'various channels' through which Islam penetrated the Afar territory. Chapter 3 centres on the establishment of Afar sultanates, most notably the Aussa Sultanate. Chapters 4 and 5 describe Islam's influence on the social organization and customary laws of the Afar people, respectively. Especially valuable is the author's analysis of the influence of Islamic law, in which he concludes that it 'left its biggest imprint on family, ritual and inheritance laws of Afar society. Its impact on the criminal aspect of the customary laws is relatively slight'. A concluding chapter summarizes the impact that Islam has exerted on Afar society. The author notes that, 'Despite all these centuries since they have converted to Islam, the religion does not seem to have thoroughly moulded Afar institutions. The influence of Islam among the Afar, aside from the coastal regions, is relatively limited'.

201 **The Christian Church and missions in Ethiopia (including Eritrea and the Somalilands).**
J. Spencer Trimingham. London: World Dominion Press, 1950. 74p. 2 maps.

A unique early perspective on the role of Christianity and mission work in Ethiopia and those areas of the Horn of Africa which came under colonial rule, including Eritrea, British and Italian Somalia (currently Somalia), and French Somaliland (Djibouti). Although primarily concerned with Ethiopia, the author notes that consideration of neighbouring areas 'is necessary in order to estimate the significance of the unfinished missionary task'. The first four chapters centre on the religions of northeast Africa and their distribution (chapter 1), the background of political and social change in Ethiopia, Eritrea and the various Somaliland territories (chapter 2), evolution of the National Church of Ethiopia (chapter 3), and the role of missions in Ethiopia (chapter 4). The final chapter deals with the 'church's unfinished task'.

Among the topics discussed are the relationship between missions and the National Church, the role of the Church on the conversion of pagans and missions among the Muslim peoples of the region.

202 The influence of Islam upon Africa.
J. Spencer Trimingham.   London; New York: Longman; Beirut: Librairie du Liban, 1980. 182p. 5 maps. bibliog.

This new edition of the author's much acclaimed 1968 study of the influence of Islam upon Africa includes a new section (chapter 6) updating Islamic developments in Africa during the 1970s. After briefly describing in an introductory section how Africa, historically, was marginal to the Islamic world, chapter 1 details the history and characteristics of six major Islamic 'culture zones' on the African continent: Mediterranean Africa; western Sudan; central Sudan; eastern or Nilotic Sudan; northeastern Ethiopic zone; and East Africa. Chapter 2 discusses the processes of religious and cultural change in Africa, including the spread and assimilation of Islam, the results of the adoption of Islam, and the effect of Islam upon African religion and society. Two subsequent chapters describe the religious life of African Muslims (chapter 3) and the influence of Islam upon social life (chapter 4). Of particular interest in this latter chapter are two sections dealing with the influence of Islam on the state and legal system, as well as the role of Arabs and Arabic in Africa. Finally, chapter 5 analyses the role of the African Muslim in what the author describes as an 'era of change'. Of particular interest in this chapter is a section dealing with the relationship between Islam and secular nationalism.

203 Islam in East Africa.
J. Spencer Trimingham.   New York: Books for Libraries, 1980. 198p. 3 maps.

Originally published in 1964, the book offers a good overview of the role of Islam in East Africa – inclusive of the Somali-speaking peoples of the region – although no specific reference is made to Djibouti. After exploring the historical background of Islamic penetration of the region (chapter 1) and the particular features of East African Islam (chapter 2), subsequent chapters focus on Islamic organization (chapter 3) and society (chapter 6). Of particular interest is a portion of the book (chapter 5) devoted to exploring the 'cycle of personal life' of the Islamic faithful. Among the topics discussed are birth, circumcision and initiation, Islamic education, marriage, and death and mourning. A glossary offers a useful summary of Swahili and Arabic words relating to the Islamic faith.

204 Islam in Ethiopia.
J. Spencer Trimingham.   London, New York: Oxford University Press, 1952. 299p. 6 maps.

A classic study of the impact of Islam in Ethiopia. After briefly introducing the reader to the peoples and religions comprising the region, emphasis is placed on describing the nature of conflict/competition between Christianity and Islam in Ethiopia. Sections centre on a historical sketch of the region before the arrival of Islam, the nature of first contacts with Islam, the Muslim conquest of the 16th century, the subsequent period of isolation and regionalism, the unification of the Ethiopian empire and the characteristics of Islamic penetration. Especially pertinent to Djibouti is the section of the book devoted to the distribution of Islam among the various ethnic groups of the Horn of Africa, including discussions of both the Afars and Somalis. A final section describes

Religion

the 'special characteristics' of Islam in the region, including the orthodox system, the dervish orders, saint worship, assimilation of Islam by pagans and the influence exerted by processes of westernization.

The Arab factor in Somali history: the origins and the development of Arab enterprise and cultural influences in the Somali peninsula.
See item no. 87.

The veneration of Sufi saints and its impact on the oral literature of the Somali people and on their literature in Arabic.
See item no. 322.

Amharic interference in ʾAfar translation.
See item no. 351.

Foreign Relations

205 **The impact of the Ethiopian and the Somali Republic linkages on the domestic structure of the French Territory of the Afars and Issas; a study on transnational politics and economics.**
Fassil Aradoum.   PhD Dissertation, Howard University, Washington, DC, 1976. 461p. 10 maps. bibliog.
The general theme of this study is that, in order to understand change in Djibouti's domestic economic and political processes, one must look to the nature of this country's linkages with Ethiopia and Somalia. It is argued that whereas Djibouti's geographical location and lack of economic resources are key to understanding Ethiopia's penetration of the economic sphere, it is Djibouti's ethnic divisions which are key to understanding Somalia's penetration in the political sphere. The first two chapters offer a summary of the project and a brief overview of the establishment of French-ruled Djibouti. Four subsequent chapters centre on Djibouti's geographical location as a factor conducive to Ethiopian influence (chapter 3), ethnic make-up as a factor conducive to Somalia's impact (chapter 4), the actual economic impact of Ethiopia (chapter 5), and the actual ideological impact of Somalia (chapter 6). It is concluded that Djibouti is a 'penetrated system' in which both the domestic economy and politics are highly susceptible to the wishes of its immediate neighbours.

206 **Somalia's relations with her neighbours: from 'Greater Somalia' to 'Western Somalia' to 'Somali refugees' to . . .**
Negussay Ayele.   In: *Proceedings of the seventh international conference of Ethiopian studies, University of Lund, 26-29 April 1982.* Edited by Sven Rubenson.   Addis Ababa: Institute of Ethiopian Studies; Uppsala, Sweden: Scandinavian Institute of African Studies; East Lansing, Michigan: African Studies Center, Michigan State University, 1984, p. 657-66.
'One of the very crucial and persistent factors that has been affecting and conditioning international relations on the Horn of Africa in the last twenty years', notes the

author, 'has been Somalia's foreign policy desideratum, otherwise known as the quest for *Greater Somalia*.' In this article the author offers a highly critical view of the evolution, consequences and future prospects of this foreign policy objective – which includes the Somali-inhabited portion of Djibouti – from an Ethiopian point of view. The author argues that Somalia could not have lost territory before 1960 to any of its neighbours, and has no legal claim to any of these territories, because it did not exist as an independent 'state' or at least as an independent 'political entity' prior to independence in 1960. The first section discusses the concept of 'Greater Somalia' from its origins in British colonial thought during the mid-1940s to its adoption by Somalia's various civilian governments (1960-69) in the aftermath of that country's independence in 1960. The second section explores what the author perceives to be merely a tactical shift by the military government of Siyaad Barre in pressing for the self-determination of 'Western Somalia' – that portion of Ethiopia inhabited largely by ethnic Somalis. Finally, the article focuses on the 1977-78 Ogaden war and the resulting hundreds of thousands of 'Somali refugees' which, the author argues, have become propaganda tools of the Somali government. In what constitutes a very one-sided argument, the author concludes that 'Greater Somalia' was a diplomatic failure; 'Western Somalia' was a military failure; and 'Somali Refugees' is an ongoing political failure.

207 **The dilemma of the Horn of Africa.**
Raman G. Bhardwaj. New Delhi: Sterling Publishers, 1979. 272p.
map. bibliog.

This general overview of conflicts within the Horn of Africa is based on primary materials gathered from the Institute of Ethiopian Studies (Addis Ababa), the University of Asmara, (Eritrea) and the National Archives in New Delhi, India. Individual sections pertaining to Djibouti focus on the socio-economic development within the country, ethnic rivalries and 'French opportunism', Djibouti's place within the Ethiopian-Somali conflict and relations with the Soviet Union. Individual sections deal with the geopolitical significance of the Horn of Africa (chapter 1), the internal dimensions of conflict (chapter 2), the growth of conflict within the region (chapter 3), the international dimension (chapter 4), and unresolved problems as of the late 1970s (chapter 5). An interesting conclusion explains that regional tensions may only be resolved through some type of confederation of Ethiopia, Somalia and Djibouti in which the Ogaden and Eritrea apparently would be equal, separate partners. Sixty-five pages of appendices reproduce twenty documents of interest.

208 **African boundaries: a legal and diplomatic encyclopaedia.**
Ian Brownlie. London: C. Hurst & Co.; Berkeley, California:
University of California Press, 1979. 1355p. maps. bibliog.

A classic work that offers a comprehensive overview and analysis of all interstate African boundaries. After briefly introducing the reader to the study of boundaries in Africa, analysis is divided into five major parts: 'States of the Mediterranean littoral' (part 1); 'States of West Africa and the western Sahara' (part 2); 'The succession of states of French Equatorial Africa, with Cameroun, Equatorial Guinea and Zaire' (part 3); 'Sudan, Ethiopia, Somalia and East Africa' (part 4); and 'Southern Africa, including Angola, Zambia, Malawi and Mozambique' (part 5). Two individual sections focus on Djibouti's borders with Ethiopia (p. 753-65) and Somalia (p. 767-74). Each section includes a general overview and map of the boundary in question, evidence of alignment (such as treaties and legislative measures), physical demarcation, current issues (such as ongoing boundary disputes) and a bibliography for further reference.

209 **The rise of Saudi regional power and the foreign policies of northeast African states.**
John Creed, Kenneth Menkhaus. *Northeast African Studies*, vol. 8, nos. 2-3 (1986), p. 1-22.

An authoritative treatment of a much neglected topic within northeast African studies: the rise of Saudi Arabian regional predominance since 1967 and its effects on the foreign policy behaviour of northeast African countries, including a brief section on Djibouti. The framework of analysis is what has been termed the 'world-system approach' in which nations are divided into 'core' (e.g. France), 'semi-periphery' (e.g. Saudi Arabia) and 'periphery' (e.g. Djibouti) countries. The authors conclude that 'Saudi Arabia has had considerable success in employing its oil wealth to "bargain" with its weaker neighbours and establish transnational ties to the governing elites of these states'. Saudi Arabia, utilizing its formidable oil wealth, is portrayed as pursuing *status quo* policies which have attempted to minimize the three threats of radical Islam, Soviet communism and Israel. Toward these ends, Saudi Arabia is described as welcoming a continued French presence in Djibouti in which France provides the military clout and Saudi Arabia provides the financial means. Moreover, the section on Djibouti describes how Djiboutian President Hassan Gouled Aptidon has 'skilfully played the Arab [read Saudi Arabian] card' by stressing Djibouti's strategic value and Islamic heritage.

210 **Cuba in Africa.**
Cuban Studies/Estudios Cubanos, vol. 10, no. 1 (Jan. 1980); vol. 10, no. 2 (July 1980).

This two-volume special edition of *Cuban Studies/Estudios Cubanos*, which centres on the Cuban role in Africa during the 1970s, is important reading for a comprehensive understanding of the international relations of the Horn. The articles contained in the January 1980 issue include: William M. LeoGrande's, 'Cuban-Soviet relations and Cuban policy in Africa' (p. 1-36); Cole Blasier's 'Comment: the consequences of military initiatives' (p. 37-42); Edward Gonzalez's 'Comment: operational goals of Cuban policy in Africa' (p. 43-48); Nelson P. Valdés' 'Cuba's involvement in the Horn of Africa: the Ethiopian-Somali war and the Eritrean conflict' (p. 49-79); Tekie Fessehatzion's 'Comment: one Eritrean view' (p. 80-84); and Said Yusuf Abdi's 'Comment: one Somali perspective' (p. 85-90). The articles contained in the July 1980 volume include: Jorge I. Domínguez's 'Political and military limitations and consequences of Cuban policies in Africa' (p. 1-35); Jiri Valenta's 'Comment: the Soviet-Cuban alliance in Africa and future prospects in the Third World' (p. 36-43); Gerald Bender's 'Comment: past, present and future perspectives of Cuba in Africa' (p. 44-54); Sergio Roca's 'Economic aspects of Cuban involvement in Africa' (p. 55-79); Jorge F. Pérez-López's 'Comment: economic costs and benefits of African involvement' (p. 80-84); and Susan Eckstein's 'Comment: the global political economy and Cuba's African involvement' (p. 85-90). Especially enlightening is a description of Cuba's original support and subsequent denunciation of the concept of pan-Somalism, as well as attempts at brokering some type of socialist federation in the Horn, both of which had significant implications for Djibouti.

Foreign Relations

211 The Horn of Africa: a map of political-strategic conflict.

James Dougherty.   Cambridge, Massachusetts: Institute for Foreign
Policy Analysis, 1982. 74p. map.

The second in a series published by the Institute for Foreign Policy Analysis on the
importance and vulnerability of the Cape route, placing special emphasis on the
security problems associated with Western and Japanese access to the oil and non-fuel
minerals of Africa and the Persian Gulf. This volume, devoted to the Horn of Africa
and its place within the geostrategic context of oil and mineral access, outlines the
major political conflicts occurring both within and between the countries of the region,
including a short chapter on Djibouti. Other chapters of particular interest delve into
the future ramifications of ongoing conflict in the Ogaden (chapter 7), implications of
the Iranian revolution, the Soviet occupation of Afghanistan and the Gulf War for
political developments in the Horn (chapter 8), and the US policy of seeking base
rights in the region, including a brief description of Djibouti (chapter 9). For further
discussion of the strategic importance of oil and mineral access, see the following two
monographs in the same series: Robert J. Hanks' (US Navy, retired) *The Cape route:
imperiled Western capeline* (1981); and Charles Perry's *The West, Japan and Cape route
imports: the oil and non-fuel mineral trade* (1982).

212 The Somali dispute.

John Drysdale.   London: Pall Mall Press, 1964. 183p. 3 maps. (Pall
Mall World Affairs Special Series, no. 1).

The author was a member of the British Overseas Civil Service in Somalia where he
served as an adviser to the Prime Minister from 1961-63. Based upon this experience,
he discusses the pan-Somali dream of uniting all the Somali peoples in the Horn of
Africa under one 'state', and the conflicts that this has caused between the Somali
Democratic Republic and its neighbours, including Djibouti. Brief mention is made of
the Djibouti–Addis Ababa railway, the Djiboutian–Ethiopian boundary, and British
assumptions prior to the beginning of the Second World War that they could count
on the French garrison in French-ruled Djibouti to aid in the defence of British
Somaliland. Short sections are also devoted to exploring the actions of Vichy-ruled
Djibouti during the Second World War and the possible future course of events
concerning the future viability of an independent Djibouti at the hands of its more
aggressive neighbours. The author presciently noted that the 'likely course of events is
neutrality [in the Ethiopian-Somali conflict] and independence with close links with
France'. In a somewhat more pessimistic tone, however, he makes the following
statement: 'It is doubtful, though, how long this vulnerable and divisive little country,
half-Danakil [Afar] and half-Somali, could maintain its independent status with
acquisitive and rival nations at its gates'.

213 Djibouti – United Nations and OAU decision – Djibouti and Ethiopia.

Ethiopia.   Addis Ababa: [no publisher], 1976. 35p.

The government of Ethiopia published this collection of documents one year before
Djibouti's independence. The first half of the booklet reproduces resolutions and
declarations of support for Djiboutian independence as promulgated by the United
Nations (UN), the Organization of African Unity (OAU) and the non-aligned
countries. Among these are: the 'UN resolution adopted on the reports of the fourth
committee: question of French Somaliland' (1975); the 'OAU declaration on the so-
called French Somaliland (Djibouti)' (three separate resolutions from 1975 and 1976);
and 'The so-called French Somaliland, Djibouti' (1975). Other documents, which spell
out the Ethiopian position, include: 'Views of the provisional military government of

Ethiopia on the independence and future of the territory of Djibouti' (26 April 1976); 'Statement by Ato Kifle Wodajo Minister for Foreign Affairs of Ethiopia, Oct. 18th, 1975'; 'Statement by the chairman of the PMG of socialist Ethiopia, Brig. General Teferi Bante at the OAU summit in Mauritius, July 1976'; and 'Statement with regard to Djibouti of the PMG of socialist Ethiopia at the summit meeting of non-aligned countries, Colombo, August 1976'. Also reproduced are a joint communiqué signed on 22 June 1976 between Kifle Wodajo, Minister for Foreign Affairs of Ethiopia, and President Hassan Gouled Aptidon of Djibouti, and the draft of a joint Somali-Ethiopian declaration recognizing Djibouti's sovereignty and territorial integrity.

214 **Which way to the sea please?**
Nuruddin Farah. *Horn of Africa*, vol. 1, no. 4 (Oct.-Dec. 1978),
p. 31-36.

The author is a renowned Somali writer whose English-language novels have explored the topics of the role of women in Somali society, the authoritarian rule of Somali leader Maxammad Siyaad Barre, and the 1977-78 Ogaden War between Ethiopia and Somalia. In this brief article the author examines Ethiopia's historic quest for an outlet to the sea, including the Djiboutian port of Tadjoura. Citing statements of previous Ethiopian rulers, it is shown that, although the names have changed, the Ethiopian quest remains the same. Whereas this quest has led to agreements with the French to import arms through their former colony of Djibouti, as well as Ethiopia's annexation of Eritrea, the ominous question of this article – published in the immediate aftermath of the 1977-78 Ogaden War – is whether Ethiopia 'might stretch its long arms' to 'grab and occupy' the Somali ports of Berbera and Zeila. The answer, hints the article, is found in the words of Ethiopia's former rulers. 'Indeed, I suggest we let Ethiopia's Kings and Emperors come out of their hiding places and speak for themselves', notes the author. 'I suggest we watch Ethiopia change her leopard's skin; that we listen to her kings contradict themselves'.

215 **War clouds on the Horn of Africa: the widening storm.**
Tom J. Farer. New York: Carnegie Endowment for International
Peace, 1979. 183p. 5 maps. bibliog.

This updated and revised version of the author's acclaimed *War clouds on the Horn of Africa: a crisis for détente* (New York: Carnegie Endowment for Peace, 1976) describes the interlocking nature of regional conflict and superpower involvement, as well as the effects that these have had in undermining détente and contributing to greater instability in the Horn. A minor section deals with Djibouti's role in the Horn's conflicts (p. 100-07). While the first section of the book describes the history and post-revolution national socialism of Ethiopia *vis-à-vis* the ongoing struggle for Eritrean independence, the second section centres on the nature and evolution of conflictual relations between Ethiopia and Somalia. Finally, section three offers policy-relevant insights, including the implications of the Ogaden war for a continued superpower policy of détente, the role of the Indian Ocean in strategic calculations, and the dilemma of idealism versus self-interest in the pursuit of policy.

216 **Djibouti: petrodollar protectorate?**
James Fitzgerald. *Horn of Africa*, vol. 1, no. 4 (Oct./Dec. 1978),
p. 25-30.

The author, after briefly questioning Djibouti's ability in 1978 to maintain political stability among competing ethnic groups, obtain a lasting national security *vis-à-vis* Ethiopia and Somalia, and achieve long term economic development and prosperity, charts out three major foreign policy options to ensure future survival as an independent mini-state. The first option, complete and unrestricted sovereignty, would entail the withdrawal of all foreign bases and facilities (i.e. French bases and facilities) and the pursuance of autocentric national development with little or no reliance on external aid. Based on Prime Minister Ahmed Dini's call for 'non-alignment and positive neutralism', the author notes that 'such an option would leave the nation with virtually no means at national defense and a permanently bankrupt economy'. In short, a non-viable option. The second option would be to accept the role of 'French subsidiary', in essence maintaining and strengthening traditional relationships with France. The drawback of this option, according to the author, is that, although the French could be counted on to repulse foreign attacks, they would not become involved in helping the government to quell domestic civil strife (perceived as a real possibility). The author concludes that the optimal foreign strategy for Djibouti to pursue is that of 'petrodollar protectorate', in which the nation would align itself with the conservative Arab states in the region, most notably Saudi Arabia. It is argued that the conservative Arab régimes not only wish to protect regional petroleum shipping (an interest as well of the major Western powers), but that they also 'have an interest in long-term political stability in the region'.

217 **The betrayal of the Somalis.**
Louis Fitzgibbon. London: Rex Collings, 1982. 113p. bibliog.

Clearly pro-Somali in argument, this offers a firm denunciation of Ethiopia's expansionist policies and the European colonial powers who, from 1897 onward, are said to have partitioned and betrayed the Somali people. The author notes that whereas the Somalis 'placed their trust' in Britain, France and Italy 'as world powers', the European powers instead 'embraced the Somalis for what could be had of them, and in return gave back the kiss of Judas'. Great Britain is especially denounced as having traded Somali territory to Ethiopia in return for Ethiopian pledges to cut off the flow of weapons to the 'mahdist' movement in the Sudan. On a contemporary scale, the United States (under the administration of President Jimmy Carter) is denounced as having wavered in its initial promise to support Somalia in the Ogaden War. Five appendices include: a 'Petition of the Somalis to the Four Power Commission'; 'Resolution of the All Somali Conference'; 'Resolution of the All African Peoples Conference 1958 and 1960'; 'In the British press and Parliament 1978-81'; and a working chronology of significant events. For an Ethiopian perspective of these events see Mesfin Wolde-Mariam's anti-Somali polemic *Somalia: the problem child of Africa* (q.v.)

218 **The evaded duty.**
Louis Fitzgibbon. London: Rex Collings, 1985. 161p. map. bibliog.

In this complementary volume to his *Betrayal of the Somalis* (q.v.), the author denounces the 'evaded duty' of the United Nations (UN) and Western powers to guarantee the right to self-determination of Somalis living in Ethiopia's Ogaden region 'as they struggle against a malignant black colonialism [Ethiopian] which has lasted for nearly one hundred years'. The author's argument for granting the right to self-

Foreign Relations

determination is backed up by over ninety-five pages of documents (contained in
nineteen appendices) spanning the 19th and 20th centuries, and which range from
treaties between the colonial powers and Ethiopia to resolutions of the UN and
Organization of African Unity. Especially useful to the student of Djibouti is appendix
6, 'Djibouti: the truth-briefing by a newly-arrived refugee from Djibouti'.

219 **Political conflict on the Horn of Africa.**
Robert F. Gorman.   New York: Praeger, 1981. 243p. bibliog.

The purpose of this book is to assess the regional and international determinants of
conflict and intervention in the Horn of Africa, centring specifically on what the author
labels the 'internationalization of a local hot spot'. The author notes, however, that
conflict in the Horn of Africa must be understood 'not only in terms of the interplay of
local and systemic factors but also as a symptom of larger shifts that are even now
occurring in the structure of international politics'. Like most general introductions to
the study of conflict and intervention in northeast Africa, only scattered references are
made to Djibouti. The contents of the book are as follows: 'Conflict on the Horn: the
internationalization of a local hot spot' (chapter 1); 'The roots of conflict in the Horn
of Africa' (chapter 2); 'Prelude to war: 1976-77' (chapter 3); 'A conflict model of the
Ethiopian-Somali war' (chapter 4); 'Foreign policy change on the Horn of Africa'
(chapter 5); 'Intervention on the Horn of Africa' (chapter 6); and 'Conclusion'
(chapter 7).

220 **Schedule of international agreements relating to the boundaries of
Ethiopia.**
David Hamilton.   *Ethiopia Observer*, vol. 16, no. 2 (1973), p. 58-69.

This chronological list offers a handy compilation of international agreements
concerning Ethiopia's boundaries with its neighbours. The author distinguishes
between the 'delimitation' and 'demarcation' of boundaries. Whereas delimitation
'involves a detailed decision as to where precisely in theory and on the map the line
will lie', demarcation refers to the 'marking out of this line on the ground with suitable
beacons and markers'. Over 150 agreements from 1827 to 1972 are cited, dozens of
which are relevant to Djibouti's evolving boundaries under French colonial rule. The
title and date of each agreement is followed by a brief description and bibliographical
reference (where it is either cited or reproduced in full). Documents relevant to
Djibouti range from the 25 December 1880 French notice respecting the limit of
French possessions of Obock to the 16 January 1954 Franco–Ethiopian protocol
confirming the delimitation and demarcation of the boundary between Ethiopia and
French-ruled Djibouti.

221 **Case studies in African diplomacy (II): the Ethiopia–Somalia–Kenya
dispute; 1960-1967.**
Edited by Catherine Hoskyns.   Dar es Salaam: Oxford University
Press for the Institute of Public Administration, 1969. 91p. map.
bibliog.

This collection of documents relating to Somalia's disputes with both Kenya and
Ethiopia from 1960 to 1967 over the self-determination of Somali inhabitants in both of
those countries was designed as a text for an international relations course at the
University College, Dar es Salaam. Unfortunately, the author neglected to deal with
the equally pressing Franco-Somali dispute over the disposition of Somalis living under
colonial rule in Djibouti during the same period. Nevertheless, the volume, in

95

conjunction with those citations dealing with the Djibouti question, is essential for a full understanding of the evolving nature of international relations in the Horn and, specifically, initial attempts at dealing with the question of ethnicity during the 1960s. This book contains study questions, brief background notes on the disputes, a timeline of significant events (1960-67) and thirty-three separate units. Documents include journal and newspaper extracts, government publications and contributions by scholars of the field, such as John Drysdale. Especially valuable are texts of speeches made by concerned parties at numerous meetings of the Organization of African Unity.

222 **The Horn of Africa in continuing crisis.**
Colin Legum, Bill Lee.   New York, London: Africana Publishing Company, 1979. 166p. 2 maps.

The chapters of this book are largely reprints from the 1977-78 edition of the highly informative *Africa contemporary record* (q.v.), edited by Colin Legum. A brief introduction summarizing the international dimensions of the Somali-Ethiopian conflict is followed by individual chapters on Ethiopia, Somalia, Sudan and Djibouti. The chapter on Djibouti summarizes the trials and tribulations of that country's first year of independence. Also included is a chapter by Zdenek Cervenka and Colin Legum on Cuba's growing role in Africa, as well as several documents pertaining to the 1977-78 Ogaden war between Ethiopia and Somalia.

223 **Superpower diplomacy in the Horn of Africa.**
Samuel M. Makinda.   New York: St. Martin's Press, 1987. 242p. bibliog.

Written by a Kenyan scholar, this provides an excellent overview of superpower involvement in the Horn of Africa primarily between 1974 and 1986. Discussion is divided into eight chapters: 'Issues and contexts' (chapter 1); 'The regional equation' (chapter 2); 'Evolution of superpower policies' (chapter 3); 'Rivalry in a changing order, 1974-76 (chapter 4); 'The 1977-78 Ogaden War' (chapter 5); 'American reassertion of force' (chapter 6); 'Soviet policy 1979-86' (chapter 7); and 'Summary and conclusions' (chapter 8). Of interest to the scholar of Djibouti are sections discussing Somalia's involvement in Djibouti's internal affairs during the 1970s and President Hassan Gouled Aptidon's mediation efforts between Ethiopia and Somalia during the 1980s. Like the majority of works on the Horn of Africa, however, the issue of Djibouti enjoys only passing references throughout the text. Two appendices reproduce the Soviet-Somali and Soviet-Ethiopian friendship treaties.

224 **Raisons de la présence française à Djibouti.** (Reasons for the French presence in Djibouti.)
Georges Malécot.   *Le Mois en Afrique*, no. 85 (Jan. 1973), p. 38-52.

In an article written four years prior to Djibouti's independence, the author succinctly summarizes French geo-strategic arguments for maintaining their presence in this small territory. First, the country's port city, described as an 'indispensable lung' to central Ethiopia, constitutes a major source of dispute in the Ethiopian–Somali conflict. Second, Djibouti commands a strategic spot in the East–West conflict, especially as concerns its geographical location astride the petroleum routes of the Persian Gulf – an economic lifeline for France. Finally, Djibouti also serves as an important strategic asset in the Arab-Israeli conflict. In short, the continued French presence is perceived as an 'indispensable factor' in a 'particularly explosive' region for maintaining regional peace and global stability. The author concludes that France has assumed a 'heavy responsibility' in Djibouti.

225 **Ethiopia, Great Britain, and the United States, 1941-1974: the problem of empire.**
Harold G. Marcus.   Berkeley, California: University of California Press, 1983. 205p. 2 maps. bibliog.

The author is a noted US scholar who has written extensively about Ethiopian history. Relying heavily on declassified documents from Great Britain's Foreign Office, as well as the US Defense Department, State Department and National Security Council, this volume describes two major trends in Ethiopia's foreign relations and domestic politics: the steady decline of Great Britain's colonial empire and, specifically, influence in Ethiopia during the 1940s and 1950s, and the parallel rise of US influence in Ethiopia during this same period, culminating with Washington's involvement in the attempted Ethiopian *coup d'état* of 14-16 December 1960. The discussion is broken down into the following chapters: 'A tale of two lions, 1941-1943' (chapter 1); 'The Anglo-Ethiopian Agreement of 1944: America intervenes' (chapter 2); 'British decline, 1944-1950' (chapter 3); 'American security and Ethiopia, 1950-1960' (chapter 4); 'The events of 14-16 December 1960' (chapter 5); 'Pathology, 1960' (chapter 6); and 'Prognosis, 1961 and thereafter' (chapter 7).

226 **Djibouti: France's strategic toehold in Africa.**
Thomas A. Marks.   *African Affairs*, vol. 73, no. 290 (Jan. 1974), p. 95-104.

Written while serving as a Second Lieutenant in the US Army, the author assesses the strategic importance of Djibouti in the aftermath of the outbreak of the October Arab-Israeli war. Asserting that the French strategic network in Africa has been 'little understood' by Western military observers, it is argued that, due to the 'historical accident' of the Arab–Israeli conflict, the French 'may find themselves the possessors of an area having a great deal more strategic importance than has been hitherto appreciated'. Two major sections describe the evolution of French defence policy in Africa and the Middle East (centring specifically on Djibouti) and those aspects of Djibouti's regional relations which have made the territory an area of strategic importance.

227 **Soviet and American influence in the Horn of Africa.**
Marina Ottaway.   New York: Praeger, 1982. 187p. bibliog.

The author is a noted scholar on African-Marxism who has frequently visited the Horn of Africa and was a lecturer at Addis Ababa University during the unfolding of the Ethiopian revolution from 1974 to 1977. Ottaway offers an excellent analysis of the changing nature of US–Soviet influence in relationships with the Horn of Africa, with Djibouti mentioned briefly at various points throughout. An especially lucid description of events is contained in eight chapters: 'The setting' (chapter 1); 'From the scramble for Africa to the cold war' (chapter 2); 'Ethiopia and Somalia before the military coups d'état' (chapter 3); 'The Soviet moment in Somalia' (chapter 4); 'Revolution in Ethiopia: challenge for the great powers' (chapter 5); 'The reversal of alliances and its impact on Somalia' (chapter 6); 'Ethiopia and the Soviet Union' (chapter 7); and 'The great powers and the Horn of Africa: an overall assessment' (chapter 8). The author concludes that 'the relationship of the great powers to the countries of the Horn cannot be looked at as one of domination and subordination.

Foreign Relations

Neither Somalia nor Ethiopia was dominated, at any point, by their much more powerful partner. They were not the helpless victims of great powers' policies. They fully contributed to US and Soviet intervention in the Horn and continue to do so'.

228 **République de Djibouti ou roue de secours d' . . . Éthiopie?** (Republic of Djibouti or spare tyre of . . . Ethiopia?)
Omar Osman Rabeh.   Ivry, France: Ateliers Silex, 1985. 140p.

During the 1960s the author was a member of the Front for the Liberation of the Somali Coast (FLCS), a pan-Somali guerrilla group committed to Djibouti's independence from French colonial rule and unification with the Somali Democratic Republic. During the 1980s, he was a founder of the Djiboutian Popular Party (DPP), an opposition party that was formed in 1981 and subsequently banned by Djibouti's one-party state. In this volume, the author offers a thought-provoking scenario of Djibouti's potential forceful incorporation as a province of Ethiopia. The scenario is one in which Ethiopia loses its major outlets to the sea (the ports of Massawa and Assab) as a result of Eritrean independence. Faced with potential economic disaster, the primary recourse would be to impose Ethiopian rule over Djibouti (although it remains unclear how, if unable to assert control over Eritrea, Ethiopia would be successful in subjugating an unwilling Djibouti). After describing French colonization and administration of the territory, both of which are ultimately perceived as serving Ethiopia's interests, an analysis is made of Djibouti's place in Ethiopian politics (chapter 1) and the pan-Somali 'vision' (chapter 2), as well as the politics of the Indian Ocean (chapter 4) and the Arab world (chapter 5). Chapter 6 is devoted to explaining Djibouti's movement toward political 'anonymity'. The author ominously warns that it remains to be seen whether Djiboutians will continue to: (1) 'shoulder a distorted history which has been imposed upon them'; (2) 'accept the passive and harmful role of simple pawns in foreign strategies directly opposed to their fundamental interests'; and (3) 'not seriously take into consideration a treacherous plot . . . of which the goal, according to all the evidence, is to strip them before long of their state, country, and liberty'. See also the author's autobiography, *Le cercle et le spirale* (The circle and the spiral) (Paris: Les Lettres Libres, 1984).

229 **The Indian Ocean and the superpowers: economic, political and strategic perspectives.**
Rasul B. Rais.   London; Sydney, Australia: Croom Helm, 1986. 215p. bibliog.

Indicative of most studies focusing on the role of the superpowers in the Indian Ocean region, the topic of Djibouti and its strategic port and rail centre of Djibouti City are largely ignored. Despite this shortcoming, the book offers a good overview of the growing involvement of the superpowers in the Indian Ocean region. After briefly explaining the conceptual framework – the 'intrusive system' paradigm – that was adopted to explain superpower involvement in the region (chapter 1), the author provides an historical overview of the geopolitics of the Indian Ocean region (chapter 2). Discussion ranges from the pre-colonial regional powers of ancient Egypt, Persia, India and the 'Arab–Islamic powers' to the retrenchment policies of Great Britain in the aftermath of the Second World War. Chapters 3-6 focus on the evolution of US involvement in the Indian Ocean, including a discussion of US naval facilities at Diego García, Oman, Somalia, Kenya and Egypt. Chapters 7-8 similarly focus on Soviet involvement in the Indian Ocean region. Of particular interest are chapters devoted to explaining regional responses to naval deployments of the superpowers (chapter 10), as well as the evolution of arms-control proposals for the Indian Ocean region (chapter

11). Special attention is paid to the regional policies of Australia, India, Iran, Pakistan and the Gulf Cooperation Council.

230 Small states & territories: status and problems.
Jacques Rapaport, Ernest Muteba, Joseph J. Therattil.   New York: Arno Press, 1971. 216p.

Sponsored by the United Nations Institute for Training and Research (UNITAR), this study 'is concerned with the problems of very small states and territories, with special reference to the question of their roles in international affairs and the assistance which can be rendered to them by the United Nations family of nations'. Although somewhat dated, the study is of significant use in understanding the evolution of Djibouti's international relations. After briefly examining the relationship between small states and international organizations, particularly the United Nations (UN), the first section of the book describes the scope of the study and the factors which have contributed to the independent existence of small states within the international system (as opposed to being absorbed by larger territorial units). The second section of the study focuses on the problems and prospects faced by the small state in the realms of foreign policy and public administration. Among the problems discussed in the realm of public administration are organization, leadership and decision-making, communication and co-ordination, civil service, local government, public finances, joint arrangements, external contact and information, and technical assistance. Section three is devoted to various actions that the UN might consider in favour of small states. Possibilities range from guarantees for security and protection to conventional international assistance. An interesting annex for the quantitatively-oriented offers a 'statistical typology of micro-states and territories towards a definition of a micro-state'.

231 The Somali dilemma: nation in search of a state.
Said S. Samatar.   In: *Partitioned Africans: ethnic relations across Africa's international boundaries, 1884-1984.*   Edited by A. I. Asiwaju.   Lagos: University of Lagos Press, 1985, p. 155-93.

The chapter comprises but one part of an excellent presentation of the effects that ethnic partition has had on African domestic, intra-regional and international relations from 1884 to 1984. The chapter offers a concise and in-depth account of the Somali 'nation's' partition among its neighbours (including Djibouti), and the Somali 'state's' subsequent irredentist efforts to unite all Somali peoples still living under foreign rule. Major sections centre on: the economy and social institutions of the Somali nation prior to imperial partition; the period of partition by Great Britain, France, Italy and Ethiopia; the impact of partitions and Somali responses prior to 1960, and the 'disappointment' of the independence period in the face of conflict with Kenya and Ethiopia. The author concludes: 'Admittedly, it will be hard on Somali sensibilities to relinquish the old dream of national reunification. Yet if in the lives of individuals, as of nations, there are times when it is prudent to question the wisdom of pursuing old dreams, the time may have come for the Somali . . . to pause for a moment of self-reflection to determine whether the prize of re-unification is worth the cost of its pursuit'.

232 Super powers in the Horn of Africa.
Madan M. Sauldie.   New York: Apt Books, 1987. 252p.

The author worked in Ethiopia for four years during the early 1970s as the Africa Correspondent of *The Hindustan Times* and All India Radio and, subsequently, in

Foreign Relations

Cologne, GFR, as editor in the Africa Service of the Voice of Germany. Unlike the majority of volumes devoted to the international relations of the Horn of Africa, this book offers a substantial chapter on Djibouti, as well as numerous references to the country and its place within the region throughout the text. Yet, in contrast to the more limited focus on the impact of the 'super powers' as implied by the title, the author also discusses the impact of regional and 'lesser' powers upon the politics of the region. Individual chapters focus on: the historical sources of tension in the region (chapter 1); Ethiopian–Somali disputes over the Ogaden region (chapter 2); the Eritrean conflict (chapter 4); the roles of Egypt and Sudan as concerns the waters of the Nile (chapter 5); the impact of foreign powers (chapter 6); and a good chapter on the role of the Organization of African Unity (OAU) as an 'impotent onlooker' in the events of the region. Chapter 3, which is devoted to Djibouti, examines the evolution of ethnic politics in the light of French influence and rival Somali and Ethiopian claims to the territory. However, discussion curiously is limited to the period preceding and including independence in 1977. A useful four-page chronology of major events in the Horn of Africa is provided at the end.

233   **Conflict and intervention in the Horn of Africa.**
      Bereket Habte Selassie.   New York; London: Monthly Review Press,
      1980. 211p. 8 maps.

The author, a renowned Eritrean scholar and former insider of the Ethiopian government, offers an historical overview and analysis of nationalism, revolution and foreign intervention in the Horn of Africa, which he defines as including Ethiopia, Somalia, Djibouti and an independent Eritrea. The seven major chapters of the book are as follows: 'Ethiopia: foundations of an empire-state' (chapter 1); 'Ethiopia: empire and revolution' (chapter 2); 'Eritrea: a forgotten colonial' (chapter 3); 'The Oromo and Tigray: national liberation and crisis of empire' (chapter 4); 'Somalia and the "lost territories"' [including a brief portion on Djibouti] (chapter 5); 'The big powers and their intermediaries' (chapter 6); and 'Neighbors and meddlers' (chapter 7). The author concludes that 'ultimately' the 'Ethiopian empire' will be 'transformed'. In his opinion, 'the most likely cause will be the success of the Eritrean freedom fighters, for a final failure of the Ethiopian military campaign will mean the same end for the Dergue that it did for Haile Selassie'. A useful chronology of events (1884-79) denotes what the author perceives as the key historical events of the Horn.

234   **French Somaliland, the infamous referendum: sequel to 'a classic
      colonial case'.**
      Somali Democratic Republic: Ministry of Foreign Affairs.
      Mogadishu: Ministry of Foreign Affairs, 1967. 20p. map.

Published in April 1967, less than one month after the French held a referendum (19 March) on Djibouti's future status within France's colonial empire, this constitutes the sequel to *French Somaliland: a classic colonial case: events leading to the referendum March 19th 1967* (Mogadishu: Ministry of Foreign Affairs, 1967). Noting that the referendum result of continued association with France was a 'predictable result' because of colonial manipulation of voting roles, the booklet, representing the official viewpoint of the Somali Democratic Republic, centres on compiling facts to both negate and condemn the outcome. After describing an incident in which an ethnic Somali was shot while protesting the outcome of the referendum, various tables document registration and population irregularities, with text centring on the official opinion and subsequent actions of the Somali government (e.g. closing of the Somali-Djiboutian border) following the referendum. Especially interesting is a compilation of nineteen international reactions to the referendum culled from newspapers from France, Great Britain and the United States, as well as various countries throughout the Middle East and Africa (all excerpts are in English). The black-and-white photographs of events surrounding the referendum are included.

235 **Memorandum on French Somaliland submitted by the government of the Somali Republic to the United Nations Special Committee on the situation with regard to the implementation of the Declaration on the Granting of Independence to Colonial Territories and Peoples.**
Somali Democratic Republic. Ministry of Foreign Affairs.
Mogadishu: Ministry of Foreign Affairs, 1965. 11p.

A Somali government pamphlet calling for the issue of Djiboutian self-determination to be placed on the agenda of the United Nations (UN) Special Committee. Initial sections present Somalia's case for French manipulation or neglect of the territory's constitutional status, political and economic structures, and educational and social system. Three final sections describe Somalia's perception of the inherently negative 'intentions' of both France and Ethiopia in relation to the future status of the territory, as well as the Somali government's desired course of action. A six-point program is presented for French withdrawal and subsequent UN administration of the territory for a period of two years to 'allow the formation of a political consensus within the territory as to its future'. The hoped-for end result is clearly stated: 'The Somali Republic's intentions are the re-integration of all territory inhabited by the Somali peoples into one nation-state, the Somali Republic, on the basis of the right of self-determination of the people of the territories'.

236 **The future of French Somaliland: the Somali viewpoint.**
Somali Democratic Republic: Ministry of Information. Mogadishu:
Ministry of Information, 1966. 16p. map.

A Somali government pamphlet outlining the official viewpoint concerning the future of French Somaliland (Djibouti). Three initial sections reproduce comments by Somali Prime Minister Abdirazak Haji Hussein concerning 'recent developments' in French Somaliland from a press conference held in Mogadishu, Somalia on 19 September 1966; an interview given by the Somali prime minister to a special correspondent of Agence France Presse (Mogadishu, 9 September 1966); and an editorial entitled 'Safeguards and guarantees' which appeared in *Somali News* on 23 September 1966 and expresses the viewpoint of the Somali government. Two annexes reproduce a circular letter sent by Ethiopia's Emperor Menelik to Britain, France, Germany, Italy and Russia in 1881 (along with an accompanying map) to underscore the fallacy of Ethiopia's historical claim to Djibouti.

237 **Ethiopia at bay: a personal account of the Haile Selassie years.**
John H. Spencer. Algonac, Michigan: Reference Publications, 1984.
397p. 5 maps. bibliog.

The author, who worked for over twenty years as a personal adviser to Ethiopia's Emperor Haile Selassie, offers an insider's account of the rise and fall of his employer. The core argument of the book is that 'external forces and crises were the primary cause of Haile Selassie's defeat and exile in 1936 and downfall and death in 1974'. The importance of Djibouti to significant events in Emperor Selassie's reign is underscored in the introduction to the book: 'Erupting in the Ogaden and followed by the invasion from Eritrea, the Italo-Ethiopian war of 1935-36 was lost by the action of France in closing off access to the sea through the Addis Ababa-Djibouti railway. The war ended with the flight of the emperor into exile. Similarly, the Ethiopian tragedy of 1974-77 was marked by the Somali invasion of the Ogaden and the continued uprising in Eritrea and was followed by the threatened loss of access to the sea through Eritrea and Djibouti'. The claim is made that French President Charles de Gaulle, in discussions with Emperor Selassie in August 1966 concerning Djibouti's independence and Ethiopian interest therein, declared: 'We have no wish to stay. You have only to move in'. It was for this reason the Emperor is said to have declared in a public statement two weeks later that Djibouti 'was one of the lost provinces of Ethiopia of which, for historical, economic, strategic and demographic reasons, it was an integral part'.

238 **Ethiopia, the Horn of Africa, and U.S. policy.**

John H. Spencer.   Cambridge, Massachusetts: Institute for Foreign Policy Analysis, 1977. 69p. map.

The author served in Ethiopia as a foreign affairs adviser to Emperor Haile Selassie for roughly twenty years, including the years 1936, 1943-60 and 1973-74. This book is devoted to analysing the rise and fall of US influence in Ethiopia. Chapter 3, 'The Greater Somaliland problem and the Djibouti territory, 1960-1977' (p. 27-30), examines Djibouti's place in Somalia's quest to unite all Somalis of the Horn of Africa within a unified state. Published in September 1977, several months after Djibouti's independence, the author forecast a gloomy outcome for the future independence of this small country (which the passing years have proven false). Consider the following: 'Thus, independent Djibouti will no doubt find itself in a financial bind, unless friendly states come to its aid – and this probably means a "bail-out" by Somalia and the Soviet Union, and eventual annexation by Somalia . . . Since the French troops in Djibouti are not likely to resist annexation, we will no doubt soon witness another step forward in the creation of a Greater Somaliland'. An integral theme of this study is that policymakers must examine conflict in the Horn of Africa as a Middle East, as opposed to an African, problem.

239 **International boundary study (no. 87). Djibouti–Somalia.**

United States: Department of State: The Geographer.   Washington, DC: US Department of State, The Geographer, 1979. 7p.

This international boundary study is one of a series of specific boundary papers prepared by the US State Department's Office of the Geographer. Included is a map of the Djiboutian–Somali border and the historical background as to how the boundary emerged in its present form. Also discussed are minor modifications of the border in 1931 and 1934 as agreed upon by an Anglo–Ethiopian boundary commission. Included at the end of the paper are Italian, French and British sources upon which the analysis is based.

240 **International boundary study (no. 154). Ethiopia–French Territory of the Afars and Issas.**

United States: Department of State: The Geographer.   Washington, DC: US Department of State, The Geographer, 1976. 15p.

This international boundary study is another in a series prepared by the US State Department's Office of the Geographer. Included is a map of the Djiboutian–Ethiopian border and the historical background as to how the boundary emerged in its present form. For example, the port of Obock and the Afar region was ceded to France in 1862 by treaty with Afar chiefs. Also included is a description of several Franco–Ethiopian protocols which formalized the Djiboutian–Ethiopian border on 16 January 1954.

241 **Somalia: the problem child of Africa.**
Mesfin Wolde-Mariam. Addis Ababa: Artistic Printing Press, 1977.
80p.

The sympathies of the author concerning the Ethiopian-Somali dispute and the tone of the manuscript are clearly portrayed by the denigrating description of Somalia in the title as a 'problem child' of Africa. Writing in the highly-charged political atmosphere of Ethiopia during 1977, the author seeks to discredit Somalia's claims to the Ogaden region. Chapters centre on: the 'obsession' of Somalis in their quest for the creation of a 'Greater Somaliland' (chapter 2); Somalia's failure to gain support for the quest in either African, Arabic, Western or communist capitals (chapter 3); the inapplicability of the international norm of self-determination as applied to the Ogaden (chapter 4); and the perceived contradictions between Somalia's 'expansionist nationalism' and 'scientific socialism'. For a noted interpretation favourable to the Somali viewpoint, see Louis Fitzgibbon's *The betrayal of the Somalis* (q.v.). See also the author's earlier work, *The background of the Ethio–Somali boundary dispute* (Addis Ababa: Haile Selassie I University, 1964).

242 **The Horn of Africa: a strategic survey.**
Lij Imru Zelleke. Washington, DC: International Security Council, 1989. 68p. bibliog.

Written by a former member of Ethiopia's diplomatic corps, this 'strategic survey' of the Horn of Africa focuses primarily on Ethiopia, as well as including three significant sections each on Somalia and Djibouti. Among the topics discussed concerning the three countries are the historical backgrounds of conflicts in the Horn of Africa, economic conditions, external relations, military role and status, strategic implications and prospects for the future. Specific topics relating to Djibouti include Ethiopia's support for Djiboutian dissidents, the country's service-related economy, and the unique role of the continued French presence as a buffer to competing Somali–Ethiopian interests in the small territory. The author concludes that 'Djibouti will probably continue to be tranquil, secure, and relatively well managed under French oversight. Its strategic location will be an ongoing magnet for Western military, as well as Ethiopian commercial, traffic'.

Djibouti: nation-carrefour. (Djibouti: crossroads-nation.)
See item no. 6.

Djibouti: pawn of the Horn of Africa.
See item no. 7.

Le regard colonial ou 'il y a peu de coloniaux qui n'aient fait escale à Djibouti au moins une fois dans leur vie'. (The colonial glance or 'there are few colonials who did not stop over at Djibouti at least once in their life'.)
See item no. 46.

The politics of repatriation: Ethiopian refugees in Djibouti, 1977-83.
See item no. 135.

Foreign Relations

Djibouti's three-front struggle for independence: 1967-77.
See item no. 166.

The right of self-determination in very small places.
See item no. 172.

Somali nationalism: international politics and the drive for unity in the Horn.
See item no. 186.

Republic of Djibouti: code of international arbitration.
See item no. 195.

EEC–Djibouti cooperation.
See item no. 245.

Geographical distribution of financial flows to developing countries.
See item no. 382.

International Development Co-operation

243 **Spécial: Djibouti.** (Special: Djibouti.)
Association Française des Volontaires du Progrès (AFVP). *Revue de l'Association Française des Volontaires du Progrès* (special edition), no. 40 (Jan. 1985), 42p.

The Association Française des Volontaires du Progrès (AFVP, French Association of Volunteers for Progress) is a non-governmental organization devoted to Third World development. This edition of the AFVP's newsletter centres on the nature and benefits of its projects in Djibouti since 1977 and, more precisely, the organization's role in aiding refugees from the 1977-78 Ogaden war between Somalia and Ethiopia and the 1980-81 drought in the Horn. The first article, 'Les maçons des nouveaux toukouls' (Builders of new toukouls) (p. 12-19), describes AFVP's efforts in teaching refugees the rudiments of masonry to build new, sedentary homes out of stone. A second set of articles – 'Le Mouloud: un périmètre devient village' (Mouloud: a perimeter becomes village) (p. 21-26), 'L'association des jardiniers du Gobaad' (Association of the gardeners of Gobaad) (p. 27-29), and 'Afar: "assez causé, maintenant je travaille"' (Afar: 'enough talk, now I work') (p. 30-34) – describes the sedentarization of displaced pastoralists within agricultural co-operatives. A final article, 'Santé: les enfants de Balbala' (Health: the children of Balbala) (p. 35-42), discusses AFVP's role in health education and maintenance among infants of Balbala, a large shantytown on the outskirts of Djibouti City.

244 **IGADD: inaugural summit in an 'oasis of peace'.**
Tom Glaser. *The Courier*, no. 96 (March-April 1986), p. 21-22.

This brief article offers a highly positive overview of the 1986 inaugural summit meeting of the Intergovernmental Authority on Drought and Development (IGADD), the headquarters of which is located in Djibouti City. After summarizing the speeches presented at the summit, two short sections outline the objectives, strategies and programmes of the organization. The author's concluding note is extremely positive and hopeful: 'It is a serious contribution to the solution of one of Africa's most serious situations. It was conceived in a spirit of collaboration and independence, prepared with care and administrative rigour, launched amid solid expressions of hope and

105

goodwill and, as such, represents for the Horn of Africa the best guarantee of progress and stability'.

245 EEC–Djibouti cooperation.
Jean-Louis Houdart. *The Courier*, no. 95 (Jan.-Feb. 1986), p. 41-42.

This brief article summarizes the European Economic Community's (EEC) development relationship with Djibouti. The EEC has provided aid in the area of rural development (such as herding, small holdings and drinking water supplies) and for improving services in Djibouti City, such as training in municipal activities and studying the potential of the town and its facilities. The EEC has been especially interested in providing funds for regional co-operation to lessen tensions in the Horn, subsequently becoming increasingly involved with the Intergovernmental Authority on Drought and Development (IGADD). A brief summary is made of EEC aid to Djibouti (1977-85), including a list of projects and funding totals.

246 Assembly of heads of state and government, first session Djibouti, 15-16 January 1986.
Intergovernmental Authority on Drought and Development (IGADD). Djibouti: IGADD, 1986. 2 vols.

The heads of state of Djibouti, Ethiopia, Kenya, Somalia, Sudan and Uganda met from 15-16 January 1986 in Djibouti City to sign an executive agreement formally establishing the Intergovernmental Authority on Drought and Development (IGADD). These two volumes document that historic agreement. The first five chapters of volume 1 include an introduction to IGADD's goals and purposes (chapter 1), a reproduction of the ten-page agreement signed by the heads of state (chapter 2), an outline of the internal rules of IGADD (chapter 3), the causes and consequences of drought (chapter 4), and the strategies necessary to combat drought (chapter 5). Chapter 6 describes the role and structure of the executive secretariat. Also discussed are the initial activities of the secretariat and its financial and budgetary implications for 1986-88. Finally, chapter 7 maps out IGADD's 'Plan of action'. The first half of volume 2 reproduces the speeches made at the opening, plenary and closing sessions of the conference, including those made by Presidents Hassan Gouled Aptidon (Djibouti), Abdou Diouf (Senegal), Mengistu Haile Mariam (Ethiopia), Daniel Arap Moi (Kenya), Tito Okello (Uganda), Maxammad Siyaad Barre (Somalia) and Abdel Rahman Mohamed Hassan Swar Al Dahab (Sudan). The second half of volume 2 reproduces congratulatory statements sent by seventeen interested countries and international organizations. A final section reproduces the 'Final communiqué' signed by the heads of state of the member IGADD countries.

247 Donor's conference.
Intergovernmental Authority on Drought and Development (IGADD). Djibouti: IGADD, 1987. 3 vols. 5 maps.

This three-volume set was provided to prospective donor countries and international organizations prior to the March 1987 meeting hosted in Djibouti of the Intergovernmental Authority on Drought and Development (IGADD). In volume 1, subtitled *General presentation*, nine chapters outline an executive summary of the proposed conference (chapter 1), background of IGADD (chapter 2), socio-economic situation of the sub-region (chapter 3), policy issues (chapter 4), main thrusts of co-operative action (chapter 5), criteria and priorities for IGADD projects (chapter 6), aid flow to IGADD countries (chapter 7), implications of the proposed projects on the future role of IGADD (chapter 8), and subregional and national projects (chapter 9). Four annexes provide twenty-two pages of excellent statistical data and flow trends of official development assistance to IGADD member countries (Djibouti, Ethiopia, Kenya, Somalia, Sudan and Uganda), a summary of the European Economic Community's (EEC) role in the region, and a background on shared water resources. Finally, five excellent colour-coded maps provide data concerning climate, soils, vegetation, desertification and population of the IGADD member countries. In volume 2, which is subtitled *Subregional projects* (and which is further subdivided into two further volumes), various data are offered on numerous subregional projects that include two or more countries. Among the sections are: 'Background and information'; 'Objectives'; 'Description'; 'Expected results and follow-up'; and related activities. In volume 3, which is subtitled *National projects*, five further subdivided volumes offer a wealth of information on numerous proposed national projects. Individual books focus on Djibouti: (volume 3-a); Ethiopia (volume 3-b); Kenya (volume 3-c); Somalia (volume 3-d); and the Sudan (volume 3-e).

248 **Donor's conference: synthesis.**
Intergovernmental Authority on Drought and Development
(IGADD). Djibouti: IGADD, 1987. 46p.

This booklet synthesizes a three-volume presentation to a donor conference held 16-18 March 1987 in Djibouti. Specifically, it summarizes the organization's goals and lists the 63 subregional projects and 154 national projects sought by the recipient countries. National and subregional projects centre around the themes of food security and early warning, desertification control, water resources, communications, agricultural research and training, and animal resources. Forty-six national projects are proposed for Djibouti.

249 **Report of the first donors conference, Djibouti, 16th to 18 March 1987.**
Intergovernmental Authority on Drought and Development
(IGADD). Djibouti: IGADD, 1987. 113p.

This is the report of the donor's conference hosted in Djibouti to enlist the support of the international community in the implementation of the Intergovernmental Authority on Drought and Development's (IGADD) plan of action, programs and projects. The conference represented a major diplomatic coup for the prestige of Djiboutian President Hassan Gouled Aptidon as promoter of regional peace and co-operation, especially concerning the Ethiopian–Somali territorial dispute and Djibouti's position therein. The first part of the report, entitled the 'Djibouti declaration', provides the final communiqué adopted by the six member countries and representa-tives of seventeen donor governments and twenty-nine international financing institutions. Section two provides a record of donor interest in projects at both the regional and subregional levels. The majority of the report constitutes the verbatim introductory remarks made by all governments and international organizations in attendance. Especially interesting are the remarks of the member nations of IGADD and the former French, British and Italian colonial powers. Four annexes summarize the agenda and timetable of the conference, and provide a list of participants and lists of the subregional and national projects.

250 **Second summit of IGADD, proceedings.**
Intergovernmental Authority on Drought and Development
(IGADD). Djibouti: IGADD, March 1988. 103p.

The second summit meeting of the heads of state and governments of the Intergovernmental Authority on Drought and Development (IGADD) took place in Djibouti during 21-22 March 1988. The bulk of the official proceedings consists of twenty-one appendices reproducing statements made by those in attendance, providing the researcher with interesting material concerning economic and political co-operation in the Horn of Africa. The sparseness and vagueness of this set of proceedings, however, as compared to the first meeting in 1986, suggest the growing stagnation of the organization amid regional conflict and donor wariness. Especially relevant appendices include: both the opening (no. 3) and closing (no. 21) addresses of Djiboutian President (and IGADD Chairperson) Hassan Gouled Aptidon; the opening speech by Moumin Bahdon Farah, Djiboutian Minister of Foreign Affairs and Minister Co-ordinator of IGADD (no. 4); statements by Somali President Maxammad Siyaad Barre (no. 7) and Ethiopian President Mengistu Haile Mariam (no. 6); the biennial report (1986-87) of the Executive Secretariat (no. 19); and the joint communiqué adopted by the heads of state and governments in attendance (no. 20).

251 **Djibouti, developing city and country.**
Republic of Djibouti: Ministry of Foreign Affairs and Cooperation.
Djibouti: Ministry of Foreign Affairs and Cooperation, 1983. 2 vols.

This two-volume set documents the donors conference that was hosted in Djibouti in November 1983. The first two chapters of volume 1, subtitled *Summary report prepared for the donor's conference*, provide a general description of the country and the nation. Chapter 3 documents the economic and social situations, including natural resources, communications, trade and services, banking system and currency, public finances, industrial production, and health and living conditions. Chapter 4 describes economic and social development undertaken since independence, while chapter 5 reproduces Djibouti's Law of Economic and Social Orientation (Act 251, 1982), or the basis of the country's sectoral policies. Finally, chapter 6 discusses five sets of intersectorial policies and ten sets of sectorial policies, while chapter 7 explains the motivations of the conference of donors. Numerous appendices contain a wealth of statistical information. The first part of volume 2 presents an economic and financial analysis of Djibouti's 1983-88 capital development program (the estimated total cost of planned projects was $570,000,000). Chapter 1 discusses the strategy, financing and absorptive capacity of the capital program, while chapter 2 examines the macro-economic (global) effects of the capital program's investment and operating phases. Chapter 3 describes the economic and financial effects of the program, judging its impact on Djibouti's trade balance, external debt, national budget, employment and gross domestic product (GDP). Four appendices to the first section include a dollar breakdown of the 1983-88 capital program investments operation as well as a diagram of secondary effects. The majority of the report, however, is devoted to a listing and description of Djibouti's capital projects (section 2). Each project listing is fleshed out in terms of description, objectives, justification, resources to be dedicated, expected results and financing. Projects are listed under the major subheadings of water-agriculture–stockbreeding, energy, industry, tourism, transport–telecommunications, urban development, training–education, culture–sports and health.

252 **VITA News.**
Arlington, Virginia: Volunteers in Technical Assistance (VITA),
1971- . quarterly.

Volunteers in Technical Assistance (VITA) is a private, non-profit international development organization which promotes self-sufficiency through the use of appropriate small-scale technologies, especially in the area of renewable energy. VITA's documentation centre in Arlington, Virginia (open to public inquiries and demands) is a storehouse for over 40,000 documents related to small- and medium-scale technologies in subjects ranging from agriculture to wind power. VITA has, since 1982, worked in Djibouti with the Institut Supérieur d'Études et de Recherches Scientifiques et Techniques (ISERST), or the science and research branch of the Djiboutian government. *VITA News*, published in Arlington, Virginia, is a quarterly publication of the organization's work abroad, and includes an update section, short feature articles, book reviews and resources section on newsletters, conferences, publications and training opportunities. Articles from time to time can be found on Djibouti. Two especially interesting articles by Jean-Yves Garnier include: 'Media campaign promotes conservation in Djibouti' (July 1986), p. 6-7; and 'Beating the heat in the maritime desert: ISERST/VITA team helps Djibouti cut energy and housing costs' (April 1987), p. 4-7. For a similar examination, see Daniel C. Dunham's 'ISERST building-energy conservation in an adverse climate' (July 1984), p. 9-13.

Djibouti: crossroads of the world. (Djibouti: terre de rencontres et d'échanges.)
See item no. 4.

British government, finance capitalists and the French Jibuti–Addis Ababa railway, 1898-1913.
See item no. 266.

Bulletin Périodique. (Periodical Bulletin.)
See item no. 313.

The United States and Africa: guide to U.S. official documents and government-sponsored publications on Africa, 1785-1975.
See item no. 409.

Economy, Trade and Transport

253 Caravan trade and history in the northern parts of East Africa.
Mordechai Abir. *Paideuma*, vol. 14 (1968), p. 103-20.
An introduction briefly assesses the impact, both positive and negative, of trade in Africa. The positive being trade's promotion of new ideas, cultural features and its role in facilitating the emergence of many African kingdoms. Adversely, caravan trade is said to have ushered in ruin and disaster through encouraging wars, carrying disease and expanding the slave trade. Three important trading systems discussed by the author include: (1) the Khartoum merchants; (2) Somali merchants from the Benadir coast; and (3) Arab/Swahili trade in Tanzania and Kenya. Of particular interest to the scholar of Djibouti is a description of the trade system of the Afar peoples from the Djiboutian port of Tadjoura into Ethiopia. However, the main emphasis is on Somali–Galla trade in the Horn of Africa, where trade in slaves and luxury items from Arabia and India were transported to Ethiopia. However, the primary focus of the article is an overview of commodities, and specifically the ethnic groups involved in caravan trade and the extent of that trade in the interior.

254 The Islamic Red Sea slave trade: an effort at quantification.
Ralph A. Austen. In: *Proceedings of the fifth international conference on Ethiopian studies: session B, April 13-16, 1978. Chicago, USA.* Edited by Robert L. Hess. Chicago: Chicago Office of Publications Services, University of Illinois at Chicago Circle, 1979, p. 443-67.
It is argued that, while the Atlantic slave trade 'forms part of the unique development pattern of Western capitalism', the Islamic slave trade, in its earlier phases, developed independently of Europe and, even in the era of European expansion into the Red Sea and adjacent areas, remained oriented toward an essentially Asian economy'. By quantifying the Islamic Red Sea slave trade, including those slaves shipped through Djibouti, the author concludes that several arguments of world systems theorists, especially their contentions about the uniqueness of Western capitalism, are subject to revision and further analysis. The author concludes that 'the evidence on the Islamic trade suggests that the needs of a preindustrial society could generate very

considerable demands for forced human mobilization, both to produce goods of various types for the market and to staff the elaborate apparatus of statecraft'.

255 History of the Franco–Ethiopian railway from Djibouti to Addis Ababa.
Owen P. C. Collier, K. M. A. Perkins. *Transport History*, vol. 10, no. 3 (winter 1979), p. 220-45.

Owen P. C. Collier, the co-author of this article, served during the Second World War with the Royal Engineers as the Chief Mechanical Engineer and, subsequently, as the General Manager of the railway that links Ethiopia's capital of Addis Ababa with Djibouti's port city. The history of the railroad is grouped into the following sections: '1894-1917: the building of the railway'; '1935-1941: the Italian invasion'; '1941-1946: British military administration'; and 'The post-war period: brief notes'. A wealth of technical data drawing largely on the pre-1946 period is offered in this history, including: topography of the rail line; civil engineering works (e.g. bridges and viaducts); a list of thirty-eight stations; description of twenty-two points of water supply; problems of communication and safety; details of serviceable locomotives and rolling stock; and amounts of imports/exports carried on the line. Especially unique are locomotive drawings and specifications of nine locomotives used on the line, as well as black-and-white photographs of the railway from the pre-1946 period.

256 Djibouti in its third year of independence.
The Courier, no. 63 (Sept.-Oct. 1980), p. 10-25.

The first three pages of this collection of articles – devoted to assessing the initial three years of Djibouti's independence – consist of an interview with Djiboutian President Hassan Gouled Aptidon in which he stresses the need to consolidate national unity and maintain the country's stature as a haven of peace and stability. Brief sections detail basic facts about the country, strengths and weaknesses of the nomadic way of life, refugee problems, and the nature of Djibouti's external relations as described by Minister for Foreign Affairs and Cooperation Moumin Bahdon Farah. The majority of the collection, however, summarizes the economic advances and problems that have accompanied three years of independence. A discussion of Djibouti's service-oriented economy is followed by an analysis of changes in foreign trade (most important a growing trade deficit), the creation of a national airline (Air Djibouti), tourist potential, geothermal prospects, and the hope of closer relations between Djibouti and the European Community.

257 Abyssinia: the Ethiopian railway and the powers.
T. Lennox Gilmour. London: Alston Rivers, 1906. 92p. map.

This small booklet highlights British fears of French economic domination of Ethiopia's markets that possibly would have resulted when the final leg of the French-financed Djibouti–Addis Ababa railway reached completion. The author is clearly opposed to the completion of the railway as an exclusively French enterprise. Rather, an argument is made for the commercialization of the line under a board of directors that would include French, British and Italian nationals. Claiming that the Ethiopian government would never support French control over such an important transportation and trade route, the author raises the spectre of the German government coming to the aid of the Ethiopian government in an attempt to justify his argument for a joint board of directors. 'Germany is strictly within her rights in seeking to increase her interests and extend her influence in Abyssinia', warns the author. 'Great Britain and France must do the same for their interests. Is it to the interest of either country that the Emperor Menelik be drawn into the arms of Germany?'

Economy, Trade and Transport

258 **World transport data. (Statistiques mondiales de transport.)**
International Road Transport Union (IRU): Department of Economic Affairs. Geneva, Switzerland: IRU, 1973- . sporadic.
Employing both English and French texts, this publication offers a wide variety of transport data for all countries of the world, including Djibouti. Among the data provided are the number of motor road vehicles, the nature and extent of the road network, the rail network and its traffic (both passengers and merchandise), and sea-borne and air traffic. Data is usually presented over several years enabling the scholar to chart transport trends and developments. Individual volumes have been published for the following years: 1973 (volume 1); 1976 (volume 2); 1980 (volume 3); and 1985 (volume 4).

259 **Djibouti: the love of liberty.**
Augustine Oyowe. *The Courier*, no. 95 (Jan.-Feb. 1986), p. 28-46.
A collection of easy-to-read articles summarizing the nature of Djibouti's economic accomplishments and future prospects nearly ten years after independence in 1977. The tone of the collection is set by an initial article discussing Djibouti's 'struggle' for greater economic self-reliance. After mapping out the history of this small country's economic development, an analysis is made of various aspects of the country's economy, including the service sector, food production (meats, vegetables, fish), mineral resources, manufacturing (with emphasis on import substitution) and urban unemployment. Three other brief articles centre on the country's port and its relationship to the service economy, the development of tourism and Djibouti's co-operation with the European Economic Community (EEC). Also included is an interview with Ismael Guedi Hared, director of the Office of the President, and a map.

260 **Ethiopia and the Red Sea and Gulf of Aden ports in the nineteenth and twentieth centuries.**
Richard Pankhurst. *Ethiopia Observer*, vol. 8, no. 1 (1964), p. 37-104.
This extremely well-documented history (408 footnotes) has two major purposes, both of which are successfully achieved. The author's first goal is 'to examine the relations between Ethiopia and the Red Sea and the Gulf of Aden coast in the nineteenth and early twentieth centuries, a period in which, as we shall see, the rulers of Ethiopia constantly reiterated their age-old claim to access to the sea while the ports which they had so long cherished changed hands between a handful of foreign powers, the Ottoman Empire and Egypt, France, Britain and Italy'. The author's second goal is 'to chronicle the various changes of status which occurred in the coastal areas of the Horn of Africa over the century or so which witnessed such varied events as the decay of the Ottoman Empire, the opening of the Suez Canal, the scramble for Africa, and the rise of fascism in Italy and other parts of Europe'. Djibouti's cities and ports of Obock, Tadjoura and Djibouti City, as well as French diplomatic manoeuvrings during the period, figure prominently throughout the text.

261 **The Franco–Ethiopian railway and its history.**
Richard Pankhurst. *Ethiopian Observer*, vol. 6, no. 4 (1963), p. 342-79.
A highly detailed history of the Djibouti–Addis Ababa railway, encompassing the period from Emperor Menelik's concession of 9 March 1894 to his Swiss adviser Alfred Ilg to establish a company (with the aim of building and operating a railway) to the Franco–Italian agreement of 7 January 1935. In this latter agreement, France

112

recognized Italian interest in the line and transferred seven per cent of its shares to Italy. The major sections of this chronological history are as follows: 'The original plan'; 'The Menelik–Ilg concession of 1894'; 'Negotiations on all sides'; 'Construction work begins'; 'Financial difficulties begin'; 'Menelik's first doubts'; 'The first train services begin'; 'Anglo–French tension'; 'The Bonhoure–Chefneux Convention'; 'Freight policy and transport costs'; 'The establishment of Dire Dawa'; 'Increasing difficulties of the Chefneux company'; 'The Tripartite Agreement of 1906'; 'Bankruptcy'; 'Menelik's second concession'; 'The Franco–Ethiopian railway'; 'The second French connection'; and 'The extension of the line to Addis Ababa'.

262 **Indian trade with Ethiopia, the Gulf of Aden and the Horn of Africa in the nineteenth and early twentieth centuries.**
Richard Pankhurst. *Cahiers d'Études Africaines*, vol. 14, no. 3 (1974), p. 453-98.
'Throughout the nineteenth century', notes the author, 'the southern Red Sea area, the Gulf of Aden and the Horn of Africa enjoyed close, and long-established, commercial contacts with the Indian subcontinent. A large portion of the trade of this part of Africa passed through the hands of Indian, or Banyan, merchants, small but vitally important colonies of whom were to be found at all principal ports of the area'. In this well documented article the author examines the extensive nature of this Indian trade with northeast Africa, including through the Djiboutian port of Tadjoura. Special attention is paid to the nature of Indian communities and the types of goods traded.

263 **The trade of the Gulf of Aden ports of Africa in the nineteenth and early twentieth centuries.**
Richard Pankhurst. *Journal of Ethiopian Studies*, vol. 3, no. 1 (Jan. 1965), p. 36-81.
A wealth of data on the nature of trade through Djibouti (including the ports of Obock, Tadjoura and Djibouti City) during the 19th and 20th centuries, as well as other ports on the Gulf of Aden. It is demonstrated that, whereas in the early part of the 19th century the ports of Berbera and Zeila were of key importance, during the latter part of the century the ports of Tadjoura and Djibouti City rose to 'considerable importance' (initially because of fire-arms trade and, subsequently, because of the construction of the Djibouti–Addis Ababa railway). Data supplied include that found in the following tables: 'Foreign trade of the French Somali coast in M. T. [Maria Theresa] dollars (1899-1907)'; 'Ethiopian imports through Jibuti in M. T. dollars (1899-1901)'; 'Trade through Jibuti in M. T. dollars (1900-1906)'; 'Coffee exports through Jibuti (1898-1906)'; 'Coffee exported via the Jibuti railway in kilos (1899-1906)'; 'Hides and skins exported via the Jibuti railway (in kilos) (1909-1935)'; 'Ivory exports through Jibuti (1899-1906)'; 'Ivory exports by rail through Jibuti, in kilos (1909-1933)'; 'Wax exports through Jibuti (1899-1905)'; 'Civet exports through Jibuti (1899-1906)'; 'Other exports through Jibuti (1899-1906)'; 'Exports of Jibuti by rail in metric tons (1909-1935)'; 'Textile imports through Jibuti in M. T. dollars (1905-1906)'; 'Textile imports through Jibuti by rail (1909-1935)'; and 'Arms imports of Jibuti by rail in metric tons (1909-1936)'.

Economy, Trade and Transport

264 **Transport and communications in Ethiopia, 1835-1935 (III).**
Richard Pankhurst. *Journal of Transport History*, vol. 5, no. 4 (Nov. 1962), p. 233-54.

In this, the final of a series of three articles on the development of transport and communications in Ethiopia from 1835 to 1935, the author focuses on the construction of the Djibouti–Addis Ababa railway. Earlier articles centred on the nature of Ethiopian hospitality and the development of inns and roads (vol. 5, no. 2, p. 69-88), as well as the extent of river crossings, bridges and the use of boats (vol. 5, no. 3, p. 166-81). In this article, detailed discussion of the events surrounding the construction of the railway include the evolving nature of internal Ethiopian politics, economic and political competition between French and British industrialists (as well as their respective governments), the nature of concessions granted to private railway concerns by the Ethiopian government, the economic dilemmas inherent in such an undertaking, and growing conflict between Ethiopia and France. The author also succinctly examines the effects that the railway exerted on the expansion of Djibouti City and the French colony in general.

265 **Le commerce des armes à Djibouti de 1888 à 1914.** (Arms trade in Djibouti from 1888 to 1914.)
Agnès Picquart. *Revue Française d'Histoire d'Outre-Mer*, vol. 58, no. 213 (1971), p. 407-32.

The author provides an extremely succinct analysis of the arms trade in Djibouti from 1888, which marked the decline of Obock as the central trading zone, to 1914, or the beginning of the First World War. The author argues that the politico-economic organization of the region, most notably endemic rivalries between opposing ethnic groups for strategic territories, was 'largely responsible for the high intake of war materials attained in these parts, and opened the way to European imperialism'. Arms came from France, Belgium, Germany, Great Britain and the Far East. The dramatic rise in arms imports to, and exports from, Djibouti is documented. For example, while in 1899 total arms imports and exports were valued at 3,279,315 (French Francs – FF) and 1,904,740 (FF) respectively, in 1914 this had risen to 28,632,145 (FF) and 43,643,215 (FF) respectively. It is shown how several countries, disturbed about the volume of the arms trade, attempted to curtail the upward spiral through international treaties, temporary halts in through-traffic, coastguard operations, decrees, councils and diplomatic manoeuvres. Yet, the author concludes: 'Apart from the basic inefficiency of certain laws, from both the legislative and practical points of views, all these measures were in reality nothing but a mobile screen of "diplomatic play" to mask some powerful stakes: European imperialism on the one hand and, on the other, economic demands (markets for the arms industry); the basic prosperity of Djibouti is proof of this'.

266 **British government, finance capitalists and the French Jibuti–Addis Ababa railway, 1898-1913.**
K. V. Ram. *Journal of Imperial and Commonwealth History*, vol. 9, no. 2 (Jan. 1981), p. 146-68.

The assumption of theories of imperialism that European governments serve as collaborators of finance capitalism in Third World areas is questioned by utilizing the case study of competing French and British finance capitalists in building the Djibouti–Addis Ababa railway during the period 1898-1913. It is argued that, although 'it is true that surplus European capital sought profitable outlets in the non-European

114

world and often solicited government intervention whenever it was threatened by European competitors and foreign governments, it was not always the case that finance capital as an imperial partner was either welcomed or supported by imperial governments'. In the case of the railway, for example, the author describes how the British government sacrificed the interests of private British investors in the line to the interests of diplomacy and strengthening Anglo–French relations.

267 **Budget de l'état, exercise 1987.** (State budget, 1987 exercise.)
République de Djibouti. Djibouti: Imprimerie Nationale, 1987.
74p.

Put together annually by the Djiboutian government, the state budget summarizes expenses for the National Assembly, the office of the President and thirteen ministries. Also included is a summary of national debt, finance laws and a brief introduction to the national budget. The 1987 Djiboutian budget totalled 22,198,950,000 Djiboutian Francs (DF) ($US 125,531,000) and represented a 3.14 per cent reduction over the 1986 budget of 22,896,267,000 DF ($US 129,474,000). The largest increase in the 1987 budget was for the National Assembly (35.55 per cent) to pay the costs of the 1987 legislative elections and increased living expenses for the deputies. State expenditures for 1987 are divided as follows: public debt (4.65 per cent); National Assembly (1.25 per cent); personnel (57.35 per cent); material (24.39 per cent); maintenance (2.18 per cent); operation subsidies (5.48 per cent); and equipment (3.79 per cent).

268 **Le rail franco–éthiopién en détresse.** (The Franco–Ethiopian railway in distress.)
Max Rosso. Paris: La Pensée Universelle, 1983. 306p.

In a very engaging style, the author, former Technical Director of the Djibouti–Addis Ababa railway, offers a very personal account of the numerous problems which have beset its operation during the late 1970s and early 1980s. The bulk of the book is devoted to the political and economic problems which have beset the railway and the impacts that these have had on Djibouti in the wake of independence in 1977. Of special importance are political developments in Ethiopia as a result of that country's revolution (such as the incarceration of the general director of the railway), acts of sabotage by the Front de Libération de la Côte Somalie (FLCS), and the Somali–Ethiopian War of 1977-78 which effectively closed the railway for over a year. A discussion of Djibouti figures prominently throughout, with numerous short sections focusing on such topics as independence ceremonies in 1977, visits to Ali Sabieh and life in general.

269 **Major ports of Ethiopia: Aseb, Jibuti, Mesewa.**
Haile Wolde-Mariam. *Ethiopian Geographical Journal*, vol. 3, no. 1 (June 1965), p. 35-47.

The article briefly discusses the physical location and historical background of Ethiopia's three major trade outlets to the outside world, including Ethiopia's ports of Assab and Massawa, as well as the Djiboutian port located in Djibouti City (which is the terminal point of the Djibouti–Addis Ababa railway). Djibouti, primarily due to its rail system, is described as the primary outlet for Ethiopia's trade. Tables clearly show Djibouti's importance as of 1965 as both an import and export centre which, however, had decreased in cargo tonnage between 1953-63. But the value of Djibouti's goods in Ethiopian dollars still overshadowed her two 'sister' ports in 1963. Also listed are the principal commodities imported (such as textiles and machinery) and exported (such as coffee and hide) for each of the three ports. Djibouti's primary export in 1963 was coffee and its primary import was mineral fuel. Other tables and maps contrast the three ports in terms of average freight-rate on principal roads and prices charged per metric ton.

270 **1977-1987: our development means economic growth.**
Paris: BCEOM, 1987. 17p.

Djibouti's international port provides capabilities for bunkering, transit of goods to neighbouring Ethiopia and Somalia, and transhipment of goods to other countries of the region. This informative booklet summarizes the valuable role that Djibouti's autonomous port has played in the country's development from 1977 to 1987. Numerous tables offer a wealth of interesting data denoting the characteristics of quays, public storage zones, traffic evolution (according to origin, destination and product), evolution of calls according to type of ship and type of operation, debarkation of goods according to destination and embarkation of goods according to origin. Also denoted are navigation conditions, service facilities, commercial installations, port departments, and contact information (e.g. telex) for local shipping agents, stevedores, oil companies, forwarding agents, shiphandlers and insurance companies.

Djibouti: crossroads of the world. (Djibouti: terre de rencontres et d'échanges.)
See item no. 4.

Arthur Rimbaud: trade and politics in northeast Africa 1880-1891.
See item no. 96.

Economic history of Ethiopia, 1800-1935.
See item no. 99.

Fire-arms in Ethiopian history (1800-1935).
See item no. 100.

The periplus of the Erythraean sea: travel and trade in the Indian Ocean by a merchant of the first century.
See item no. 107.

Qat: changes in the production and consumption of a quasilegal commodity in northeast Africa.
See item no. 110.

Table ronde sur la création de petites entreprises 4 mai 1986, interventions et débat. (Round table on the creation of small enterprises 4 May 1986, interventions and debate.)
See item no. 121.

Which way to the sea please?
See item no. 214.

Le secteur non-structuré à Djibouti: charactéristiques des entreprises et de la main-d'oeuvre du secteur. Contribution à l'emploi et la formation des revenus. (Djibouti's non-structured sector: characteristics of the sector's

enterprises and handicrafts. Contribution to employment and the formation of revenues.)
See item no. 294.

Bulletin Périodique. (Periodical Bulletin.)
See item no. 313.

International trade statistics yearbook.
See item no. 388.

Handbook of international trade and development statistics.
See item no. 393.

Energy

271 **Technical-economic studies of geothermal projects: the Djibouti case.**
A. Abdallah, A. Gandino, C. Sommaruga. *Geothermics*, vol. 14, nos. 2/3 (1985), p. 327-34.

A summary of the prospects for geothermal exploration and development in Djibouti. The authors argue that Djibouti's great geothermal potential, if properly put to use, 'can meet most of the country's energy requirements, both in the production of electrical power . . . and in agriculture, tourism and mining'. A map points out the most promising geothermal fields throughout the country. A figure provides what the authors perceive to be the necessary steps in fleshing out a technical-economic pre-feasibility study of geothermal development. Among the topics are production costs and potential profitability of a geothermal project, cost-benefit analysis and the prospects of integrated development in Djibouti.

272 **Étude sur les combustibles domestiques dans les districts de Djibouti.**
(Study of domestic combustibles in the districts of Djibouti.)
Dominique Briane. Djibouti: Institut Supérieur d'Études et de Recherches Scientifiques et Techniques (ISERST) and Volunteers in Technical Assistance (VITA), 1986. 60p. 2 maps.

The purpose of this study was to investigate the possibilities of enhancing the use of domestic combustibles (primarily wood and charcoal) in the cooking of food in Djibouti. The study also concerned itself with the use of kerosene as a means for preparing food. The report is divided into five major sections: introduction (section 1); study of wood combustibles (section 2); the use of kerosene in cooking food (section 3); identification of improved techniques for the burning of wood and charcoal, adapted to the case of Djibouti (section 4); and final recommendations (section 5). Useful appendices outline the methodology of the study, including the questionnaire used to determine usage of domestic combustibles in Djibouti.

273 **Conventional electricity in Djibouti: challenges and opportunities for the future.**
Shibu Dhai. Arlington, Virginia: Volunteers in Technical Assistance (VITA), 1985. 107p.

The report was prepared by Djibouti's National Energy Service, the National Institute for Higher Scientific and Technical Research (ISERST), Volunteers in Technical Assistance (VITA) and the United States Agency for International Development (USAID). The report offers estimates on the impacts of energy conservation on future electricity demand and capacity planning. Specifically, the report 'quantifies the impacts of demand reduction programs and conservation measures for the 1985-2000 time period in terms of system expansion and revenue requirements. For load management and conservation programs, short-range, medium-range, and long range "best estimate" scenarios were developed to evaluate the impacts on system capacity and revenue requirements'. The first two chapters discuss the nature of Djibouti's electricity supply system, demand forecasting and capacity expansion requirements. Chapter 3 centres on energy conservation and load management potentials, while chapter 4 outlines supply scenarios of electricity production.

274 **Building for the maritime desert: climate, construction, and energy in Djibouti.**
Daniel C. Dunham. Arlington, Virginia: Volunteers in Technical Assistance (VITA), 1983. 53p. bibliog.

This handbook was prepared as part of the Djibouti Energy Initiatives Project to provide the necessary background material for developing patterns of construction for Djibouti that are energy efficient, economical and functional. As the author notes: 'Designing specifically for climate has yet to be done in many areas where it is most acutely needed. It first requires a recognition of how present or historic buildings succeed or fail in providing comfortable interior spaces. It means organized experimentation with climatic design and a willingness on the part of clients to accept the risks that experimentation entails'. An extensive analysis of Djibouti's climate (temperature, humidity, radiation, wind and rainfall) is followed by sections describing how to protect interior spaces from exterior heat and types of building materials one must use. Chapter 5 examines aspects of environmental modifications (exterior and interior environment, air movement and daylighting), with a final chapter providing conclusions and recommendations, including designer, client and government responsibilities.

275 **Djiboutian urban development project: energy conserving design for salines-ouest housing.**
Daniel C. Dunham. Arlington, Virginia: Volunteers in Technical Assistance (VITA), 1985. 23p. bibliog.

The report 'represents an attempt to utilize the climate studies and building experience gained by the VITA/ISERST Renewable Energy Project in Djibouti. The purpose was to provide practical assistance in climatic and energy conserving design during the planning of the housing which will be built as part of the Djibouti Urban Development Project'. An introductory background and summary of the study is followed by an analysis of 'add-on features' to basic housing design to conserve energy. Discussion centres around the cost and potential for add-on features, add-on features to reduce radiant temperatures and augment ventilation and air movement, and further research potential. Chapter 4 outlines a cost benefit analysis of electricity consumption, aiming at lighting, refrigerators, air conditioning and ceiling fans. Finally, research recommendations are offered.

276 **Reducing energy consumption in Djibouti: the potential for conservation in Djibouti.**
Seymour Jarmul.   Arlington, Virginia: Volunteers in Technical Assistance (VITA), 1984. 81p. bibliog.
The author claims that there currently exists in Djibouti the potential for reducing energy consumption in existing buildings by over twenty per cent, and in future construction by over fifty per cent below present levels. It is argued that these reductions can be realized at minimal cost, with the investment being recouped in less than one year. The first section of the report outlines present energy consumption in Djibouti's buildings, with a second section discussing recommendations aimed at reducing energy consumption in existing and planned construction. Section three provides the options necessary for implementation of energy-conserving construction. Two appendices detail how to conduct energy audits and provide typical energy audit findings for Djibouti.

277 **Djibouti energy initiatives: national energy assessment.**
Matthew Milukas, Jesse Ribot, Peter Maxson.   Arlington, Virginia: Volunteers in Technical Assistance (VITA), 1984. 435p. bibliog.
The purpose of this report is to analyse energy demand in Djibouti and the possibilities of conserving energy in all sectors of the economy. It is argued that any future energy policy for Djibouti – a country heavily dependent on oil imports and offering limited biomass resources and non-existent hydroelectric potential – must offer some combination of fuel importation, geothermal energy production (potential of which is in abundance), energy conservation and renewables. The current project is the result of collaboration between the Institut Supérieur d'Études et de Recherches Scientifiques et Techniques (ISERST), the United States Agency for International Development (USAID) and Volunteers in Technical Assistances (VITA). The first section provides general information on Djibouti and prior achievements of the project. Section two analyses energy supply and demand in Djibouti. Section three discusses energy policies, prices and institutions. Sections four and five describe future energy demand and supply scenarios, respectively. A final section offers detailed recommendations for the future. Excellent appendices include: 'Energy conversions' (appendix A); 'National energy balances 1982 and 1983' (appendix B); 'Data received from petroleum countries' (appendix C); 'Petroleum fuel prices' (appendix D); 'Impacts of future development projects' (appendix E); 'Wind resources of Djibouti' (appendix F); 'Solar energy resources of Djibouti' (appendix G); 'History of renewable energy applications in Djibouti' (appendix H); 'Water pumping and supply' (appendix I); 'End use efficiency' (appendix J); 'Household energy use survey' (appendix K); 'Calculation: fuel use efficiency for railroad' (appendix L); 'Electric price structures' (appendix M); 'Projection of building energy conservation potential' (appendix N); 'Electric utility conservation and load management' (appendix O); 'Calculation: local share of aviation fuels' (appendix P); 'Temperature data for Djibouti' (appendix Q); 'Economic indicators for Djibouti' (appendix R); 'Historical data: petroleum products' (appendix S); and 'Suggested program for the completion of the energy initiatives project' (appendix T). This is by far the most comprehensive work on energy in Djibouti.

278 **Perspectives de développement du système éléctrique et tarification de l'éléctricité.** (Development perspectives of the electrical system and electricity tariffs).
Mihai Petcu.   Djibouti: Institut Supérieur d'Études et de Recherches Scientifiques et Techniques (ISERST), 1986. 105p.

Carried out in co-operation with Volunteers in Technical Assistance (VITA) and the United Nations Development Program (UNDP), the primary goals of the study were to examine the various elements necessary to comprise a development program for electricity use within Djibouti, and to respond to a current problem in Djibouti through the reorganization of electricity rates. The study documents that Djibouti in 1986 boasted twelve electrified localities with a total of 19,000 subscribers, of which 15,000 were domestic homes. Thus, the part of the population having access to electricity does not surpass twenty-five per cent. Yet the study asserts that electricity potential is immense (noting that the urbanization rate is nearly seventy-five per cent), making reorganization of the electrical sector an important aspect of any energy policy in Djibouti. Five major sections include: an introduction (summary and conclusions of the study); general characteristics of the electricity sector in Djibouti; analysis of demand for electricity; current situation and development perspectives for future exploitation of the resource (including four possible options); cost analysis of future projects; and current electricity costs and possibilities for their future reorganization. Six annexes document: the production and consumption of electricity in Djibouti (annex 1); the structure of consumption (annex 2); equipment (annex 3); the development of an electrical system from 1986 to 1995 (annex 4); the structure of costs (annex 5); and financial projections (annex 6).

279 **National energy plan. (Plan énergique national.)**
Volunteers in Technical Assistance (VITA).   Arlington, Virginia: The Author, 1987. 567p.

The volume was put together under the auspices of the Institut Supérieur d'Études et de Recherches Scientifiques et Techniques (ISERST), along with specialists from Volunteers in Technical Assistance (VITA), the United Nations Program for Development (UNDP) and the United States Agency for International Development (USAID). The purpose of the study is to provide a comprehensive, long-term energy plan for the government of Djibouti. Specifically, the project sought to identify long- and short-term energy actions and objectives and to encourage financial support for the realization of the plan by international donor agencies and countries. The first five chapters centre on Djibouti's energy demand balance for 1985 (chapter 2), the nature of primary energy (fuelwood, solar, geothermal and wind) (chapter 3), the nature of secondary energy (charcoal, imported oil and electricity) (chapter 4) and final energy products (e.g. lighting) (chapter 5). Chapters 6 and 7 summarize the methodology of the study, including the application of the 'Medee-S' computer model for forecasting energy demand in Djibouti. The final three chapters centre on the evolution of Djibouti's energy supply and demand (chapter 8), energy conservation and demand management (chapter 9) and recommendations for the future (chapter 10).

Volcanic formations of the Republic of Djibouti: geochemical and petrological data.
See item no. 22.

Energy

Eastern Africa regional studies: trends and interrelationships in food, population, and energy in Eastern Africa: a preliminary analysis.
See item no. 285.

Agriculture and Development

280 **L'agriculture maraichère et fruitière traditionnelle en République de Djibouti.** (Traditional market and fruit agriculture in the Republic of Djibouti).
J. P. Amat, M. Esquerre, Silah Eddine (with the collaboration of Kamil Daoud and J. Prini). Paris: Agence de Coopération Culturelle et Technique, 1981. 131p.

Although somewhat dated (the research was carried out in 1979), this offers the best summary of the nature and development of agriculture in Djibouti. The first section provides a brief overview of climatological givens and constraints, dividing the country into four major zones: coastal region, interior plains, plateau areas and mountain chains. The second section, the largest of the monograph, summarizes various aspects of agriculture in various districts of the country, including Djibouti City, Dikhil, Ali Sabieh, Tadjoura and Obock. Among the topics discussed are infrastructure associated with agricultural development, the nature of soil and fertilizers employed, methods of cultivation, irrigation systems, vegetable production and the evolution of production in general. A third section centres on how agriculture can be further advanced. Topics include the strengthening of traditional methods and the cultivation of greater surface areas. A brief conclusion places Djibouti's agricultural development in perspective.

281 **Plan d'action.** (Action plan.)
Association Nationale pour le Développement Économique et Social (ANDES). Djibouti: The Author, 1987. 21p.

The National Association for Economic and Social Development (ANDES) is a Djiboutian organization which was inaugurated on 24 January 1987. The primary purpose of this organization is to provide an appropriate framework for development by supporting private sector initiatives, especially those targeted toward small and medium enterprises. The organization is especially targeted toward Djibouti's youth. This booklet provides ANDES' plan of action, including its objectives, strategies and priorities, as well as short- and long-term programs. In a final section, ANDES outlines its perspective concerning development.

Agriculture and Development

282 Eastern Africa country profiles: Djibouti.
Leonard Berry. Worchester, Massachusetts: Program for
International Development, Clark University, 1980. 43p. 4 maps.
bibliog.

At the request of the United States Agency for International Development (USAID),
this country profile of Djibouti was prepared as one in a series of eastern African
country profiles. Others in the series include Sudan, Tanzania, Kenya, Somalia,
Ethiopia and Uganda. An introductory section provides an overview of Djibouti's
natural resources, history, culture and economics. Section two examines the issues of
economic stability and growth, possible national strategies for the future, problems and
possibilities of rural growth, and the problems associated with urban growth, drought
and refugees. A final section discusses the nature and distribution of poverty in
Djibouti. Topics discussed include the nature of poverty, refugees, unemployment,
employees in the informal sector, the rural areas and the context of poverty.

283 Afar pastoralists in transition and the Ethiopian revolution.
Jeferra-Worg Beshah, John W. Harbeson. *Journal of African Studies*,
vol. 5, no. 3 (1978), p. 249-67.

This article addresses the relationship between Ethiopia's northeastern Afar pastoral/
semi-nomadic communities and the central government since the 1974 Ethiopian
revolution, with possible implications for Djibouti's Afar populations. The authors
argue that substantial socioeconomic transformation had already affected the Afar
peoples since the end of the Second World War, and that the revolution which toppled
Ethiopian Emperor Haile Selassie had not initiated but, instead, altered the
'complexion and the character of their fundamental political struggles and processes of
socioeconomic change'. Three separate phases, according to the authors, distinguish
the strained relationship between the Afar peoples and the Ethiopian government: (1)
the pre-revolutionary régimes' encouragement of private commercial farming; (2)
experimentation with settlement schemes and grazing programs for the Afar in the
years just preceeding the revolution; and (3) the revolutionary government's initiation
of new settlement schemes, nationalization of commercial farms and state farm
creation to exemplify the newly formulated principles of Ethiopian socialism.

284 People and capitalism in the north-eastern lowlands of Ethiopia.
Lars Bondestam. *Journal of Modern African Studies*, vol. 12, no. 3
(1974), p. 423-39.

The author wrote this article in the aftermath of his departure as a demographer at the
Central Statistical Office of Ethiopia's Planning Commission in Addis Ababa, where he
served from 1969 to 1971. He examines the process of 'underdevelopment' among
Ethiopia's north-eastern lowlands – largely inhabited by the Afar ethnic group – as a
result of the 'profit incentive' of international capitalism. This process, according to the
author, is not an isolated Ethiopian case and, therefore, should have important
implications for the neighbouring Afar peoples in Djibouti. Individual sections analyse
the mode of production among the Afar, the impact of capitalism and the benefactors
of commercial production.

285 **Eastern Africa regional studies: trends and interrelationships in food, population, and energy in eastern Africa: a preliminary analysis.**
Clark University: Program for International Development.
Worchester, Massachusetts: The Author, 1980. 3 vols. bibliog.

This three-volume set, prepared at the request of the United States Agency for International Development (USAID), analyses the linkages and interactions between the issues of food, population and energy in Eastern Africa, including Djibouti. Volume 1, entitled *Overview* (47p.), provides a concise assessment of food, population and energy problems in East Africa. Volume 2, entitled *Background papers* (195p.), examines in much greater depth specific issues concerning the topic under study. Finally, volume 3, entitled *Literature summaries and reviews* (191p.), provides annotated bibliographies for Burundi, Ethiopia, Kenya, Rwanda, Somalia, Sudan, Tanzania, Uganda and, most important for this study, Djibouti.

286 **Occupation de l'espace périphérique de la ville de Djibouti: évolution des genres de vie traditionnels et sédentarisation des pasteurs nomades.**
(Occupation of peripheral space in Djibouti City: changes in traditional ways of living and settlement of pastoral nomads.)
Pierre-Marie Decoudras. *Cahiers d'Outre-Mer* (Bordeaux), vol. 40, no. 158 (1987), p. 93-126.

The purpose of this article is to examine changes in traditional ways of living – most notably the settlement of pastoral nomads – in the regions immediately peripheral to Djibouti City. Five major sections detail infrastructural development and distribution of populations within the region studied, the nature of pastoralism among the Issa Somali, causes and mechanisms of the sedentarization process, economic activities and organization of the populations studied and, finally, the problems of development faced by the Djiboutian government. 'In the vicinity of the capital [of Djibouti]', concludes the author, 'the railroad stations, military camps and water sources are all important points which encourage nomads to settle down. They no longer hesitate about abandoning their usual way of life and voluntarily sacrifice their independence for national and international aid'.

287 **Development of fishing and fisheries in Djibouti – phase I.**
Paul A. DeRito, Robert W. Campbell, Keith W. Cox, Dee W. McFadden, Theodore McNeill. Placerville, California: Resources Development Associates (RDA), 1985. 4 vols. map.

This four-volume report, prepared by Resources Development Associates (RDA) at the request of the United States Agency for International Development (USAID), is a continuation of the project described in *Development of fishing and fisheries in Djibouti* (q.v.). Volumes 1 and 2 (342p.) contain an executive summary of the fisheries project and progress and results achieved, including improved fishing methods, production, small boat construction and repair, co-operative and national fisheries production, handling, storage, processing, marketing, administration, management and research. The last two volumes (non-paginated) comprise twenty-five appendices which provide a wealth of data concerning fisheries development in Djibouti. Especially useful are the following: 'Fiscal management system' (appendix B); 'FAO socio-economic study' (appendix C); 'An analysis of fisheries efforts and environmental assessment' (appendix E); 'Fish inventory report' (appendix F); 'Retail outlet contract' (appendix

Agriculture and Development

I); 'Cooperative by-laws' (appendix L); 'Cooperative internal by-laws' (appendix M); 'Price study' (appendix N); and 'Cooperative 1983-84 financial statements' (appendix O).

288 **Development of fishing and fisheries in Djibouti.**
Paul A. DeRito, Dee W. McFadden, Robert W. Campbell, Keith W. Cox. Diamond Springs, California: Resources Development Associates (RDA), 1982. 125p.

Resources Development Associates (RDA) prepared this report at the request of the United States Agency for International Development (USAID). As in Ethiopia and Somalia, Djibouti has vastly underutilized fisheries potential. The purposes of the fisheries project were to assist the Djiboutian government with a viable system for the improved marketing of fish, as well as strengthening the institutional capacity of the Fisheries Division, Ministry of Agriculture, to support private sector initiatives in the fishing industry. The first two chapters outline the successes already achieved by the fisheries project and the development of the project idea. Chapter 3 elaborates on contract tasks such as surveys of demand and consumption and existing marketing facilities, promotional demonstrations, new retail outlets and improved transportation, and potential for co-operative development. The remainder of the report examines contract sub-activities (such as boatbuilding and repair and oyster culture development) and interaction with other donors associated with the project, including the International Fund for Agricultural Development (IFAD), Catholic Relief Services (CRS) and the Red Sea Regional Project.

289 **Djibouti water resources and soils analysis: final report.**
Joseph E. Goebel, Aboubaker Douale, Farah Omar. Diamond Springs, California: Resources Development Associates (RDA), 1983. 5 vols.

This is by far the most comprehensive water resources and soils analysis of Djibouti. The report was prepared for the United States Agency for International Development (USAID) by Resources Development Associates (RDA). The purpose of the project was to: institutionalize the capacity to analyse ground and surface water quality; compile, catalogue and disseminate hydrological information; and classify soils, prepare soils maps and provide evaluations concerning the proper utilization of soils. In short, the primary goal of the project was to expand Djibouti's agricultural production through irrigated gardens to obtain self-sufficiency in food products, especially vegetables and fruits. The first volume centres on a full-scale analysis of agricultural development in Djibouti (including history, background, and nature of the water resources and soils analysis project), personnel and training requirements, and technical assistance required. Over 300 pages of appendices (not enumerated consecutively throughout) contained in the remaining four volumes provide a wealth of data on agriculture in Djibouti. Of special importance are the following: 'Report on the soils of the Sabbalou and Chekheti region' (appendix J); 'Report on the soils and watersheds of the Dey Dey region' (appendix K); 'Study on land ownership of Houmbouli and Douda agricultural areas' (appendix N); and 'Water salinity investigation of Houmbouli and Grande Douda agricultural areas' (appendix G). The report has become the basis of all water and soil projects in Djibouti.

290   **Conflict resolution in fisheries development: the case of Djibouti.**
Michael K. Kelleher, Ray N'T. Tshibanda.   In: *Proceedings of the international conference of the Groupe d'Étude des Ressources Maritimes (GERMA) on small-scale fisheries and economic development and of the International Institute of Fisheries Economics and Trade (IIFET) on fisheries trade, development and policies held at the University of Quebec Rimouski, Canada, August 10-15, 1986.* Edited by GERMA.   Rimouski, Quebec: The Editor, 1986. p. 1127-38.

A very authoritative article on the nature of fisheries development in Djibouti. Since Djibouti is a resource-poor country and imports upwards of ninety per cent of what it consumes, its largely untapped 8,000 sq. km. exclusive economic zone can provide the basis for a thriving, future fishing industry. Firstly, presentation is made of various statistics summarizing the nature of fisheries development in Djibouti, especially concerning the national Livestock and Fisheries Service (SEP) and the Marine Fisheries Cooperative Association (ACPM). The policy objectives and conflicts between the four major institutional actors involved in the fisheries projects (government, fishermen, vendors and international funding agencies) subsequently are analysed. The conflicts and issues of contention include the following: government-versus-fishermen (prices/employment), government-versus-vendors (prices/mark-up), fishermen-versus-vendors (prices/volume of purchases) and government-versus-international funding agencies (priorities/strategies). In order to resolve these conflicts, several institutional and technical approaches are outlined. The authors conclude that 'the basic solution is to establish constructive dialogue among the stakeholders so that each is aware of the requirements of the others, so that a national consensus on fisheries objectives and priorities can emerge and so that fisheries development policies and plans can be agreed upon by all parties'. Also suggested are the creation of a forum for dialogue, organizational structures for implementing an attained consensus, and measures for improving the cost efficiency of fishery sector operations.

291   **Development, drought, and famine in the Awash valley of Ethiopia.**
Helmut Kloos.   *African Studies Review*, vol. 25, no. 4 (Dec. 1982), p. 21-48.

Sponsored in part by a grant from the United States Agency for International Development (USAID), the study examines the interrelationships between development, drought and famine in the Awash valley of Ethiopia, an area heavily populated by Afar pastoralists. In this regard, the author's results have direct relevance to the Afar population in neighbouring Djibouti. Specifically, the author seeks to understand the adaptive responses of pastoralists in the region to drought and famine induced by physico-environmental and politico-economic factors. Several sections describe the traditional economies of the indigenous populations inhabiting the Awash valley (including the Afar), the relationship between government-induced development and drought, local responses to drought and famine, and drought-related morbidity and mortality. In terms of the Afar people, the author concurs with earlier studies that 'Afar society contains structures of a cooperative and communal nature which are amenable to development of small clan-owned and clan-managed farms and livestock ranches'. In short, the author argues that a prerequisite for development is greater understanding of the social and economic organization of the pastoral groups in the region that aids them in 'defining and achieving their objectives and restores a sense of responsibility and control over their own lands'.

Agriculture and Development

292 **Origin and early development of food-producing cultures in north-eastern Africa.**
Edited by Lech Krzyzaniak, Michael Kobusiewicz. Poznan, Poland: Polish Academy of Sciences (Poznan Branch), Poznan Archaeological Museum, 1984. 503p.

This important volume represents the published proceedings of an international symposium organized by the Archaeological Commission of the Polish Academy of Sciences (Poznan Branch) and held under the auspices of the Commission on Terminology of the Prehistory of the Near East and North Africa of the International Union of Prehistoric and Protohistoric Sciences, 9-13 September 1980. Although not specifically centring on Djibouti, this compilation – the result of fieldwork by seventy-seven participants from fourteen countries – constitutes an invaluable contribution to our understanding of the origins and early development of food-producing cultures in northeast Africa. In this regard, special attention is focused on the development of food-producing cultures in the ancient Nubian and Egyptian societies. Interested scholars are directed to the introductory essay by anthropologist J. Desmond Clark, 'The domestication process in northeast Africa: ecological change and adaptive strategies' (p. 25-41). Papers are divided into six major sections: 'General themes' (section 1); 'Late palaeolithic and early neolithic of Egypt' (section 2); 'Egyptian varia' (section 3); 'Late palaeolithic, "early Khartoum" and the neolithic of the Sudan' (section 4); 'The terminal palaeolithic and neolithic of the Sahara and the Maghreb' (section 5); and 'The neolithic of East Africa' (section 6).

293 **Institution strengthening in rural development: the case of Djibouti.**
J. Mullen. *Agricultural Administration and Extension*, vol. 28, no. 3 (1988), p. 181-89.

Agricultural specialists have long lamented that Djibouti will forever be dependent on significant levels of food imports due to the country's barren landscape and harsh climatic conditions. In a unique departure from this viewpoint, the author argues that recent advances in sedentary agriculture during the 1980s – such as a growth in the number of small-scale farms producing vegetables and fruits, from 180 in 1980 to 930 in 1985 – have been severely hampered by ineffective administrative policies. Specifically, an assessment is made of the divisions between competing departments within Djibouti's Ministry of Agriculture and Rural Development. Calling for an integrated approach to agricultural, pastoral, fisheries and forestry development, two concluding sections assess the possible impact of intended government reforms.

294 **Le secteur non-structuré à Djibouti: charactéristiques des entreprises et de la main-d'oeuvre du secteur. Contribution à l'emploi et la formation des revenus.** (Djibouti's non-structured sector: characteristics of the sector's enterprises and labour. Contribution to employment and the formation of revenues.)
Les Nations Unies: Bureau International du Travail (BIT), Programme des Emplois et des Compétences Techniques pour l'Afrique (PECTA). Addis Ababa, Ethiopia: BIT & PECTA, 1982. 162p.

This detailed analysis by the International Labour Organization examines how Djibouti's rather substantial and 'non-structured' informal sector provides substantial opportunities for development at low cost. After briefly introducing the nature and objectives of the study, the first six chapters detail the initial results. Among the topics discussed are the geographical distribution of economic activities throughout the country (chapter 1), characteristics of employment (chapter 2), the role of training and apprenticeships (chapter 3), technical capital (chapter 4), revenues (chapter 5), and productivity (chapter 6). The second section of the study analyses the nature of Djibouti's informal economic sector. Various chapters define exactly what is meant by 'informal' in the context of Djibouti (chapter 1), the integration of this sector with other components of the economy (chapter 2), problems and constraints associated with the sector (chapter 3) and, finally, the necessary political components for any development efforts targeted toward this sector. A final section makes an argument for a program of 'integrated development'. Numerous charts offer a host of valuable statistics.

295   **Djibouti: urban development with a social slant.**
      Emilio Pérez-Porras.   *The Courier*, no. 118 (Nov.-Dec. 1989),
      p. 79-82.

This short article offers interesting insights into the evolution of official Djiboutian government policy concerning the development of Djibouti City. After briefly summarizing the origins of the city, emphasis is placed on describing the principles and institutional organs which guided urban development. Of special interest are various statistics concerning the ethnic and class divisions prevalent in various portions of the city, such as the shantytown portion of the capital known as Balbala. A final section analyses the future of Djibouti's urban expansion and development.

296   **Plan de développement économique et social, 1982-1984.** (Economic and
      social development plan, 1982-1984.)
      République de Djibouti: Direction de la Planification.   Djibouti:
      The Author, 1981-82. 3 vols.

The first volume of this ambitious development plan, subtitled *Situation économique et sociale à la veille du plan 1982-1984* (Economic and social situation prior to the plan 1982-1984), is divided into two parts. The first section (94p.) places Djibouti's socio-economic situation within a global context, while the second section (125p.) offers a sectoral analysis (including numerous statistics) of Djibouti's progress prior to 1982. Various sectors discussed include agriculture, herding, fisheries, water resources, industry, energy, transport, telecommunications, urbanization, housing, tourism, artisanry, social conditions, education and health. The second volume (113p.), subtitled *Loi d'orientation économique et sociale, 1983-1989* (Law of social and economic orientation, 1983-1989), underscores the nationally legislated outlines for social and economic development, while volume 3 (57p.), subtitled *Annexe, cadre général d'application, 1983-1989* (Annexe, general context for application, 1983-1989), outlines the long-run potential and goals of Djibouti's development plans. The volumes and their projected outcomes are especially interesting when compared against actual levels of development achieved.

Agriculture and Development

297 **Elaboration du schéma directeur d'Ali-Sabieh – note d'accompagnement.** (Elaboration of a guiding plan for Ali Sabieh – accompanying note.)
République de Djibouti: Ministère des Travaux Publics de l'Urbanisme et du Logement. Djibouti: Direction de l'Urbanisme et du Logement, 1986. 69p. maps.

Ali Sabieh, a town nearly 100 kilometres southwest of Djibouti City, owes its birth and continued existence to the Djibouti–Addis Ababa railway, construction of which began in 1897 and reached the town in 1900. The document details future plans for managed growth and enhancement of life within the town. An introductory section describes Ali Sabieh's relationship *vis-à-vis* the national context and general program of urban development. The following two sections describe the physical characteristics and constraints of the town and region, and general context for instituting the development plan. Section four explains the specific functions of Ali Sabieh's urban space, while subsequent sections discuss food production and availability of potable water, enhancement of electricity, and perspectives of development for short-, medium- and long-term perspectives. The text is complemented by several maps and figures.

298 **Elaboration du schéma directeur de Dikhil – note d'accompagnement.** (Elaboration of a guiding plan for Dikhil – accompanying note.)
République de Djibouti: Ministère des Travaux Publics de l'Urbanisme et du Logement. Djibouti: Direction de l'Urbanisme et du Logement, 1986. 73p. maps.

Dikhil is a town southwest of Djibouti City, and, like Ali Sabieh, owes much of its lifeblood to the nearby Djibouti–Addis Ababa railway. An introductory section describes Dikhil's relationship *vis-à-vis* the national context and general programs of urban development. Two subsequent chapters outline the general context for implementing the development plan, as well as the physical characteristics and constraints of the town and region. Subsequent sections discuss food production and availability of drinking water, enhancement of electricity output and future perspectives of development from short-, medium- and long-term outlooks. The text is complemented by several detailed maps and figures.

299 **Djibouti aujourd'hui, structure à long terme, mise en oeuvre du développement urbain.** (Djibouti today, long-term structure, implementation of urban development).
République de Djibouti: Ministère des Travaux Publics de l'Urbanisme et du Logement, Cellule d'Urbanisme et d'Habitat. Djibouti: The Author, 1983. 307p. maps.

The volume constitutes Djibouti's long-range goals and implementation of urban development. The first section outlines the basic contours and structure of urban Djibouti in 1983, including the port, railway, airport, education, health, highways public transportation, drinkable water and electricity. Section two examines these same topics from a long-term perspective, with section three detailing the implementation of the development plan. A presentation is first made of project goals to be obtained in the 1983-86 period, comprising: expansion of the port, railway and airport; construction and rehabilitation of Balbala, the old quartiers and West Salines; enhancement and extension of highways, electricity capacity and water supplies; and protection against the flooding of the 'oeud Ambouli'. A plan is then outlined for the 1987-93 period, comprising: the extension of East Salines; expansion of the city centre; designation and intensification of industrial centres; zoning of Dorale; and construction of an all-weather road to Somalia. The volume contains dozens of coloured maps concerning all aspects of the above-noted topics.

300   **Rejection of fish as human food in Africa: a problem in history and ecology.**
      J. S. Simmons. *Ecology of Food and Nutrition*, vol. 3 (1974), p. 89-105.

The primary purpose of this article is to examine the rejection of fish as human food in Africa, with particular reference to the Cushitic peoples of northeast Africa who are recognized as the key to understanding the history of African fish avoidance. In particular, the author identifies: the context and rationale of fish avoidance; the distribution of the trait in Africa today and in the past; its spread from one part of the continent to another; and the ecological and other factors that may have contributed to its development. For example, the extent of disdain for fish among the Somali peoples of the Horn is noted by the following saying: 'Speak not to me with that mouth that eats fish'. In contrast, the Afar peoples of the Horn are described as 'one group who seem to lack prejudice against eating fish'. Individual sections include: 'Northeast Africa: the Cushitic center of fish avoidance'; 'The question of Nubia'; 'Sacred fish and fish avoidance in ancient Egypt'; 'A Berber area of avoidance'; 'East Africa: Cushites, Nilotes, and Bantu'; and 'Bantu of southern Africa'. Of particular usefulness is a map and accompanying list identifying eighty-one groups demonstrating evidence of fish avoidance, as well as a fairly extensive bibliography for further reference.

301   **Urbanismes et gestions urbaines de Djibouti.** (Town planning and urban administration of Djibouti.)
      Jean-François Tribillon. *Le Mois en Afrique* (Paris), nos. 207/208 (April-May 1983), p. 69-76.

In this brief article, the author critically analyses the non-co-ordinated and partial methods of urban planning and administration in Djibouti. The result of differences between social formations constituting Djibouti City, as well as the diversity of institutional and legal instruments, Djibouti's urban problems are also described as deriving from the country's colonial past. After discussing four historical types of town planning, an analysis is made of 'new paths' and 'recent endeavors'.

The development of a middle class in British Somaliland, French Somaliland and in Somalia under trusteeship (with some reference to Ethiopia and the Sudan).
See item no. 111.

Public health, pastoralism, and politics in the Horn of Africa.
See item no. 120.

Les femmes djiboutiennes dans le processus de développement; situation et besoins. (Djiboutian women in the process of development: situation and needs).
See item no. 127.

Agriculture and Development

An analysis of Afar pastoralism in the northeastern rangelands of Ethiopia.
See item no. 154.

Workers, capital and the state in the Ethiopian region, 1919-1974.
See item no. 174.

Ethiopia, revolution, and the question of nationalities: the case of the Afar.
See item no. 183.

Problems of political development in a ministate: the French Territory of the Afars and the Issas.
See item no. 185.

Donor's conference.
See item no. 247.

Djiboutian urban development project: energy conserving design for salines-ouest housing.
See item no. 275.

Perspectives de développement du système éléctrique et tarification de l'éléctricité. (Development perspectives of the electrical system and electricity tariffs.)
See item no. 278.

A developmental bibliography for the Republic of Djibouti.
See item no. 399.

Periodicals and
Official Publications

302 **Africa Research Bulletin. Economic Series.**
Exeter, England: Africa Research Ltd., 1964- . monthly.
This monthly bulletin of economic events in Africa has undergone several name changes in its history: *Africa-Economic, Financial and Technical* (vol. 1, 1964); *Africa Research Bulletin. Africa – Economic, Financial and Technical Series* (vol. 2, nos. 1-2, Jan.-March 1965); *Africa Research Bulletin. Economic, Financial and Technical Series* (vol. 2, no. 3-vol. 21, April 1965-Jan. 1985); and the current title, starting with vol. 22, no. 1 (Feb. 1985). The bulletin often cites economic developments in Djibouti. Economic briefs are divided into seven major sections: continental developments; policy and practice; development plans; commodities; industries; economic aid; and statistical supplement. Each issue indexes its citations by country title for easy reference. A similar annual index is compiled for each volume.

303 **Africa Research Bulletin. Political Series.**
Exeter, England: Africa Research Ltd., 1964- . monthly.
This monthly bulletin of political events in Africa has undergone several name changes in its history: *Africa – Political, Social and Cultural* (vol. 1, 1964); *Africa Research Bulletin. Africa – Political, Social and Cultural Series* (vol. 2, nos. 1-2, Jan.-Feb. 1965); *Africa Research Bulletin: Political, Social and Cultural Series* (vol. 2, no. 3-vol. 21, March 1965-84); and the current title, starting with vol. 22, no. 1 (Feb. 1985). Brief blurbs on political events on the African continent offer one (albeit limited) means of monitoring political events in Djibouti. Political briefs are divided into five major sections: continental alignments; internal developments; national security; overseas relations; and social and cultural events. Each issue indexes its citations by country title for easy reference. A similar annual index is compiled for each volume.

304 **Country report: analysis of economic and political trends every quarter.**
London: Economist Intelligence Unit, 1955- . quarterly.
The purpose of this publication is to 'regularly monitor political, economic and business conditions in over 165 countries for those who need to constantly keep in

Periodicals and Official Publications

touch'. Annual subscriptions include four quarterly issues on the country of your choice, plus a *Country profile* volume at the end of the year. The quarterly country report on Djibouti also includes the countries of Uganda, Ethiopia and Somalia. Each issue offers a brief one-paragraph summary on events in each country, a table of the latest available economic statistics and a brief analysis of that country's future outlook. In the fourth issue of 1988, for example, the outlook on Djibouti was detailed under this three-part heading: 'Ethnic tensions mount – and the economic situation is still precarious – while the (flagship of development) may be sinking'. The main section of each issue is devoted to numerous one-paragraph summaries of the most recent political and economic events occurring in each country, and offers an invaluable source for those wishing to remain on top of current events in Djibouti.

305 **Horn of Africa.**
Summit, New Jersey: Horn of Africa Journal, 1978- . quarterly.

The primary purpose of this journal was succinctly stated by editor Osman Sultan Ali when the first issue was published in 1978: 'We seek specific policy recommendations on crucial issues that, in one form or another, confront policy makers; and we hope the discussions of these issues will affect their actions, or at least their thinking. Our long-term goal is to help bring about an eventual, broad reconciliation in the Horn of Africa – that is, a genuine conciliation between Ethiopians and Somalis, Ethiopians and Eritreans, Kenyans and Somalis, and so on'. The journal has definitely contributed to much debate as concerns the Horn through brief articles, book reviews, editorials and 'open letters'. Unfortunately, financial problems contributed to the sporadic publishing of issues in the 1980s and, finally, a temporary cancellation of publication. Yet, the journal was launched anew in 1990. The premier issue focused on the Somali civil war. Articles of particular interest to scholars of Djibouti prior to the journal's resumption of publication include Said Yusuf Abdi's 'The mini-republic of Djibouti' (q.v.); Claire Brisset's 'Djibouti's refugee hoards' (q.v.); James Fitzgerald's 'Djibouti: petrodollar protectorate?' (q.v.); Ethiopian Refugee Committee's 'From the Ethiopian Refugee Committee' (vol. 3, no. 3, 1980, p. 32-35); 'Kenya & Djibouti: politics and economics' (vol. 4, no. 1, 1981, p. 52-54); and Osman Sultan Ali's 'Djibouti: the only stable state in the Horn?' (q.v.).

306 **The Indian Ocean Newsletter. (La Lettre de l'Océan Indien.)**
Paris: Indian Ocean Information and Documentation Bank (BIDOI), 1981- . weekly.

Established in 1981, this is a weekly publication (fifty times a year) on the diplomacy, politics, strategy and economics of the African countries and islands which border the Indian Ocean, especially Djibouti, Ethiopia, Somalia and Kenya. Although extremely expensive, the publication provides a wealth of up-to-date data on current events in Djibouti. Each issue is generally seven to eight pages in length and sometimes is augmented by 'special reports'. An index is provided at the end of each year and the Indian Ocean Information and Documentation Bank (BIDOI) often publishes books derived from information collected, such as *Djibouti: les institutions politiques et militaires* (q.v.).

307 **Africa contemporary record: annual survey and documents.**
Edited by Colin Legum.   New York; London: Africana Publishing, 1970- . annual.

This distinguished and authoritative annual is divided into three major sections: essays devoted to thematic topics (e.g. crisis in the Horn of Africa); a country-by-country review; and the reproduction of documents of particular importance for the year. The country-by-country review is an especially good and concise overview of the yearly political, economic and social developments in each African state, including Djibouti. The following subtitles of the sections on Djibouti during the 1980s indicate the various themes centred upon in each volume. 'Pragmatic path to stability' (vol. 13, 1980-81); 'The politics of survival' (vol. 14, 1981-82); 'Balancing act on the tip of the Horn' (vol. 15, 1982-83); 'Economic progress impeded by refugees' (vol. 16, 1983-84); 'Games of position' (vol. 17, 1984-85); 'A port in many storms' (vol. 18, 1985-86); 'The approaching end of the president's rule brings new uncertainties' (vol. 19, 1986-87); and 'Political and economic uncertainties continue to plague the Gouled regime' (vol. 20, 1987-88).

308 **La Nation.** (The Nation.)
Djibouti: Republic of Dijbouti, 1968- . weekly.

La Nation is the official newspaper of Djibouti. Distributed once a week on Thursday (4,000 distribution), fifty issues in French are printed each year. The paper comprises sections centring on domestic politics, Africa, the international scene, culture and society, economy and sports. Originally entitled *Le Réveil de Djibouti* (The Awakening of Djibouti), the paper took on its current title on 3 July 1980. An interesting aspect of the paper is the addition in 1987 of a cartoon strip entitled 'Les aventures de Samireh' ('The adventures of Samireh'). The comic strip is significant in that it regularly criticizes/satirizes government policies and social ills of Djiboutian society such as the chewing of khat (*catha edulis*) and the introduction of a national lottery.

309 **Northeast African Studies.**
East Lansing, Michigan: African Studies Center, Michigan State University, 1979- . three times a year.

Incorporating the former *Ethiopianist Notes*, (1977–79) this journal is an excellent source of scholarly written articles that deal with the countries of northeast Africa, including Djibouti. Initially appearing in 1979, the journal publishes three issues a year and accepts submissions in both English and French (although the majority of articles are in English). The editor of the journal is Harold G. Marcus, noted historian of Ethiopian studies. An emphasis is placed on historical analyses, although the interested reader will also find articles devoted to the politics, economics, language and current relations of countries comprising the region, as well as book reviews of recent publications devoted to northeast African studies. Articles of particular interest include Didier Morin's 'Aspects du multilinguisme en République de Djibouti' (q.v.) and Theodore Natsoulas' 'Arthur Rimbaud: trade and politics in northeast Africa 1880-1891' (q.v.).

310 **Pount.**
Djibouti: Société d'Études de l'Afrique Orientale-Connaissances de Djibouti (SEAO-CD), 1968- . trimester review.

The journal was originally published by the Société d'Études de l'Afrique Orientale (SEAO), an organization created on 20 January 1964, and committed to examining the topics of biology, culture, history, language and medicine of the countries of the Horn of Africa, especially Djibouti. Although listed as a trimester review, the SEAO published only sixteen issues on a sporadic basis from 1966 to 1982. The journal underwent a rebirth in 1986 with issue number 17, the result of a joint initiative between the SEAO and Connaissances de Djibouti (CD). The CD was formed on 14 January 1985 by forty-five persons interested in resurrecting the journal and providing a scholarly outlet for recording various aspects of Djiboutian culture and history. The current editorial staff emphasizes the 'apolitical' nature of the enterprise, claiming that it is 'above all a precious tool for research on the culture and environment of East African populations'. Two excellent articles on Djibouti appear in issue number 17 (the only one published as of this writing): 'Un example du pouvoir traditionnel Afar: le sultanat de Tadjourah' (An example of traditional Afar power: the Tadjoura Sultanate) by Aramis Houmed Soule (q.v.), and 'Le Xeer Issa: étude d'un contrat social' (The Issa xeer: study of a social contract) by Ali Moussa Iyé (q.v.).

311 **Proceedings of the international conferences of the Ethiopian Studies Association.**

The Ethiopian Studies Association has held several international conferences, seventy papers from the 1982 conference comprising the most recent volume (see below). The scope of the organization ensures that the interested scholar can find numerous articles of direct relevance to Djibouti in the vast proceedings. Especially useful in this pursuit is an appendix in the 1982 proceedings compiled by Rita Pankhurst, 'International conferences of Ethiopian studies I-VI, 1959-1980: author and subject bibliography' (p. 681-705), which lists all the papers of the first six meetings of the association. Scholars in search of material on Djibouti may also consult the proceedings of the individual conferences as follows: (1st) *Atti del convegno internazionale di studi Ethiopici (Roma 2-4 Aprile 1959)*. Rome: Accademia dei Lincei, 1960; (2nd) *Ethiopian studies. Papers read at the second international conference of Ethiopian studies (Manchester University, [8-11] July 1963*, edited by C. F. Beckingham, Edward Ullendorff, *Journal of Semitic Studies*, vol. 9, no. 1 (spring 1964); (3rd) *Proceedings of the third international conference of Ethiopian studies, Addis Ababa (3-7 April) 1966*. Addis Ababa: Institute of Ethiopian Studies, Haile Selassie I University, (1969-70), 3 vols.; (4th) *IV congresso internazionale di studi Etiopici (Roma 10-15 Aprile 1972*. Rome: Accademia dei Lincei, 1974, 2 vols.; (5th) (A) *Modern Ethiopia from the accession of Menelik II to the present: proceedings of the fifth international conference of Ethiopian studies, Nice, 19-22 December 1977*, edited by Joseph Tubiana. Rotterdam, Belgium: Balkema, 1980; (5th) (B) *Proceedings of the fifth international conference of Ethiopian studies, session B, April 13-16, 1978, Chicago, U.S.A.*, edited by Robert L. Hess. Chicago: University of Illinois at Chicago Circle, 1979; (6th) *Proceedings of the sixth international conference of Ethiopian studies, Tel Aviv, 14-17 April 1980* (not yet published); (7th) *Proceedings of the seventh international conference of Ethiopian studies, University of Lund, 26-29 April 1982*, edited by Sven Rubenson. Addis Ababa, Ethiopia: Institute of Ethiopian Studies; Uppsala, Sweden: Scandinavian Institute of African Studies; East Lansing, Michigan: African Studies Center, Michigan State University, 1984. See also *Proceedings of the international congresses of the Somali Studies Association* (q.v.).

312 **Proceedings of the international congresses of the Somali Studies Association.**

In comparison to its Ethiopian counterpart, the Somali Studies Association has enjoyed fewer international conferences and a more haphazard publication record of these proceedings. The proceedings of the first international conference held in 1980, for example, have yet to be published. However, the four-volume set that emerged from the second international conference held in 1983 represent a significant advance of Somali studies. See *Proceedings of the second international congress of Somali studies, University of Hamburg, August 1-6, 1983*, edited by Thomas Labahn (Hamburg, GFR: Helmut Buske Verlag, 1984). Individual volumes focus on linguistics and literature (volume 1), archaeology and history (volume 2), aspects of development (volume 3), and studies in humanities and natural sciences (volume 4). See also *Proceedings of the third international congress of Somali studies*, edited by Annarita Puglielli (Rome: Il Pensiero Scientifico, 1988). As of this writing, the papers of the fourth international congress held in Mogadishu, Somalia in 1989 have yet to be published. See also *Proceedings of the international conferences of the Ethiopian Studies Association* (q.v.).

313 **Bulletin Périodique.** (Periodical Bulletin.)
République de Djibouti: Chambre Internationale de Commerce et d'Industrie de Djibouti. Djibouti: The Author, 1971- . monthly.

Published on a sporadic basis by Djibouti's Chamber of Commerce, this official government publication offers a variety of useful information on trade and investment. However, quality of issues and topics of discussion vary widely from issue to issue, with issues sometimes adopting a unifying theme. In this regard, two issues of particular interest focus on the structure and activities of Djibouti's Chamber of Commerce (no. 6, Sept. 1987) and that country's role within the Preferential Trade Area (PTA) of Eastern and Southern Africa (special issue, no date).

314 **Le Progrès.** (Progress.)
République de Djibouti: Rassemblement Populaire pour le Progrès (RPP).
Djibouti: The Author, 1980- . sporadic.

Le Progrès is the official publication of Djibouti's sole recognized political party, the Rassemblement Populaire pour le Progrès (RPP) (Popular Union for Progress). The first issue was published on 27 June 1980, the third anniversary of Djibouti's independence from France. Published on an irregular basis, issues tend to centre around major events of political and economic significance, such as the donor's conference of 21-23 November 1983 and the legislative elections of 24 April 1987.

315 **Periodicals from Africa: a bibliography and union list of periodicals published in Africa.**
Standing Conference of Library Materials from Africa. Boston, Massachusetts: G. K. Hall, 1977. 619p. bibliog.

This volume provides a comprehensive listing of periodicals published in Africa. In addition to magazines and journals, the text includes reference to government annuals, daily official bulletins, non-commercial newspapers and yearbooks. Although the majority of citations are in European languages, over a dozen African languages (including Swahili, Amharic and Somali) appear as well. The periodical titles are listed alphabetically by country of publication. Titles of publications banned by a government are also included.

316 **World refugee survey.**
Washington, DC: US Committee for Refugees, 1961- . annual.

This yearly publication, published by the privately funded US Committee for Refugees (USCR), a public information and advocacy program of the American Council for Nationalities Service (ACNS), serves as a useful summary of the world's growing refugee populations, including those in Djibouti. Each year a review includes numerous articles, statistical tables and graphs, and individual country reports on those countries hosting refugee populations. Also included are a list of selected international, governmental and private US organizations providing information about or assistance for refugees, and a select listing of publications pertaining to populations. The 'country reports' section of the survey is especially valuable to those desiring a summary of the current refugee population in Djibouti. The ACNS and USCR also publish a monthly newsletter entitled *Refugee Reports*, as well as an occasional *Issue Paper* series, one issue of which pertained to Djibouti: *Beyond the headlines: refugees in the Horn of Africa* (q.v.).

Africa south of the Sahara.
See item no. 1.

Amnesty International report.
See item no. 108.

Country reports on human rights practices: report submitted to the Committee on Foreign Relations, U.S. Senate and Committee on Foreign Affairs U.S. House of Representatives by the Department of State.
See item no. 128.

Journal Officiel de la République de Djibouti. (Official Journal of the Republic of Djibouti.)
See item no. 196.

VITA News.
See item no. 252.

Bulletin semestriel de statistique. (Biannual statistical bulletin.)
See item no. 383.

Annuaire statistique de Djibouti. (Statistical annual of Djibouti.)
See item no. 384.

Direction générale de l'éducation nationale, annuaire statistique. (General direction of national education, statistical annual.)
See item no. 385.

Current African directories.
See item no. 397.

Official publications of Somaliland, 1941-1959; a guide.
See item no. 401.

Literature and Folklore

317 The art of the miniature in Somali literature.
B. W. Andrzejewski. *African Language Review*, vol. 6 (1976), p. 5-16.

The art of 'miniature' poetry was introduced in 1944 by a young Somali poet and lorry driver named Abdi Deeqsi (nicknamed 'Cinema'). This pop genre of Somali verse entitled *balwo* consists of a short poem generally one or two lines in length. The subject of the *balwo* is usually love, with themes encompassing unrequited affection, the sorrows of separation and the agonies of passion. The author discusses the rise and nature of this genre of Somali poetry, providing samples in their original Somali script with English translations.

318 The art of the verbal message in Somali society.
B. W. Andrzejewski, Muse H. I. Galaal. In: *Neue Afrikanistische Studien*. Edited by Johannes Lukas. Hamburg, GFR: Deutsches Institut für Afrika-Forshung, 1966, p. 29-39.

The first half of the article describes the art of the verbal message which flourishes among Somali nomads. The second half is devoted to the recording of an oral tradition about an episode in the life of Raage Ugaas, a renowned Somali poet. The story, which is provided in original Somali along with an English translation, is about the exchange of messages between Raage Ugaas and his father.

319 Modern and traditional aspects of Somali drama.
B. W. Andrzejewski. In: *Folklore in the modern world*. Edited by Richard M. Dorson. Paris: Moutin, 1978, p. 87-101.

After a brief overview, it is shown how Somali theatre makes extensive use of traditional folklore. Examples of how modern Somali drama incorporates exchanges, riddles and allusions to folktales are provided in their original Somali text along with English translations.

Literature and Folklore

320 **Reflections on the nature and social function of Somali proverbs.**
B. W. Andrzejewski. *African Language Review*, vol. 7 (1968),
p. 74-85.

Andrzejewski asserts: 'In Somali society, proverbs are part of everyday life, and as one
observant Somali once remarked, "they put spice into speech"'. This article serves as
an introduction to the nature and social function that proverbs play in Somali culture.
Numerous examples are given in their original Somali text accompanied by English
translations.

321 **The rise of written Somali literature.**
B. W. Andrzejewski. Mogadishu: Academy of Somali Culture, 1975.
23p.

The author presented this lecture at the Somali Institute of Development Administration and Management (SIDAM), a training institute located in Mogadishu, Somalia.
The speech, which provides a general overview of the rise of written Somali literature,
classifies authors as being either 'preservers', 'transmuters' or 'innovators'. Andrzejewski's later and more easily available essay, 'Somali prose fiction writing, 1967-1981',
in *Proceedings of the second international congress of Somali studies vol I*, edited by
Thomas Labahn (Hamburg, GFR: Helmut Buske Verlag, 1984, p. 379-410), provides
further commentary.

322 **The veneration of Sufi saints and its impact on the oral literature of the
Somali people and on their literature in Arabic.**
B. W. Andrzejewski. *African Language Studies*, vol. 15 (1974),
p. 15-54.

The veneration of the Sufi saints (extremely widespread in Somali society) has greatly
contributed to Somali oral literature and literature in Arabic. The veneration of Sufi
saints is said to have 'acted as an intellectual and emotional stimulus to creativity, and
in fact, among Somali prose narratives, legends of the saints occupy a major position,
perhaps even exceeding, in their number and variety, accounts of the lives and deeds
of secular prominent men'. The author compares the oral literature to Somali
hagiographies in Arabic entitled *manqabas*, or a 'short, transposable account of an
event in the life of a saint or of his particular virtue or gift'.

323 **Somali poetry: an introduction.**
B. W. Andrzejewski, I. M. Lewis. Oxford: Clarendon Press, 1964.
167p. bibliog.

The first half of the book highlights the social and cultural setting of Somalia, the
nature of the Somali language, the characteristics of Somali verse and bibliographical
notes on poets. The second half of the book reproduces thirty-one Somali poems (in
Somali and Arabic) along with their English translations. Major categories include
classical poetry, traditional and modern songs, and religious poetry in Arabic.

324 **Somali literature in European languages.**
David F. Beer. *Horn of Africa*, vol. 2, no. 4 (Oct.-Dec. 1979),
p. 27-35.

The article provides a worthwhile overview of Somali literature written in the former
colonial languages of English, French and Italian. The author provides a simple

summary and brief analysis of the majority of works cited. Somali literature cited includes oral poetry translated into English by Margaret Laurence, I. M. Lewis and B. W. Andrzejewski, plays translated into English (Hassan Sheikh Mumin), and poetry written in English and French (William J. F. Syad) and Italian (Mohamed Said Samatar). Also, the works of Somalis who have written short stories in English (Yusuf Duhul and Abdi Sheik-Abdi) and novels in English (Nuruddin Farah) are examined. Similar material will be found in Beer's essay, 'Aspects of Somali literature in European languages' in the *Proceedings of the second international congress of Somali studies, vol. I*, edited by Thomas Labahn (Hamburg, GFR: Helmut Buske Verlag, 1984, p. 411-28).

325 **Afar songs.**
Loren F. Bliese. *Northeast African Studies*, vol. 4, no. 3 (1982-83), p. 51-76.

The Afar, one of the two major ethnic groups in Djibouti, have orally passed down through the generations highly sophisticated poetic songs that follow strict rules concerning metre. Songs can be classified according to syllables per line and melody patterns. The author analyses six types of Afar songs, providing numerous examples of each type in both original Afar text and English translation. The various melodies of each song (*gabba* or *korsiyya*) are illustrated by the addition of musical notes 'which match closest on the piano'. The six types of songs described within the text are as follows: (1) *kalluwalle*: 'traditionally sung in a circle around a woman oracle . . . the songs involve statements of prowess and bravery by the men and of slander' to the oracle; (2) *sadda*: sung at weddings and markets attended by both sexes, the contents of these songs 'are largely sexual propositions with compliments, playful slander and refusals'; (3) *horra*: 'heard at markets, weddings and evening get-togethers', these are sung by groups of men and serve as 'boasting songs'; (4) *tirtira*: these are 'war shouts', and are performed as 'short interruptions of the horra'; (5) *saare*: these serve as 'praise songs', whether that of a man describing the beauty of his girlfriend or the recounting of a tale of bravery in time of war; (6) *kassow*: these are 'challenging songs' and are utilized if, for example, one clan has a grievance against another.

326 **The lexicon – a key to culture; with illustrations from Afar word lists.**
Loren F. Bliese. *Journal of Ethiopian Studies*, vol. 8, no. 2 (1970), p. 1-19.

The purpose of the article, using the case study of the Afar language, is to demonstrate the numerous ways in which lexicon can be of aid to the ethnographer. 'Both in suggesting fruitful areas of research and in giving supporting evidence for ethnographic observations, the lexicon contains indispensable data'. The first three sections describe the development of what the author terms 'ethno-linguistics' (the relationship between language and culture) and its importance in both synchronic and diachronic studies. The majority of the article, however, is devoted to describing the cultural inferences that one can make about the Afar based on the Afar lexicon. Discussion is divided into four sections: 'Lexical elaboration as an indication of cultural interests'; 'General terms as an indication of a lack of cultural focus'; 'Genetic relationship indicated by vocabulary'; and 'Lexical borrowing as ethnographic data'.

327 **Ignorance is the enemy of love (Aqoondarro waa u nacab jacayl).**
Faarax M. J. Cawl, translated by B. W. Andrzejewski. London: Zed
Books, 1984. 104p.

Not only was this the first novel published in the Somali language since a Latin script
was adopted by the Somali Democratic Republic in 1972, but it is also significant
because it engenders an adaptation of the rich oral tradition of the Somali peoples of
the Horn of Africa. The novel, which is set in 1915, is the love story of a Dervish
fighter named Calimaax who rescues a woman (Cawrala) from a sinking ship. The
couple is soon afterwards separated because of the Dervish struggle, with Cawrala
eventually expressing her love for Calimaax in a letter. Both die before they are able to
be reunited.

328 **Heellooy heelleellooy: the development of the genre heello in modern
Somali poetry.**
John William Johnson, foreword by B. W. Andrzejewski.
Bloomington, Indiana: Indiana University Press, 1974. 209p. (African
Series, vol. 5).

Heello oral poetry is one genre of the several comprising Somali oral poetry and it is
the least documented. The 'family of miniature genres' and the emergence of the
belwo within Somali oral poetry are first examined in terms of their contribution to the
evolution of the genre *heello*. Second, the evolution of the genre *heello* is divided into
three periods, with common characteristics of all three periods being described.
Finally, a summary is made of the historical inheritance of the *heello* and the forces
behind the success and development of modern oral poetry.

329 **Research in Somali folklore.**
John William Johnson. *Research in African Literatures*, vol. 4, no. 1
(spring 1973), p. 51-61.

The article represents the first published effort summarizing the state of folklore
research on the Somali peoples of the Horn of Africa. The author lists and provides a
brief description of the various Somali and foreign scholars and their respective
institutions involved in Somali folklore research. A bibliography at the end of the
article lists those works which were not originally included in, or published
subsequently to, the appearance of Johnson's earlier article 'A bibliography of the
Somali language and literature', *African Language R view*, vol. 8 (1969), p. 279-97.

330 **Somali prosodic systems.**
John William Johnson. *Horn of Africa*, vol. 2, no. 3 (July-Sept.
1971), p. 46-54.

This essay provides a detailed textual description of four classical genres of Somali
poetry: *gabay*, *jiifto*, *geeraar* and *buraambur*. These four genres are 'scanned
quantitatively' (counting temporal units on the line). Examples are given of foot and
scansion patterns of original Somali texts accompanied by English translations. Further
research is reported in Johnson's essay, 'Recent researches into the scansion of Somali
oral poetry' in *Proceedings of the second international congress of Somali studies, vol. I*
edited by Thomas Labahn (Hamburg, GFR: Helmut Buske Verlag, 1984, p. 313-32).

142

331 **A tree for poverty: Somali poetry and prose.**
Collected by Margaret Laurence. Hamilton, Canada: McMaster
University Press; Shannon, Ireland: Irish University Press, 1976.
Reprint. 146p.

This reprint was originally published in 1954 (Nairobi: Press for the Somaliland
Protectorate), and although some of the information in the text is a little dated,
it constitutes the pioneering work in the English language on Somali poetry and prose.
The title of the book is derived from a Somali poem which states, 'On the plain Ban-
Aul there is a tree/For poverty to shelter under'. After briefly describing two major
types of Somali poetry (*belwo* and *gabay*), English translations of ten Somali stories
are reproduced in full. The majority of the text, however, consists of twenty-six
paraphrased stories which have been translated into English from either Arabic or
Somali.

332 **Somali liberation songs.**
Colin Legum. *Journal of Modern African Studies*, vol. 1, no. 4 (1963),
p. 503-19.

The author argues that the two major weapons employed by the Somali Democratic
Republic to further its pan-Somali quest were diplomacy and the radio. This article
examines the radio side of Somalia's efforts, concentrating on the various Somali songs
and poems broadcast regularly between September and December, 1963, from Radio
Mogadishu and Radio Cairo. Numerous Somali songs discussed (and reproduced in
English) include those directed against Kenya's Northern Frontier District (NFD), the
Ethiopian regions of the Ogaden, Haud and Reserved Area, and, most important for
scholars of Djibouti, the French-ruled colony of Djibouti. The author outlines five
major themes that the Somali liberation songs emphasize: (1) need for Somali
unification; (2) the injustice of Ethiopian and French colonial policies towards Somalis;
(3) modern political events; (4) the importance of intra-Somali unity and forgiveness;
and (5) the demand for the reunification of Kenya's NFD with Somalia.

333 **Somalia: in word and image.**
Edited by Katherine S. Loughran, John L. Loughran, John William
Johnson, Said Sheikh Samatar, foreword by Samuel Hamrick.
Bloomington, Indiana; Washington, DC: Indiana University Press for
the Foundation for Cross Cultural Understanding, 1986. 175p. map.
bibliog.

This book is the result of the first major exhibition of Somali material art and artifacts
in the United States. The catalogue not only documents the artifacts shown in the
exhibit, but includes descriptive essays by noted Somali scholars centring on various
aspects of Somali oral and material art. Essays include: John William Johnson's
'Introduction: word and image on the Horn of Africa'; Jo Arnoldi's 'The artistic
heritage of Somalia'; Said Sheikh Samatar's 'Somali verbal and material arts'; B. W.
Andrzejewski's 'The literary culture of the Somali people'; Lee V. Cassanelli's 'Society
and culture in the riverine region of southern Somalia'; Vinigi L. Grottanelli's 'Somalia
wood engravings'; and I. M. Lewis's 'Islam in Somalia'. The combination of essays and
photos provides the most comprehensive and enjoyable overview of Somali art and
culture.

Literature and Folklore

334 **Somali games.**
G. Marin. *Journal of the Royal Anthropological Institute of Great Britain and Ireland*, vol. 61 (1931), p. 499-511.

Offers brief descriptions of various types of games played among the Somali peoples of the Horn, including Djibouti. Among the aspects described of each game are the rules, number and ages of the players, objectives and required instruments of play. The games are divided into eight categories (including numerous subcategories of play): games of pretence; winning games; games of strength and agility; games of nimbleness; games of attention and celebrity; searching games; games of calculation; and games of chance. The majority of the article is devoted to describing seven different types of games of calculation, inclusive of diagrams of play.

335 **Leopard among the women: shabeelnaagood – a Somali play.**
Hassan Sheikh Mumin, translated from Somali by B. W. Andrzejewski. London: Oxford University Press, 1974. 230p.

This translated play and associated notations by B. W. Andrzejewski, the most renowned scholar of the Somali languae, represent an important contribution to Somali literature. Somali drama, unlike its Western counterpart, before 1973 had no written scripts, but rather relied on oral traditions. The play itself, written by a celebrated Somali author, censures the evils within Somali society during the early 1960s. Andrzejewski provides both the original Somali version and an English translation of the sixteen-act play. Also included are general descriptions of Somali drama, social and cultural settings of the play, and specific notes on unique aspects of the play (i.e. stage directions).

336 **Contes de Djibouti.** (Djibouti tales.)
Hassan Sheikh Mumin, Hamad La'Ade, Ibrahim Ahmed Dini, collected and translated into French by Didier Morin. Paris: Conseil International de la Langue Française, 1980. 170p.

The book is a collection of stories written in the Afar language (narrated by Hamad La'Ade in collaboration with Ibrahim Ahmed Dini) and in the Somali language (narrated by the renowed Somali poet and playwright Hassan Sheikh Mumin). Morin has transcribed the stories in their indigenous languages and provides French translations. The stories are targeted toward children and young people, with animal fables being one of the primary types of tales included. The book is illustrated by Loita Abbas.

337 **Somali folktales.**
Aki'o Nakano. Tokyo: Institute for the Study of Languages and Cultures of Asia and Africa, 1980. 58p.

Nakano studied in Somalia between July 1980 and March 1981 under the auspices of the Japanese Ministry of Education and as a member of a project entitled *Comparative Survey on Islamic Societies and their Cultural Change*. The author has recorded twenty-four Somali folktales (in Somali) falling under the broad categories of 'Tales of animals', 'Tales of human beings', 'Long stories' and 'Religious and hagiographical tales'. Although English translations are not provided, the tales should serve as a useful source for scholars of the Somali language and folklore.

144

338 **Musique traditionnelle de l'Afrique noire, discographie: Djibouti.**
(Traditional music of black Africa, discography: Djibouti.)
Chantal Nourrit, William Pruitt.   Paris: Radio-France Internationale,
Centre de Documentation Africaine, 1983. 64p. 2 maps. bibliog. (Series
no. 17).

This is but one of a general series collected and published by the African
Documentation Centre of Radio-France International, the purpose of which is to
preserve the traditional music of sub-Saharan Africa. A brief introduction to the
project is followed by an essay written by Christian Poche, entitled 'La musique
traditionnelle à Djibouti' (Traditional music in Djibouti), p. 1-28. Poche introduces the
reader to the instruments, songs and dances of Djibouti's various ethnic groups. The
essay is followed by a listing of forty-four records containing traditional Djiboutian
music, including titles of songs, origins, where it can be obtained and description, when
felt necessary, of the specific song named. Several indexes centring around various
headings, including ethnic group, instrument, interpreter, origin of music, theme, title
and type of chant, provide easy access to the records for the specialist. Major themes
discussed include animals, love, hunting, dancing, blacksmiths, war, initiation rites,
marriage, rain, religion and work.

339 **Board games of the Horn of Africa.**
Richard Pankhurst.   *Horn of Africa*, vol. 3, no. 4 (1980/81), p. 41-45.

Board games, based on some variation of dropping pebbles or some other type of
counter into holes, are common to all ethnic groups and countries of the Horn of
Africa, including Djibouti, and constitute the subject of this brief overview. In
mountainous areas these games may be played in holes chiselled in stone or dug in the
ground, and in desert areas in holes carved in the sand, while some may instead use
gabata-boards fashioned of wood or moulded in sundried clay. *Gabata*-balls may be
pebbles (in Amharic, *teter*), balls of mud, seeds, dry goatdung (in Bilan, *til*) or camel-
droppings (in Somali, *salo*). The variation of games in northeast Africa is underscored
by the detailed description of rules for six different games. The author notes that 'the
descriptions should enable readers wishing to do so actually to play these games'.

340 **Gabata and other board-games of Ethiopia and the Horn of Africa.**
Richard Pankhurst.   *Azania: Journal of the British Institute in Eastern
Africa*, vol. 17 (1982), p. 27-42.

Gabata is a game of skill, the variants of which are widely distributed throughout
Africa and, particularly, the Horn of Africa. Dating back to the 6th to 8th centuries in
the Horn, *gabata* is played by dropping a rounded object (counter) into holes dug in
the ground, carved into a wooden board or chiselled out of rock. In this article the
author discusses the similarities and differences of the various games found in the
Horn, noting that the distribution of game types, far from being random, falls within
'definable, and culturally significant, geographical areas'. It is concluded that the
variations in games (and their subsequent diffusion) 'in some instances appears to
reflect the ethnic history of the region, as well as, conceivably, varying attitudes to
life'. Variations in the game which are discussed include arrangement of the board,
differences in the number of holes per board, method of distributing balls, direction of
play, opening gambits, method of capture and the procedure at the end of play.

Literature and Folklore

341 **Afar stories, riddles and proverbs.**
Enid Parker. *Journal of Ethiopian Studies*, vol. 9, no. 2 (1971),
p. 219-87.

After briefly introducing the reader to Afar phonology and the orthographic system
(which utilizes characters), recreational activities and games (such as *radoyta*, a ball
game), original texts and English translations are provided for Afar riddles, stories
and proverbs. In all examples, the literal translation of the Afar characters is followed
by a 'free translation'. Twenty-five riddles of varying lengths are followed by eight
stories, the titles of which are as follows: 'Punishment of evil'; 'The story of the deaf
family'; 'The two friends'; 'The story of the ostrich and the elephant'; 'The story of two
men, a selfish and a stingy'; 'The story of the pelican and the jackal'; 'The hyena and
lion story'; and 'The crocodile story'. A discussion of seven types of Afar songs,
including the reproduction of 'A type of patriotic song', is followed by 115 Afar
proverbs. The author notes that 'where English proverbs are similar, or nearly so,
these have been written in'.

342 **Quatres amis à Djibouti.** (Four friends in Djibouti.)
République de Djibouti. Bureau Pédagogique du Service du Premier
Degré. Ministère de l'Éducation Nationale, de la Jeunesse, des Sports
et de la Culture. Paris: Nouvelles Éditions Africaines
(NEA)/EDICEF Jeunesse, 1986. 160p.

This handy school manual/children's book was put together by Djibouti's Bureau
Pédagogique du Service du Premier Degré from works begun by the students of
Djibouti's Ecole Normale d'Instituteurs. Fifty-three short stories designed for
secondary-school children, twelve years and older, centre around the lives of four
children in school together in Djibouti. Two of the children, Philippe and Sophie, have
just arrived from France, while the two other children, Ali and Fatima, are Djiboutian
nationals. The children become good friends and the book focuses on their travels,
stories and exploits. The book is an expanded, updated version of an earlier edition:
Quatre amis à Djibouti, (Dakar: Les Nouvelles Éditions Africaines, [n.d.]).

343 **2ème forum culturel, 20-27 Juin 1983.** (2nd cultural forum, 20-27 June
1983.)
République de Djibouti: Rassemblement Populaire pour les progrès
Commission Culturelle. Djibouti: Republic of Djibouti, 1983. 56p.

Fifty-eight colour and black-and-white photographs and accompanying text offer an
excellent introduction to Djiboutian music, dance and culture as recorded at the
second cultural forum held 20-27 June 1983. According to the proceedings, 528
dancers, 158 singers and musicians, 173 poets and 9 primary-school children (229 of
whom represented the four interior districts of the country) took part in the
celebration. Glowing speeches by members of the government are followed by
descriptions of the performing of various dances and the playing of numerous
instruments. The various dances include the following: *dabal, dabbal, hafat malabo,
barrimo, nacna, horra, falo, laale, zailai, sadexleey, gobley, wilwileh, siliko*, and *hella
yar yar*. Other sections note the recipients of competitive prizes and the role of
traditional artistry in daily life.

344 **Gabay-Hayir: a Somali mock heroic song.**
Said S. Samatar. *Research in African Literature*, vol. 11, no. 4 (winter 1980), p. 449-78.

The chief purpose of the *gabay-hayir* genre of Somali oral poetry 'is to imitate in syntax and subject a serious poem for the purpose of trivializing it'. The origins, setting and purposes of the *gabay-hayir* are examined, with the poetry of Abdisalaam H. Aadan (a master satirist of the Dervish poets) being discussed at length. Examples of his poems are provided in Somali, accompanied by English translations and analysis. An informative table shows the form employed and general characteristics of all fifteen genres of Somali poetry. A more general survey of the role of poetry in Somali arts is contained in the essay by the same author in *Somalia: in word and image* (q.v.).

345 **Oral poetry and Somali nationalism: the case of Sayyid Mahammad Abdille Hasan.**
Said S. Samatar. Cambridge, England: Cambridge University Press, 1982. 232p. bibliog.

This unique application of the rich oral history and literature of the Somali peoples of the Horn of Africa provides an analysis of how the oratory skills of Somali nationalist Sayyid Mahammad Abdille Hasan were instrumental in fostering the Dervish nationalist struggle and the acquisition of his personal political power. The first two chapters describe the structure, forms, and methods of transmission and dissemination of oral poetry within Somali society. The following two chapters present the historical rise of the Dervish movement and the role of oral poetry in that process. The final chapter, which is entitled 'Myth and mullah', describes the changing images of Sayyid, his roles as 'master polemicist' and 'mystic warrior', and an appraisal of his historical legacy.

346 **Naufragés du destin.** (Castaways of fate.)
William J. F. Syad. Paris: Présence Africaine, 1978. 123p.

The author is a renowned Somali poet who was born in Djibouti and writes poetry in both French and English. In this volume, a lengthy poem written in French casts a critical eye on the politics of the Somali peoples and, particularly, the succession of régimes in the Somali Democratic Republic. The first section of the book, entitled 'Aperçu historique de la Somalie' (Historical glimpse of Somalia), is an essay describing the general history of the Somali, including a section on their 'dismemberment' at the hands of various colonial powers such as France. The second part of the book is a thirty-two verse poem describing 'La Somalie des années sombres' (The somber years of Somalia). The poem focuses on the 1960-69 period of multi-party politics in Somalia. Finally, part three of the book is an essay entitled 'Retrospective historique, politique, économique, sociale et cuturelle depuis la révolution du 21 Octobre 1969 à ce jour' (Historical, political, economic, social and cultural retrospective from the revolution of 21 October 1969 to this day). For earlier collections of poems written in French and English by the same author, see *Cantiques* (Canticles) (Dakar, Abidjan: Les Nouvelles Éditions Africaines, 1976); *Harmoniques* (Harmonics) (Dakar; Abidjan: Les Nouvelles Éditions Africaines, 1976); and *Khamsine* (Paris: Présence Africaine, 1959).

Literature and Folklore

347 **The Horn of Africa: Ethiopia, Sudan, Somalia & Djibouti.**
Harold Woods, Geraldine Woods.   New York; London; Toronto;
Sydney: Franklin Watts, 1981. 64p. 2 maps.

A unique series of books whose goal is to offer an introduction to the 'history, geography, climate, people, and politics of the African countries in an interesting and accessible format for young readers'. In this sixth volume of the series, the young reader is introduced to the countries of the Horn of Africa, including a separate chapter on Djibouti. Four chapters discuss the region's geography and climate (chapter 1), history and colonial relations with Europe (chapter 2), independence movements (chapter 3) and future prospects (chapter 8). The chapter on Djibouti (chapter 7) describes the meaning of the country's flag, ethnic relations, religion and education, and industry and trade. The book and series is a welcome and much needed introduction for younger readers interested in the region.

Proceedings of the second international congress of Somali studies, University of Hamburg, August 1-6, 1983. Volume I, linguistics and literature.
See item no. 365.

Somali language and literature.
See item no. 404.

Language

348 **The use of Somali in mathematics and science.**
B. W. Andrzejewski. *Afrika und Übersee*, vol. 63 (1980), p. 103-17.
This brief article sheds light on how the Somali language has expanded since an official orthography was adopted in Somalia in 1972 to meet the needs for mathematical and scientific terms. Initiated by the Somali Language Commission in 1972-73, the expansion was carried out by the authors of schoolbooks and teachers' manuals, and was financed and guided by the Curriculum Department of the Somali Ministry of Education. The author notes that official efforts concerning expansion of the Somali language are praiseworthy when one realizes that 'within a period of seven years the Somali vocabulary has had to pass through a process of expansion which in some European languages took more than two centuries'.

349 **Language in Ethiopia.**
Edited by Marvin L. Bender, J. Donald Bowen, Robert C. Cooper, Charles A. Ferguson. London: Oxford University Press, 1976. 572p. map. bibliog.
The volume constitutes the final report of the language survey on Ethiopia, a project sponsored by the Ford Foundation as part of a five-nation survey of language use and language teaching in eastern Africa (the other countries studied were Kenya, Tanzania, Uganda and Zambia). Although essential for understanding the full breadth and scope of language distribution in the Horn of Africa, Afar and Somali – two minority languages in Ethiopia which are two of the major languages of neighbouring Djibouti – are given short shrift. Numerous essays are divided into three major categories: 'The languages of Ethiopia' (part 1); 'Language use in Ethiopia' (part 2); and 'Language and education in Ethiopia' (part 3). Of particular interest is an extremely well-conceived, colour, wall-size map of language distribution in Ethiopia.

Language

350 **Afar.**
Loren F. Bliese. In: *The non-semitic languages of Ethiopia.* Edited
by M. Lionel Bender. East Lansing, Michigan: African Studies
Center, Michigan State University, 1976, p. 133-65. (Occasional
Papers, series no. 5).

This chapter, a shortened version of the author's more substantial *A generative grammar of Afar* (q.v.), offers a useful introduction to the grammar of the Afar language. After briefly summarizing previous investigations of the Afar language, the author divides his discussion of Afar grammar rules into five major sections: phrase structure rules; subcategorization rules; transformation component; lexicon; and phonology. Examples are provided in Afar with English translations. Two general essays on Cushitic languages (including Afar) which are included in this volume nicely complement Bliese's essay on the Afar. For an overview of studies of the Cushitic languages, see Andrzej Zaborski's 'Cushitic overview' (p. 67-85). For the history of the Cushitic languages, see Christopher Ehret's 'Cushitic prehistory' p. 85-96).

351 **Amharic interference in 'Afar translation.**
Loren F. Bliese. *Bulletin of the School of Oriental and African
Studies,* vol. 43, no. 2 (1980), p. 345-56.

The authors note that by 1978 the Afar translation team of the Ethiopian Bible Society had translated about two-thirds of the New Testament into the Afar language. Yet, since English was 'difficult' for the Afar members of the translation team, 'the language used to translate from was the popular Amharic version' in preparation by the Bible Society. The net result of this 'translation utilizing a translation' was that 'the use of Amharic as the source language resulted in interference in the 'Afar draft, as subsequent testing revealed'. Problem areas of translation are demonstrated through numerous examples in which both the Afar and Amharic texts are provided along with English translations. Discussion is grouped under the following headings: 'Passives'; 'Series of imperatives'; 'Subordinating and co-ordinating conjunctions together'; 'Series of co-ordinating conjunctions'; 'No propositions before conjunctions'; 'Contrastive conjunction "or" '; 'Postposition "to" for motion towards'; 'Class nouns preferred to plurals'; 'Number agreement'; 'Plural verbs changed to feminine singular'; 'Person agreement in relatives'; 'Separation of relatives in "Afar" '; 'Verbs and case'; 'Verbal nouns or finite verbs'; 'Marking quotations'; 'Use of "say" with conjunctions'; and 'Semantic interference'.

352 **A generative grammar of Afar.**
Loren F. Bliese. Arlington, Texas: Summer Institute of Linguistics,
University of Texas at Arlington, 1981. 306p. bibliog. (Summer
Institute of Linguistics Publications in Linguistics, no. 65).

The book is the result of the culmination of over fifteen years of living and working in Ethiopia, and represents a revised and updated version of the author's 1977 doctoral dissertation of the same title. Seeking to exact a discipline of 'generative' (i.e. transformational) grammar rules, the book provides an excellent introduction to the grammar of the Afar language. A brief introduction centring on orthography, parts of speech and roots of the Afar language is followed by twelve chapters on grammar. 'The sentence' (chapter 1); 'Noun phrase' (chapter 2); 'Sentence (verb phrase) complement' (chapter 3); 'Postpositional phrase' (chapter 4); 'Conjunctives' (chapter 5); 'Other sentence construction types (quotations, negation, questions, deletions, movements)' (chapter 6); 'Verbals' (chapter 7); 'Nominals' (chapter 8); 'Pronouns'

150

(chapter 9); 'Adverbs' (chapter 10), 'Phonology' (chapter 11); and 'Morphologically determined alternatives' (chapter 12). Three appendices provide phrase structure rules, subcategorization rules, and transformational components. A good bibliography directs the reader to numerous detailed subjects concerning the Afar language.

353 **The modernization of Somali vocabulary, with particular reference to the period from 1972 to the present.**
John Charles Caney.   Hamburg, GFR: Helmut Buske Verlag, 1984.
389p. bibliog. (Hamburg Philologische Studien, no. 59)
The purpose of this book is to document the accelerated vocabulary expansion and lexical modernization of the Somali language since the determination of an official orthography by the government of Somalia in 1972. This process has obvious ramifications for Djibouti's Somali-speaking population. Part 1 places the expansion of the Somali language within an overall theoretical framework of vocabulary expansion in general. Part 2 centres on the lexical modernization of the Somali language, including a detailed analysis of selected vocabulary within the following groupings: agriculture, armed forces, banking and finance, chemistry, commerce and industry, communications, education, geography, language, law, mathematics, medicine, office equipment, physics, politics and public affairs, printing and publishing, sport, town and facilities, vehicles and vehicle parts, and work. Subsequent sections are devoted to examples of vocabulary expansion in selected extracts from news bulletins broadcast by Somalia's Radio Hargeisa (part 3), the roles played by the Somali daily newspaper *Xiddigta Oktoobar* (part 4), and school text-books (part 5) in the modernization of Somali grammar.

354 **La soco af Somaaliga.** (Go along with the Somali language.)
Joy Carter.   Nairobi: Mennonite Board in East Africa, 1984. 114p.
The book is an excellent companion to John Warner's three-volume set *Somali grammar* (q.v.). The text, which emphasizes the mastery of oral skills in the Somali language, includes sixteen dialogues, greetings, fifteen sets of useful expressions, and thirteen summary sheets of Somali grammar. The majority of the text, however, is comprised of seventy-five work sheets designed to aid oral mastery. The text includes hundreds of illustrations which are integrated into tne lessons. Cassettes and a teachers' manual are also available.

355 **Manuel de conversation somali–français: suivi d'un guide de Djibouti.**
(Somali–French conversation manual: followed by a guide of Djibouti.)
Véronique Carton-Dibeth.   Paris: Éditions l'Harmattan, 1988. 80p.
map.
This handy little guide was designed for both French tourists and inhabitants of Djibouti who desire to know the basics of the Somali language for everyday living purposes. A brief discussion of twenty-two important rules of Somali grammar is followed by a short section describing the nature of names in Somali society. The remainder of the booklet is divided into two major sections. The first section groups useful phrases according to situations most likely to be encountered by the French speaker, such as seeking directions, going shopping and speaking on the telephone. The second section provides the Somali equivalent for groups of French vocabulary especially relevant to the traveller or newcomer to the language. Among these are fruits and vegetables, the bakery and the butcher, prominent things around the house, and going on a trip. A final section constitutes a small travel guide.

Language

356 Notes on the northern dialect of the 'Afar language.
James G. Colby. *Journal of Ethiopian Studies*, vol. 8, no. 1 (Jan. 1970), p. 1-8.

This brief article is simply a list of various unique aspects of the northern dialect of the Afar language and does not include an accompanying essay or text. A chart of the phonology of the dialect is followed by English–Afar examples grouped under the following headings: 'Formational statement of phonemes'; 'Non-phonemic phonetic features'; 'Distribution of phonemes'; and 'Morpho-phonemics'.

357 Arabic script for Somali.
Muuse Haaji Ismaa'iil Galaal. *Islamic Quarterly*, vol. 1, no. 1 (1954), p. 114-18.

A case for the writing of the Somali language in Arabic script (as opposed to the Osmania or Latin scripts) prior to Somalia's official adoption of a Latin script in 1972, by one of Somalia's most recognized authorities on that country's folklore and culture. Noting the technical difficulty of writing Somali using Arabic letters, the author presents a modified version of the Arabic vowel system to facilitate its use. The author argues that his compatriots should 'realize that the Arabic script, already well established in our country, has the greatest chance of becoming a medium of rapid educational progress and the spreading of literacy'. The vast expansion of the Somali language since 1972 and obvious success as a medium for literacy and education have rendered this argument moot.

358 Iska wax u gabso (self help): a Somali language learning manual.
Joseph Gleason, Omar Awad, David Rorick, revised and adapted by Adam J. Farax, Naomi Smoker, introduction by Douglas Biber. Nairobi: Mennonite Board in East Africa, 1981. 76p.

Designed for beginners in the Somali language, this text is written employing the standard orthography adopted in 1972. Each section is comprised of short drills and dialogues. The book is designed for oral teaching purposes and concentrates on the student achieving oral skills necessary for day-to-day living.

359 The Sam languages: a history of Rendille, Boni, and Somali.
Bernd Heine. *Afroasiatic Linguistics*, vol. 6, no. 2 (Dec. 1978), p. 1-93.

The 'Sam' languages, which include Rendille, Boni and the various dialects of Somali, are spoken in the East African countries of Djibouti, Somalia, Kenya and Ethiopia. The term Sam refers to 'the closely-knit unit of Cushitic languages within the Omo-Tana (formerly called "Somaloid" or "macro-Somali") branch of the Lowland East Cushitic'. The book recreates the historical development and evolution of the Sam languages, which are said to have their origin among the Ethiopian peoples who migrated and spread their language. A section entitled 'Comparative vocabulary' includes a list of 'reconstructed proto-Sam roots' with English translations. An appendix provides an alphabetical list of English words with their proto-Sam equivalents.

360   **Tonal accent in Somali.**
      Larry H. Hyman.   *Studies in African Linguistics*, vol. 12, no. 2 (1981),
      p. 169-203.

Somali is a 'tonal accent' language in that it assigns accents to vowels rather than
syllables. The author develops a model which includes rules of accent placement (on
either the final or penultimate vowel of a word), accent modification (shifts,
reductions), and tone and pitch assignment.

361   **The modern English–Somali phrase book.**
      Ahmed F. Ali 'Idaaja', Omar au Nuh.   Mogadishu: National Printing
      Agency, 1975. 91p.

This English–Somali phrase book is designed for the beginner in the Somali language
or the tourist traveller. The text is written employing the standard orthography
adopted in 1972. Sections are constructed around topical headings such as 'People and
occupations', 'Telling the time' and 'Colours'. A phrase or word in English is
accompanied by its Somali equivalent. Unfortunately, the manual lacks an index.

362   **A Somali newspaper reader.**
      Abdullahi A. Issa, John D. Murphy.   Kensington, England:
      Dunwoody Press, 1984. 186p.

This has been designed for intermediate students of the Somali language who have
already completed an elementary course. The first half of the book comprises fifty-one
Somali newspaper selections (in Somali). The majority of the newspaper articles come
from Somalia's daily newspaper *Xiddigta Oktoobar*, with the selections stressing
political, economic, military and human interest themes. Each selection is accompanied by English translations of select vocabulary terms and grammatical notes when
necessary. The second half of the book comprises complete English translations of all
fifty-one newspaper selections. A Somali/English glossary is provided which includes
all the Somali words employed within the text.

363   **A survey of materials for the study of the uncommonly taught languages:**
      languages of sub-Saharan Africa.
      Dora E. Johnson et al.   Washington, DC: Center for Applied
      Linguistics, 1976. 79p.

An annotated bibliography of basic tools of access for the study of uncommonly taught
languages in sub-Saharan Africa. Designed for native English speakers who have
knowledge of modern linguistic terminology, the text consists of annotated bibliographic entries for topics such as grammars (both reference and linguistic), readers
(literary, history, social science, folklore, newspaper), dictionaries (comprehensive,
student dictionaries and glossaries) and teaching materials (audio-visual, radio
recordings). The citations are organized under the following linguistic groups on
country/regions: Germanic (Afrikaans), Ethiopia and Somalia, West Africa, Bantu,
Khoisan, Interior Africa and Malayo–Polynesian. A complete alphabetical listing of
the various languages is listed in the index.

Language

364 **A glossary of botanical terms: explanations in English and Somali.**
S. M. A. Kazmi, A. A. Elmi. Mogadishu: National Herbarium,
National Range Agency, 1983. 47p.

A useful compilation of over 500 technical terms for those interested in botany. Each term is listed alphabetically in English and is followed by both English and Somali language descriptions. Nine pages of plates contain dozens of hand-drawn pictures referring to key terms in the text. Although a useful beginning in this much neglected field, Somali equivalents are often not given for the English terms (although descriptions in Somali are almost always provided).

365 **Proceedings of the second international congress of Somali studies,
University of Hamburg, August 1-6, 1983. Volume I, linguistics and
literature.**
Edited by Thomas Labahn. Hamburg, GFR: Helmut Buske Verlag,
1984. 449p. map.

This volume is the first of a four-volume set of papers delivered at the second international congress of Somali studies held at the University of Hamburg, 1-6 August 1983. The articles contained in this volume, which centres on Somali linguistics and literature, are of direct relevance to Djibouti and its Issa population. Relevant articles include Richard J. Hayward and John Saeed's 'NP focus in Somali and Dirayta: a comparison of *baa* and *pa*'; Lucyna Gebert's 'Absolute constructions in Somali'; Jacqueline Lecarme's 'On Somali complement constructions'; Annarita Puglielli's 'Derived nouns in Somali/part I'; Biancamaria Bruno's 'Notes on denominal verbal derivation in Somali'; Roberto Ajello's 'Substantives as predicates in Somali'; David L. Appleyard's 'Possessive pronoun suffixes in Somali and their cognates in other Cushitic languages'; Giorgio Banti's 'Possessive affixes in the Somali area'; Marcello Lamberti's 'The linguistic situation in the Somali Democratic Republic'; Christopher Ehret and Mohamed Nuuh Ali's 'Soomaali classification'; Cabdalla C. Mansur's 'Some traces of Somali history in Maay dialect'; Didier Morin's 'À propos des emprunts: à l'Arabe et au Français en Afar et en Somali à Djibouti' (q.v.); Isse Mohamed Siyad's 'A semantic field: the camel'; John William Johnson's 'Recent researches into the scansion of Somali oral poetry'; Ahmed Adan Ahmed's 'Maanso structure and content (an application of Guuleed's Maanso scansion system to the meaning of *dardaaran*)'; and John Charles Caney's 'The role of the newspaper and the school textbook in the modernization of Somali vocabulary'.

366 **Somali–English dictionary.**
Virginia Luling. Wheaton, Maryland: Dunwoody Press, 1987. 605p.

The author modestly notes that this is but a 'preliminary edition' still embodying 'editorial problems', but that 'the current need for useful lexical aids for Somali outweighs further delay in publication'. The dictionary contains over 18,000 entries of Somali words with precise English translations, with the primary source being Yaasiin C. Keenadiid's *Qaamuuska Af-Soomaaliga* (A dictionary of the Somali language) (Mogadishu: State Printing Agency, 1976). A brief appendix describes irregular verbs. Unfortunately, the dictionary only centres on Somali–English translations, and not vice versa.

367   **Dictionnaire français–somali, qaamuus faransiis–soomaali.**
(French–Somali dictionary, qaamuus Faransiis–Soomaali.)
Maxamed Cabdi Maxamed.   Paris: Institut National des Langues et
Civilisations Orientales, 1985. 598p. 2 vols.

Utilizing the orthography adopted by the government of Somalia in 1972, this dictionary provides brief definitions in the Somali language for French terms. The text contains roughly 15,000 words and 2,500 French expressions, and is seemingly geared toward the translation of materials from French and Somali. Volume 1 is devoted to words from A to M, while volume 2 is devoted to words from N to Z. For a Somali–French dictionary by the same author, see *Eraybixin soomaali–faransiis, lexique somali–français* (q.v.).

368   **Eraybixin soomaali–faransiis, lexique somali–français.** (Eraybixin
Soomaali–Faransiis, Somali–French lexicon.)
Maxamed Cabdi Maxamed.   Besançon, France: Imprimerie Stalactite
Sucrée, 1987. 128p. bibliog.

Published through the financial aid of the United Nations Educational, Scientific and Cultural Organization (UNESCO), the volume constitutes a limited companion to the author's *Dictionnaire français–somali, qaamuus faransiis–soomaali* (q.v.). French equivalents are given for Somali terms arranged alphabetically. An extremely limited dictionary except for the beginning scholar, a brief introductory section offers basic notes on the Somali language. It is unclear why the author did not offer a much more complete Somali–French dictionary along the lines of his much more extensive French–Somali work.

369   **Aspects du multilinguisme en République de Djibouti.** (Aspects of
multilingualism in the Republic of Djibouti.)
Didier Morin.   *Northeast African Studies*, no. 4, vol. 1 (1982), p. 1-8.

The author briefly describes the major aspects of Djibouti's multilingual society. Although Arabic is described as the oldest foreign language to be implanted in Djibouti, as well as one of the official national languages of the country, its usage is mainly limited to religious purposes, whereas Afar and Somali are shown to be the dominant maternal languages of the majority of the population. French, to the contrary, is described as the foreign language whose continual growth is assured by its implantation within society as the language of education. The author briefly describes how the various languages interact (i.e. how usage of one language is affected by another) and provides statistics documenting the repartition of maternal languages in the country. For example, out of a total population estimated at 259,570 in 1979, 64,170 spoke Afar, 180,200 spoke Somali and 15,200 spoke Arabic as their maternal language.

370 **À propos des emprunts: à l'arabe et au français en afar et en somali à Djibouti.** (Concerning loan-words: from Arab and French to Afar and Somali in Djibouti.)
Didier Morin. In: *Proceedings of the second international congress of Somali studies*, vol. 2. Edited by Thomas Labahn (Hamburg, GFR: Helmut Buske Verlag, 1984), p. 277-86.

A brief but highly informative analysis of loan-words (i.e. borrowed words) from French and Arabic and how they have affected the names of persons, places and modern technical vocabulary in Djibouti's indigenous Afar and Somali languages (thus making the Afar and Somali languages of Djibouti somewhat different from their linguistic cousins in Ethiopia and Somalia, respectively). For example, it is demonstrated that often the name of a place (in either the Somali or Afar languages) in Djibouti derives from French administrative terminology, which, in turn, is derived from the Arabization of an original Afar or Somali name. In short, the accepted usage of the name of a place in either Afar or Somali, rather than proceeding from its original usage, has evolved as follows: Somali or Afar name of a place (leads to) Arabic form (leads to) French form (leads to) current usage in either Afar or Somali. As concerns proper names, those of the Afar group are said to be subtlely changed because of French, Somali and Arabic linguistic influences. Finally, word-borrowing as concerns modern technical vocabulary, especially that in the political domain, is shown to be heavily influenced by the French language, despite the modernization of the Somali vocabulary in neighbouring Somalia (which, according to the author, finds 'only a faible echo in the Djiboutian Somaliphone population schooled in French').

371 **Propositions pour la transcription de l'Afar.** (Propositions for the transcription of Afar).
Didier Morin. In: *Proceedings of the fifth international conference of Ethiopian studies, session B, April 13-16, 1978, Chicago, U.S.A.*
Edited by Robert L. Hess. Chicago: University of Illinois at Chicago Circle, 1979, p. 125-29.

The Afar language, unlike its Somali counterpart, still lacks an agreed-upon form of transcription. In this brief article, a noted French scholar of language use in Djibouti examines the various approaches to ultimately settling the still elusive issue of transcription. Individual sections examine differences concerning the transcription of consonants, vowels and accent marks, with the author ultimately proposing one means for overcoming these differences. Using an Afar language extract from a publication in Djibouti, the author demonstrates how his proposed method for transcription would be employed.

372 **An English–Afar phrase book.**
Enid M. Parker, introduction by Maureen N. D. B. Yeates. London: [no publisher], 1981. 59p. map.

A handy booklet for students of the Afar language. An introductory section offers a description and map of that region referred to as Afar, as well as simple notes concerning the Afar language, including alphabet and pronunciation, stress, restrictions on consonants and modification of words. A second section provides English phrases and Afar equivalents within various categories, such as 'seasons and months', 'shopping' and 'medical matters'. A third section centres on Afar grammar (grouped under the headings 'word classes', 'nouns' and 'verbs'), while a concluding section

Language

offers an eighteen-page English–Afar listing of commonly used words. Although utilizing the Latin script, the following letters are used for what are termed the three 'problem' consonants: retroflex 'd' (p); and voiced (c) and voiceless (x) pharyngeal fricatives.

373 **An Afar–English–French dictionary (with grammatical notes in English).**
Enid M. Parker, Richard J. Hayward.   London: School of Oriental and African Studies, University of London, 1985. 306p. bibliog.

The dictionary is the result of extensive field research among the Afar, including the year 1980 in Djibouti, and utilizes what the authors denote as the 'Dimis and Reedo' orthography. Two introductory sections describe the genesis of the work, methodological problems contained therein, competing orthographies for a written Afar language in Djibouti, and a short summary on how to use the dictionary correctly. Each full entry begins with the Afar word in bold-face print, followed by the English translation. The French equivalent is then provided in brackets. An appendix concisely describes the major aspects of Afar grammar as it relates to pronunciation and composition of words, including a four-page index for quickly finding material related to a specific question. A second appendix describes the major aspects and structural features of Afar kinship. A useful bibliography outlines the major works done in reference to the Afar language. Although utilizing the Latin script, the following letters are used for what are termed the three 'problem' consonants: retroflex 'd'(x); and voiced (q) and voiceless (c) pharyngeal fricatives. This method of transcription, said to be the most favoured and used ('as amply demonstrated by the wide practical use to which this is now being put both within the Djibouti Republic and abroad'), is spelled out in the following Afar texts written by Dimis and Reedo and published in Paris by l'Imprimerie de la Réunion: *Qafar Afih Baritto* (1975); and *Yabti Rakiibo* (1975).

374 **English–Somali phrase book of common and medical terms (for travellers, health field workers, etc.).**
Wayne F. Peate, MD, assisted by Hersi Mohammed.   Tucson, Arizona: Anglo-American Press, 1982. 83p. map.

This handy language booklet is a must for doctors, midwives, nurses, dentists and other medical personnel who will be working among Somali-speaking peoples in Djibouti, Ethiopia, Somalia and Kenya. Somali language equivalents are provided for the most common and useful English words and phrases that will be needed by medical personnel who, for example, will be working in refugee camps. Medical terms and phrases are divided into the following groupings: 'Parts of anatomy'; 'Body products'; 'Medical conditions' (signs, symptoms and diseases); 'Health worker to patient phrases'; 'Obstetrics/midwifery'; 'Dentistry'; 'Medical supplies'; 'Procedures'; and 'Instructions to community health workers'. Other brief sections can offer a guide to pronunciation and a brief grammar of the Somali language, common words and phrases divided by functional category (e.g. eating out), Somali proverbs and metric/English conversion tables. Since the booklet is primarily targeted toward those seeking work in Somalia proper, two sections offer general information on Somalia, as well as simple phrases in other languages commonly found in the region (Arabic, Italian and Swahili).

Language

375 **Petit lexique somali–français.** (A small Somali–French vocabulary.)
Christophe Philibert. Paris: Librairie C. Klincksieck, 1976. 55p.

A small, handy dictionary which generally offers one-word definitions in the French language of Somali terms utilizing the official orthography chosen by the government of Somalia in 1972. The dictionary's size obviously limits its scope, and the lack of a reverse French–Somali conversion of terms limits its versatility. For a much larger French–Somali dictionary, see the two-volume work by Maxamed Cabdi Maxamed, *Dictionnaire français–somali, qaamuus fransiis–soomaali* (q.v.).

376 **Language reform in Somalia: the official adoption of a vernacular.**
John Ibrahim Saeed. *N. E. A. Journal of Research on North East Africa*, vol. 4, no. 2 (1982), p. 95-107.

The adoption of a written script for the Somali language was debated for decades by partisans who made cases for using Arabic, Latin and Osmania scripts, each, of course, engendering certain benefits and drawbacks, depending on one's point of view and maternal language. This article summarizes the successful adoption in 1972 and continued modernization and spread of the Somali language as the official medium for government administration and instruction in schools. Although the emphasis of the article is Somalia, the official selection and modernization of the Somali language utilizing a Latin script obviously has enormous ramifications for Djibouti – a country where a large portion of the population speaks Somali as the primary language and where the institutionalization of French as one of the official languages makes the choice of a Latin script logical. Emphasis is placed on who was responsible in each case for directing the modernization of the vocabulary and how the use of modernized Somali was encouraged.

377 **Somali reference grammar.**
John Ibrahim Saeed, foreword by B. W. Andrzejewski. Wheaton, Maryland: Dunwoody Press, 1987. 275p. bibliog.

Noted scholar B. W. Andrzejewski correctly asserts in the preface that the author 'has a remarkable talent for explaining the complexities of grammar in a simple and readily accessible manner without lowering the standards of accuracy in description. His approach is particularly successful when he deals with those aspects of Somali grammar which have no parallels in English and which often intimidate the learner by their unfamiliarity'. This book is by far the best work on Somali grammar currently available in the English language, although it does not contain practice exercises or a working bibliography and, thus, is to serve as a complement to other texts and exercises. A brief introduction is followed by discussions of various aspects of grammar, under the following chapter headings: 'Sounds & orthography' (chapter 2); 'Verbs' (chapter 3); 'Nouns and simple noun phrases' (chapter 4); 'Adjectives' (chapter 5); 'Propositions' (chapter 6); 'Simple sentences' (chapter 7); 'Subordinate clauses' (chapter 8); 'Coordination' (chapter 9); and 'Time expressions' (chapter 10). A useful bibliography and comprehensive index of grammatical terms is also included.

378 **Somali grammar.**
John Warner. Nairobi: Mennonite Board in Eastern Africa, 1983. 3 vols.

This three-volume set serves as an excellent beginners' course for those interested in learning the Somali language. Employing the standard Somali script as adopted in

158

1972, the set is comprised of sixty-nine separate lessons. Each lesson presents a particular aspect of Somali grammar and is accompanied by examples, a list of relevant vocabulary and short exercises (such as translating English sentences into Somali or vice versa). The author warns that 'due to the demand for this to be ready for duplicating' it was not possible to check each section thoroughly with Somali informants, 'particularly those in the latter half of the course'. See also the companion oral textbook by Joy Carter, *La soco af Somaaliga* (q.v.).

379 English–Somali dictionary.
Saciid Warsame Xirsi, Cabduraxmaan C. Oomaar. Mogadishu: National Printing Agency, 1975. 272p.

This dictionary allows the scholar of the Somali language to find the Somali meaning(s) for a given English word. The Somali equivalents are written employing the standard orthography adopted in 1972.

380 Arabic loan-words in Somali: preliminary survey.
Andrzej Zaborski. *Folia Orientalia*, vol. 8 (1966), p. 125-75.

An interesting portrayal of the effect of Arab culture on Somalia through the documentation of 'loan-words' (i.e. borrowed words) from Arabic that have been assimilated into the Somali language. Limitations of the work include concentration on only 'classical Arabic' as a source of loan-words and the transcription of Somali equivalents without the benefit of an accepted orthography. The lexical assimilation of Arabic loan-words is illustrated by the alphabetical listing of hundreds of Somali words (with definition and Arabic equivalent) within the following categories: 'Religion'; 'Law'; 'Administration and politics'; 'Writing and reading, education'; 'Time and calendar'; 'Kinship terminology'; 'Social relations'; 'Nationality'; 'Human body, health and medicine'; 'Trade'; 'Tools, utensils, clothes, etc.'; 'Professions'; 'Building'; 'Jewelry'; 'Minerals'; 'Plants, meals and cooking'; 'Animals'; 'Navigation, sea'; 'Geography'; 'Gambling, alcoholism, prostitution'; 'Measures'; 'Adverbs, prepositions, particles'; and 'Verbs, adjectives and abstract nouns not mentioned previously'. Especially useful is a substantial section noting twenty-eight areas of phonological assimilation of Arabic into Somali.

Bible translation from SVO to SOV languages in Ethiopia.
See item no. 197.

The rise of written Somali literature.
See item no. 321.

The lexicon – a key to culture; with illustrations from Afar word lists.
See item no. 326.

Somali language and literature.
See item no. 404.

Statistics

381 **Statistics Africa: sources for social, economic, and market research.**
Edited by Joan M. Harvey. Beckenham, England: CBD Research,
1978. 374p.

An extensive listing of sources of statistical data for all African countries including
Djibouti. Each reference consists of statistics dealing with: (1) general information
(such as climate, demography and health); (2) production, including mining,
agriculture, industry and construction; (3) external trade; (4) internal distribution and
service trades, (5) population; (6) social indicators (such as standard of living, welfare
and education); (7) finance (banking, public finance and investment); and (8) transport
(road, air, rail, shipping, telecommunications and postal service). Among the sources
for the data are central statistical offices, statistics collection agencies, principal
libraries, major statistical publications and information services. Sources are indexed
numerically, along with a brief description of what information the reference contains.
A general index is included for each of the citations used throughout the text, as well
as an alphabetical listing of all titles (a total of 1,461 entries are listed.)

382 **Geographical distribution of financial flows to developing countries.**
Organization for Economic Cooperation and Development (OECD).
Paris: OECD, 1956- . annual.

A comprehensive statistical series which focuses on the volume and sources of financial
flows to developing countries, including Djibouti. The bulk of the publication is a
country-by-country display, in millions of US dollars, of financial allocations in terms
of net and gross loans and disbursements, as well as grants, debt and debt service. In
addition to noting financial flows from individual Development Assistance Council
(DAC) countries, tables also include the flow of resources from groupings of countries
such as the Organization of Petroleum Exporting Countries (OPEC). Included in the
statistics is a breakdown of resources allocated to areas such as technical co-operation,
food aid and emergency aid. Recipient countries are broken down into the following
four categories: least-developed countries (LDCs), low-income countries (LICs), low-
middle income countries (LMICs) and upper middle-income countries (UMICs).

383 **Bulletin semestriel de statistique.** (Biannual statistical bulletin.)
République de Djibouti: Direction Nationale de la Statistique
(DINAS).   Djibouti: The Author, 1970- . sporadic.

Previous to 1981 this official Djiboutian government publication was issued under two
different titles: *Bulletin de statistique et de documentation* (nos. 1-31); and *Bulletin
trimestriel de statistique* (nos. 32-36). Published on a sporadic basis, it contains a host of
data on Djibouti ranging from climate, transport and communications, to teaching and
education. The bulletin has two supplements. One, entitled *Bulletin de statistique et de
documentation. Numéro spécial, annuaire*, summarizes various economic data over a
four-year span. The second, entitled *Bulletin de statistique et de documentation.
Numéro spécial, statistiques détaillées des importations spéciales pour l'année*, offers
annual statistics on imports and trade.

384 **Annuaire statistique de Djibouti.** (Statistical annual of Djibouti.)
République de Djibouti: Ministère du Commerce, des Transports et du
Tourisme: Direction Nationale de la Statistique (DINAS).   Djibouti:
DINAS, 1977- . annual.

Published under the title *Annuaire statistique* prior to 1981, this annual provides a rich
assortment of statistics on numerous topics of interest to the scholar of Djibouti. For
example, the 1986 volume, which comprises 150 pages, is divided into eight sections.
Section 1 summarizes demographic and geoclimatic givens of Djibouti, while section 2
discusses the population of the country and conditions of life (e.g. employment,
salaries, health, education, mass media and sports). Section 3 outlines production
statistics, including agriculture, ranching, fishing, water, electricity, housing, public
works and commercial enterprises, Section 4 provides statistics on road, rail, maritime
and air transportation, telecommunications and tourism. Section 5 documents domestic
consumption and internal and external trade, and section 6 outlines public finances and
banking. Section 7 provides data on the national budget and 'national energy balance'.
Finally, section 8 offers a description of Djibouti's system of social security, a fiscal
summary of the republic and an outline of the country's investment code.

385 **Direction générale de l'éducation nationale, annuaire statistique.**
(General direction of national education, annual statistics.)
République de Djibouti: Ministère de l'Éducation Nationale, de la
Jeunesse, des Sports et de la Culture (ENJSC).   Djibouti: The Author
[n.d.]. annual.

Published annually by Djibouti's Ministry of National Education, Youth, Sports and
Culture, the volume provides very precise data on the nature of education in Djibouti,
both within the capital and the outlying rural areas. Two introductory charts provide
the structure of the Ministry and system of education (which is heavily influenced by
the French educational system). The data offers insights on such topics as
characteristics of primary- and secondary-school children, number of classes taught in
primary and secondary schools, types of personnel teaching in the primary and
secondary state school system, private education and exams.

Statistics

386 **The statesman's yearbook: statistical and historical annual of the states of the world.**
London: Macmillan, 1864- . annual.
A detailed country-by-country analysis for all members of the United Nations (UN). Each case study follows a similar outline that includes a brief discussion of numerous topics of interest. Among these are the history of the country, area and population, climate, constitution and government structure (including a list of current government officials and their offices), defence (size of army, navy, air force), international relations (membership status within the UN and other international and regional bodies), economy (budget, currency, banking), energy and natural resources (electricity, minerals and agriculture), industry and trade (imports and exports) and communications (roads, railways and aviation). Each country brief also includes a general overview of education (degree of illiteracy/number of learning institutions), welfare and religion.

387 **Demographic yearbook.**
United Nations (UN). New York: The Author, 1948- . annual.
A comprehensive collection of international demographic statistics. However, since data is collected from official government sources without any modification on the part of the United Nations (UN) Secretariat, the statistics are often of questionable validity. Among the statistics are the size, distribution and trends in population growth, mortality, nuptiality and divorce. Other topics include natality (such as ages of mother and father, birth order, type of birth and birth weight) and fertility (such as foetal deaths and legally-induced abortion).

388 **International trade statistics yearbook.**
United Nations (UN). New York: The Author, 1950- . annual.
Formerly entitled *Yearbook of international trade statistics*, this series provides basic economic statistics for all countries' external trade performance in terms of the overall trends in current value, as well as in volume and price. Statistical data for each country illuminates: (1) historical trends since 1950 in such diverse categories as merchandise trade and gold trade (in both national currencies and US dollars); and (2) imports and exports by broad economic category (such as food and industry). The text also provides data concerning trade by principal countries of provenance and destination, which is given in terms of US dollars. This data is given for a selected group of fifty trading partners, as well as general regions such as Africa, Europe and North America.

389 **National accounts statistics.**
United Nations (UN). New York: The Author, 1957- . annual.
This series contains statistical data of national accounts for individual countries and regions. All of the tables are designed to facilitate international comparisons, that is, countries within regions, country groupings based on developed and developing economies, type of economic system (market or centrally planned), as well as global aggregations, all of which are presented in millions of US dollars and national currencies. Statistics outline capital transactions and capital accumulation, as well as what portion of the gross domestic economy is spent by the government and by the private sector in areas such as investment. Other tables list economic activity in terms of the Gross Domestic Product (GDP) as they relate to areas such as agriculture, construction, and wholesale and retail trade. The yearbook also reflects trends in economic development expressed in rates of growth at constant prices of GDP.

162

390 **Statistical yearbook.** (Annuaire statistique.)
United Nations (UN). New York: UN, 1948- . annual.

Provides a comprehensive range of socioeconomic statistics for all United Nations (UN) member countries. Among the topics included are mining, manufacturing, employment, inflation, distribution of income, development of new energy sources, supply of food, external debt, education, illiteracy, dwelling availability, improvement in living conditions, and foreign assistance. The values listed in the tables are based on the national currency of each country.

391 **African statistical yearbook.** (Annuaire statistique pour l'Afrique.)
Addis Ababa: UN, Economic Commission for Africa, 1974- . annual.

Published annually by the Economic Commission for Africa, each yearbook comprises four volumes devoted to a particular region of Africa: North Africa (volume 1); West Africa (volume 2); eastern and southern Africa (volume 3); and central Africa (volume 4). Statistics on Djibouti fall under the volume devoted to eastern and southern Africa. Although there is a significant lag time in publication, the wide diversity of statistics are of great use to the interested scholar, especially as the tables usually span 8-10 years. The tables are grouped by country and are subdivided under the following nine major headings: 'Population and employment'; 'National accounts'; 'Agriculture, forestry and fishing'; 'Industry'; 'Transport and communications'; 'Foreign trade'; 'Prices'; 'Finance'; and 'Social statistics'. Each volume contains both English and French texts.

392 **Survey of economic and social conditions in Africa.**
United Nations (UN), Economic Commission for Africa. Socio-Economic Research and Planning Division. New York: UN, 1983- . annual.

The text, containing general social and economic statistics for all African states including Djibouti, is divided into three general categories: (1) overall review and outlook for that year, including international economic situation, economic trends, external sectors of African economies, and fiscal and monetary policies; (2) main economic sectors, including agriculture, forestry, mining, manufacturing, transport, communications and tourism; and (3) social sectors, such as population growth, education and public health. Each of these three parts and their respective subdivisions include both current information and projections for the coming year. For a summary of this data from 1970 to 1983, see *African socio-economic indicators* (New York: United Nations, 1985).

393 **Handbook of international trade and development statistics.**
United Nations Conference on Trade and Development (UNCTAD).
New York: The Author, 1964- . annual.

Published annually in recent years, this handbook offers a general summary of world trade and development statistics. Countries are divided into four major categories: (1) developed market economy countries; (2) socialist countries of Eastern Europe; (3) socialist countries of Asia; and (4) developing countries and territories (including all African states except South Africa, which is included in the first category.) In addition, countries are also classified according to economic grouping, such as major exporters of manufactures and major petroleum exporting countries. These are placed at the end of the text. Each of the above classifications are incorporated under seven major headings and figures constitute millions of US dollars. Among the seven major

163

Statistics

categories are: (1) value, growth and shares of world trade in current prices; (2) volume, unit value and terms of trade indices; (3) network of world trade (including summary by selected regions of origin and destination, and export and import structure by selected commodity groups); (4) export and import structure by commodity and country; (5) balance of payments, financial resource flows and external indebtedness; (6) basic indicators of development (such as population growth rates); and, finally, (7) special studies.

394   **UNCTAD commodity yearbook.**
United Nations Conference on Trade and Development (UNCTAD).
New York: The Author, 1984- . annual.

Statistics are provided at world, regional and country levels for trade and consumption in selected agricultural primary commodities and minerals for all countries of the world, including Djibouti. Among the commodities and minerals listed are cereals, vegetables, iron ore, bauxite and copper. Countries are grouped by region (such as West Africa) and economic organization (such as European Economic Community). African countries, such as Djibouti, are listed under 'least developed countries'.

395   **UNESCO statistical yearbook.**
United Nations Educational, Scientific and Cultural Organization
(UNESCO).   Paris: The Author, 1963- . annual.

Detailed statistics cover a wide range of topics for all members of the United Nations (UN), including Djibouti. The publication is written in English/Spanish/French with appendices in Arabic and Russian. The information presented is from official government responses to questionnaires and special surveys distributed by the United Nations Educational, Scientific and Cultural Organization (UNESCO). In addition, official reports, publications and information available to the UN Secretariat are also included. Statistics are offered on a range of topics including: libraries (national, public, special); book production (numbers of translations, titles, authors most frequently translated); newspapers (daily general-interest, number and circulation per 1,000 inhabitants); cultural heritage (number of museums and archival institutions); film and cinema (number of cinemas and number of films produced and imported); broadcasting (radio and television, number of receivers, transmitters, expenditures and state revenue); and international trade in printed matter (import and export of books and pamphlets). Other topics in the educational field include enrolment, expenditure, faculty, illiteracy and sex ratio. Finally, a section on science and technology offers data on numbers of scientists, research facilities, engineers and overall expenditure.

396   **Foreign economic trends and their implications for the United States.**
United States: Department of Commerce.   Washington, DC: The Author,
1979- . irregular.

These economic briefs are periodically prepared for every country of the world. Key economic indicators dealing with the domestic economy include population growth, Gross Domestic Product, consumer price indices, industrial production index and government operating budget. Key economic indicators dealing with balance of payments include exports, imports, foreign debt, debt service and foreign exchange reserves. Figures are given in millions of US dollars for a period of three to four years. Depending on the report, other information may be included such as agricultural production, foreign investment, US bilateral aid (economic and military), and principal US exports and imports. Some briefs also discuss political issues such as the economic

164

effects of elections, constitutional changes and nationalization. Each brief includes an analysis of projected economic implications for US businesses.

Étude sur la sous-alimentation en côte française des Somalis. (Study of malnutrition in the French Somali Coast.)
See item no. 116.

Résultats de l'enquête sur la mortalité infantine dans la ville de Djibouti.
(Results of the survey on infant mortality in Djibouti City.)
See item no. 117.

Djibouti.
See item no. 153.

Donor's conference.
See item no. 247.

Djibouti, developing city and country.
See item no. 251.

World transport data. (Statistiques mondiales de transport.)
See item no. 258.

The trade of the Gulf of Aden ports of Africa in the nineteenth and early twentieth centuries.
See item no. 263.

1977-1987: our development means economic growth.
See item no. 270.

Plan de développement économique et social, 1982-1984. (Economic and social development plan, 1982-1984.)
See item no. 296.

Bibliographies

397 **Current African directories.**
Edited by I. G. Anderson. Beckenham, England: CBD Research
Ltd., 1972. 200p.

A list of directories published in, or relating to, all the independent and dependent
territories of Africa, including island states. The book includes: yearbooks; almanacs;
gazetteers; general industrial and commercial directories; research, library and
bibliographic directories; and regional, specialized and technical directories. Listings
also include publishers and bibliographic data, description of content, languages used,
frequency, date published, price and size. The book contains two parts. The first is an
alphabetical list of directories by title. The second is a country-by-country listing of
sources of business information, responsible offices, legal forms required, official
gazette, sterling exchange information and an index to directories for each country
listed in the first section.

398 **Bibliographie de la République de Djibouti.** (Bibliography of the
Republic of Djibouti.)
Centre de Documentation du Centre Culturel Français de Djibouti.
Paris: République Française, Ministère de la Coopération, 1980. 77p.

Assembled by the well-established French Cultural Center of Djibouti, this
bibliography is intended to be selective in nature, citing what are considered to be the
most important works written on Djibouti. Although the vast majority of the 944
citations are in the French language, a few English-language citations are also to be
found. The works are listed alphabetically by author's last name within ten functional
categories, with a useful annex providing an alphabetical list of all authors cited (with
corresponding page numbers). The functional categories include: general works
(section 1); history (section 2); economy (section 3); geography (section 4); earth
sciences (section 5); natural sciences (section 6); medicine and social life (section 7);
ethnology and ethnography (section 8); linguistics (section 9); and literature (section
10). Each category is further subdivided. For example the section on Djibouti's
economy is subdivided into general works, infrastructure, resources and commerce.

399 A developmental bibliography for the Republic of Djibouti.
W. Sheldon Clarke.   Djibouti: Institut Supérieur d'Études et de
Recherches Scientifiques et Techniques (ISERST), 1979. 242p. map.
The author was the first US chargé d'affaires to be accredited to the newly independent
Republic of Djibouti. The bibliography is arranged in twenty functional categories,
including an index to authors who are said to have 'contributed in one way or another
to our understanding of the area now known as Djibouti'. Works of the English and
French languages are included. Unfortunately, all the documented works are not
indexed, making it difficult to determine if and where specific works are noted. Works
are grouped under the following twenty chapters: 'General works' (chapter 1); 'Early
accounts and travel' (chapter 2); 'Historical studies' (chapter 3); 'Anthropology,
ethnography, and archaeology' (chapter 4); 'Language studies' (chapter 5); 'Modern
politics (chapter 6); 'Local political literature' (chapter 7); 'Relations with neighbours,
international relations' (chapter 8); 'Economics, trade and development issues'
(chapter 9); 'Agriculture, rural development, fisheries' (chapter 10); 'Medicine,
biology and other natural sciences' (chapter 11); 'Earth sciences, geography' (chapter
12); 'Climate, meteorology' (chapter 13); 'Maps, cartographic studies' (chapter 14);
'Cultural figures, literature and fiction' (chapter 15); 'Travel, tourism, pictorial
materials' (chapter 16); 'Official publications' (chapter 17); 'Publications by other
countries, international organizations' (chapter 18); 'Bibliographies and general
reference materials' (chapter 19); and 'Index to authors' (chapter 20).

**400 The Republic of Djibouti – an introduction to Africa's newest state and a
review of related literature and sources.**
W. Sheldon Clarke.   *Current Bibliography of African Affairs* (New
York), no. 1, vol. 10 (1977-78), p. 3-31.
This bibliography was compiled to correspond with Djibouti's independence in 1977
and serve as a starting point for scholars interested in carrying out research on the
country. Citations, which are largely in the French language, are listed chronologically
by date of publication within major subheadings. The subheadings are as follows:
'General works'; 'Early accounts and travel'; 'Historical studies'; 'Anthropology,
ethnography and archaeology'; 'Social and urban studies'; 'Modern politics'; 'Foreign
relations, regional affairs'; 'Economics, trade and agriculture'; 'Climate, geography';
'Science, medicine'; 'Literature, cultural life, fiction'; 'Administrative and legal
studies'; 'Language studies, linguistics'; 'Travel, tourism'; 'Official publications of the
French territory of the Afars and Issas'; 'Foreign official publications'; and 'General
reference and bibliography'. For a much more substantial volume by the same author,
see *A developmental bibliography for the Republic of Djibouti* (q.v.).

401 Official publications of Somaliland, 1941-1959; a guide.
Helen F. Conover.   Washington, DC: Library of Congress, General
Reference and Bibliography Division, 1960. 41p.
This bibliography lists 169 official publications of French, British and Italian colonial
administrations in the Horn of Africa published during 1941-59. Works are listed
alphabetically by author's last name within four major sections: 'Bibliographies';
'Somaliland under Italian administration'; 'British Somaliland'; and, of most interest to
scholars of Djibouti, 'French Somaliland'. Yet, as the author notes in the introduction,
'The last section on French Somaliland is very short; apparently little is published
relating to this sparsely inhabited country, the only one in French Africa that in the
referendum of 1958 voted to retain its previous status of an overseas territory of
France'. An index provides quick access to topics of particular interest to the reader.

Bibliographies

402 **A Soviet view of Africa: an annotated bibliography on Ethiopia, Somalia and Djibouti.**
Colin Darch. Boston, Massachusetts: G. K. Hall, 1980. 200p.
This annotated bibliography of Russian-language literature devoted to Djibouti, Ethiopia and Somalia is a much needed addition to scholars interested in the Horn of Africa. Literature is separated into dozens of categories and four appendices introduce the reader to Russian-language 'Book reviews', 'Soviet Ethiopiana in languages other than Russian', 'Selected Soviet press reports about Ethiopia in Soviet newspapers, 1945-1978', and 'Incomplete, unverified or doubtful citations'. The 1,207 citations are indexed accordng to subject and author. However, the title of this work is misleading as only ninne works are listed in the index as centring specifically on Djibouti (although obviously numerous works are related to the topic in question). This state of affairs is no doubt reflective of the minor attention given to the topic of Djibouti among Soviet scholars (similar to the attention focused on the country by English-speaking researchers).

403 **Somalia.**
Mark W. DeLancey, Sheila L. Elliott, December Green, Kenneth J. Menkhaus, Mohammed Haji Moqtar, Peter J. Schraeder. Oxford, England: Clio Press, 1988. 191p. map. (World Bibliographical Series, 92).
This fully-annotated bibliography is the ninety-second volume of the World Bibliographical Series, a project which will eventually include every country in the world. Although the topic of this book is Somalia, the 584 articles, books and other reference materials cited are often of direct relevance to the Horn of Africa and, particularly, Djibouti's Issa (Somali) population. Works are cited alphabetically by author within twenty-six functional categories, including: 'The country and its people'; 'Geography'; 'Travellers' accounts'; 'Flora and fauna'; 'Anthropology'; 'History'; 'Language'; 'Religion'; 'Population, health and welfare'; 'Urbanization and Migration'; 'Politics'; 'Administration'; 'Constitution, legal system and land tenure'; 'Foreign relations'; 'Economy and economic development'; 'Trade'; 'Industry, power, transport and communications'; 'Agriculture and animal husbandry'; 'Education'; 'Art and music'; 'Literature and folklore'; 'Statistics'; 'Printing, publishing and broadcasting'; 'Libraries, museums and archives'; 'Periodicals'; and 'Bibliographies'. The volume is complemented by a brief introductory essay and three convenient indexes (divided by authors, titles and subjects) for locating items of particular interest.

404 **Somali language and literature.**
Marcello Lamberti, foreword by B. W. Andrzejewski. Hamburg, GFR: Helmut Buske Verlag, 1986. 106p. (African Linguistic Bibliographies, no. 2).
This is an excellent bibliography of the rapidly expanding literature on Somali language and literature. The bibliographical references are ordered alphabetically according to authors' names, with an index of subject matter (divided by topical groupings such as 'historical linguistics') providing easy access to a desired topic. The editor states: 'As far as a fairly reliable level of completeness is concerned, the compiler's final date is 1980. We have added, unsystematically, a number of titles which have appeared between 1980 and 1984 and we have changed most of the entries which by 1980 referred to manuscript and should now refer to publications'. See also the author's

Map of Somali dialects in the Somali Democratic Republic (Hamburg, GFR: Helmut Buske Verlag, 1986).

405 **The modern history of Ethiopia and the Horn of Africa: a select and annotated bibliography.**
Harold G. Marcus.   Stanford, California: Hoover Institution, 1972. 541p.

The noted scholar of Ethiopian studies, Harold Marcus, oversaw a four-year project of culling material from little-known publications of European and US geographic societies of the 19th and 20th centuries found primarily in the US Library of Congress. As the author notes, the term geography was 'so elastic' in the 19th century that the result of this archival foray – the present volume – includes entries ranging from (but not limited to) ethnology, geology, cultural history, material culture and linguistics. Although primarily focused on Ethiopia, numerous works centre on the Horn of Africa in general and, of direct interest to the scholar of Djibouti, the role of French colonialism, 19th-century travellers' accounts, and regional and international trade routes. Over 2,000 fully-annotated entries are arranged chronologically within five major sections divided by language: English, French, Italian, German and Russian (including other European languages). Two appendices list the geographical journals consulted and a partial listing of books mentioned in the bibliography. Four indexes – divided by author's name, geography, proper noun and subject – offer easy access to topics of particular interest.

406 **Somalia: a bibliographical survey.**
Mohamed Khalief Salad, series foreword by Daniel G. Matthews, foreword by Ali Khalief Galied.   Westport, Connecticut: Greenwood Press, 1977. 468p. (African Bibliographic Center, Special Bibliographic Series, no. 4).

This collection provides the most comprehensive collection of documentary materials concerning Somalia to date. The collection comprises nearly 4,000 books, journal articles, and newspaper and cartographical materials. The author has included works from five languages: English, Italian, French, German and Somali. The materials are divided according to seventeen major topical headings and forty-three subheadings, with works being listed alphabetically by author's name. Numerous references centre on Djibouti and its relationship with Somalia.

407 **Bibliographies for African studies: 1980-1983.**
Yvette Scheven.   New York; London; Paris: Hans Zell, 1984. 300p. bibliog.

This general reference to recent bibiographies of Africa contains 1,192 annotated entries. Items with a specific Djibouti section are listed in the index. Earlier bibliographies are included in two previous editions covering the periods 1970-75 and 1976-79 (published by Crossroads Press in 1977 and 1980, respectively).

Bibliographies

408 **An annotated bibliography on the climate of French Somaliland.**
Charles S. Vitale.   Silver Spring, Maryland: US Environmental Data
Service, 1968. 34p.

Although dated, the bibliography offers a wealth of data concerning climatological and meteorological data for Djibouti. This was but one of a continuing series prepared by the Foreign Branch, Climatology Division, of the US Environmental Data Service. The author fully annotates over fifty sources (both French and English), specifically summarizing extensive passages when they pertain to Djibouti. Author and subject indexes facilitate searches for specific topics of interest. Citations are arranged alphabetically by author's last name under the following chronological headings: '1911-1920'; '1921-1930'; '1931-1940'; '1941-1950'; '1951-1960'; and '1961- . . .'.

409 **The United States and Africa: guide to U.S. official documents and**
government-sponsored publications on Africa, 1785-1975.
Julian W. Witherell.   Washington, DC: Library of Congress, 1978.
949p.

An annotated compilation of 8,827 unclassified documents both prepared and sponsored by the US government and its various agencies from 1785 to 1975. Works are grouped into five major chronological sections (1785-1819; 1820-63; 1863-1921; 1921-51; 1952-75), and each section is further subdivided by region or country. The last section (1952-75) contains over eighty per cent of all the annotated works and is further subdivided by subject. While the first four sections are 'limited primarily to congressional and presidential documents, commercial reports, diplomatic papers, and treaties', the final section 'also features translations issued by the Joint Publications Research Service and printed and mimeographed studies concerning American assistance programs prepared by or for federal government agencies'. An extensive 131-page index facilitates easy access to topics of particular interest. See also the 5,047 annotated entries in a companion volume that covers the 1976-80 period: Julian W. Witherell's *The United States and Sub-Saharan Africa: guide to U.S. official documents and government-sponsored publications, 1976-1980* (Washington, DC: Library of Congress, 1984).

Historical dictionary of Somalia.
See item no. 75.

Historical dictionary of Ethiopia.
See item no. 103.

Periodicals from Africa: a bibliography and union list of periodicals published in Africa.
See item no. 315.

A generative grammar of Afar.
See item no. 352.

A survey of materials for the study of the uncommonly taught languages: languages of sub-Saharan Africa.
See item no. 363.

Somali reference grammar.
See item no. 377.

Statistics Africa: sources for social, economic, and market research.
See item no. 381.

Index

The index lists, in alphabetical sequence, authors (personal and corporate), titles, and subjects. Index entries refer both to the principal citations and to further works mentioned in the annotations. Titles of books and articles are italicized. Numbers refer to bibliographic entries.

Algeria 189
Algiers 52
Ali Abdirahman Hersi *see*
  Hersi, Ali
  Abdirahman
Ali Aref *see* Aref, Ali
Ali Sabieh 12, 13, 31, 268,
  280, 297
Ali, Mohamed Nuuh 365
Ali Moussa Iyé *see* Iyé, Ali
  Moussa
Ali, Osman Sultan 2, 305
All African Peoples
  Conference 217
All India Radio 232
All Somali Conference 217
almanacs 397
Amat, J. P. 280
Ambouli 69
American Council for
  Nationalities Service
  see ACNS.
*Amharic interference in
  'Afar translation* 351
Amnesty International 108
*Amnesty international
  report* 108
*An analysis of Afar
  pastoralism in the
  northeastern
  rangelands of Ethiopia*
  154
*Ancient civilizations in
  Africa* 89
Anderson, David M. 115
Anderson, Gaylord W. 124
Anderson, I. G. 397
ANDES (National
  Association for
  Economic and Social
  Development)
  long-term programs of
  281
  objectives of 281
  priorities of 281
  short-term programs of
  281
  strategies of 281
Andrew, R. B. W. G. 41
Andrzejewski, B. W. 317-
  24, 327-28, 333, 348,
  377, 404
Anglo-Ethiopian
  Agreement (1944) 225

Anglo-Ethiopian Boundary
  Commission (1931 &
  1934) 240
Angola 134, 173
*Animals of the French
  Territory of the Afars
  and Issas* 68
*Les animaux du Territoire
  Français des Afars et
  des Issas* 68
ANLM (Afar National
  Liberation Movement)
  183
*Annexe, cadre général
  d'application,
  1983-1989* 296
*Annexe, general context for
  application, 1983-1989*
  296
*An annotated bibliography
  on the climate of
  French Somaliland* 408
Annuaire Statistique 384,
  390
*Annuaire Statistique de
  Djibouti* 384
*Annuaire Statistique pour
  l'Afrique* 391
*Anthropological
  comparison between
  the Afars and Issas of
  Djibouti* 147
anthropology
  bibliographies 399-400
Antigua and Barbuda 168
Antilles 169
Antoine, Major 82
Appadurai, Arjun 110
Appleyard, David L. 365
*The approaching end of the
  president's rule brings
  new uncertainties* 307
Aptidon, President Hassan
  Gouled 2, 74, 105,
  188, 196, 209, 213,
  223, 246, 249, 256, 307
*Aqoondarro waa u nacab
  jacayl* 327
aquatic sports 13
*The Arab factor in Somali
  history: the origins and
  the development of
  Arab enterprise and
  cultural influences in*

the Somali peninsula
  87
Arab League 105
Arab World 228
Arabia 157, 253
Arabian Bustard 71
Arabian peninsula 114, 147
Arabic language 182, 203,
  300, 357
*Arabic loan-words in
  Somali: preliminary
  survey* 380
Arabic script for Somali
  357
Arab–Israeli conflict 224
Arab–Israeli War (1973)
  226
Arabs
  blood relationships with
  the Somali 182
  cross-breeding with
  Afars 147
  geographers 87
  historians 87
  immigrant communities
  in East Africa 98
  in Somali history (1500-
  1800) 87
  influence in the Horn 87
  influence on Somali
  culture 87
  influence on Somali
  economics 87
  influence on Somali
  migration 140
  literature concerning the
  Horn 87
  settlements in the Horn
  87
Aradoum, Fassil 205
Aramis Houmed Soule *see*
  Soule, Aramis
  Houmed
arbitration 195
Archaeological
  Commission of the
  Polish Academy of
  Sciences (Poznan
  Branch) 292
archaeology
  bibliographies 399, 400
  burial sites 57
  caravan routes 57
  cemeteries 159

D

dabal 343
dabbal 343
DAC (Development
    Assistance Council)
    382
Le Dain, Anne-Yvonne 17
Damer Kadda'-Alayli
    Dadda formation 20
*The Danakil: nomads of
    Ethiopia's wasteland*
    151
*Les Danakils du cercle de
    Tadjourah* 145
dance
    Afar 145
    barrimo 343
    dabal 343
    dabbal 343
    falo 343
    gobley 343
    hafat malabo 343
    hella yar yar 343
    horra 343
    laale 343
    music associated with
        338
    nacna 343
    sadexleey 343
    siliko 343
    wilwileh 343
    zailai 343
Danzig 93
'A Danzig solution'? 93
Daoud, Kamil 280
Dar es Salaam 221
Darch, Colin 402
dardaaran 365
Daroud 149
Dars, R. 20
*Dating of Quaternary
    tectonic movements in
    the Republic of
    Djibouti* 39
Day Forest 4, 12, 69, 70
Dead men do tell tales 57
Debon, F. 20
debt 251, 382, 393, 396
decolonization 172
Decoudras, Pierre-Marie
    286
Deeqsi, Abdi 'Cinema' 317
Deflez, Gilbert 170

Dehedin, J. 149
Deighton, Len 189
Delaloye, M. 20, 24, 25, 34
DeLancey, Mark W. 403
Democratic Front for the
    Liberation of Djibouti
    see FDLD
Demographic Yearbook
    387
demography statistics 387
dengue 123
Denis, F. 23
dependency 186
Derains, Yves 195
Dergue 233
DeRito, Paul A. 287, 288
*Derived nouns in
    Somali/part I* 365
*Dermatoglyphes digitaux et
    palmaires d'Afar
    (Danakil) et d'Issa
    (Somali), et le
    problème du
    peuplement de la
    Corne de l'Afrique* 150
dervishes 327
    dervish orders 204
    nationalist struggle 345
    poetry 344
Detre, G. 117
development
    agriculture 118, 251,
        280, 293
    Awash valley 291
    bibliographies 399-400
    capital program 251
    cultural 251
    Djibouti City 301
    economic 216, 296, 302,
        389
    educational training 251
    electricity 278
    energy 251, 279
    fisheries 287-88, 290, 293
    foreign perspectives 42
    forestry 293
    government policy
        toward urban
        development 295
    historical influences 6
    history 259
    impact of autocentric
        national policies 216
    in Africa 302, 307

    in Ali Sabieh 297
    in Dikhil 298
    indicators of 393
    industry 251, 302
    informal sector 294
    medium private
        enterprises 281
    of pastoral groups 154
    origins of agricultural
        development in
        northeast Africa 292
    pastoral sector 293
    post-independence
        period 251, 256, 259
    problem of 286
    role in promoting ethnic
        rivalry 186
    role of nutrition in
        economic
        development 118
    role of nutrition in social
        development 118
    role of women 127
    small private enterprises
        281
    socio-economic 207, 251,
        296
    statistics 390, 393
    telecommunications 251
    tourism 251
    underdevelopment,
        northeastern Ethiopia
        284
    urban projects 99, 137,
        251, 275, 295, 298-99
Development Assistance
    Council *see* DAC
*Development, drought, and
    famine in the Awash
    valley of Ethiopia* 291
*Development of fishing and
    fisheries in Djibouti*
    287
*Development of fishing and
    fisheries in Djibouti –
    phase I* 287
*The development of a
    middle class in British
    Somaliland, French
    Somaliland and in
    Somalia under
    trusteeship (with some
    references to Ethiopia
    and the Sudan)* 111

185

186

impact on Somali
  pastoral nomadic
  settlement 138
induced by the
  environment 291
induced by politics 291
local responses to 291
mortality 291
northeast Africa 115
pastoralist responses to
  291
problems with 282
role in increasing the
  flow of Ethiopian
  refugees 135
Drysdale, John 80, 212,
  221
*Dualism in Somali notions
  of power* 155
Ducros, Jacqueline 150
Duhul, Yusuf 324
Dunham, Daniel C. 252,
  274-75
dysentery 109, 124

E

*Earthquake history of
  Ethiopia and the Horn
  of Africa* 30
East Africa 72, 73, 83, 88,
  98, 114, 118, 202, 203,
  292
  neolithic food-producing
    cultures 292
  rejection of fish diet in
    300
*East Africa and the Orient:
  cultural syntheses in
  pre-colonial times* 137
*The East African coast:
  select documents from
  the first to the earlier
  nineteenth century* 83
East African holiday 16
East African Hong Kong
  95
East Prussia 93
East Salines 299
Eastern Afar 36
*Eastern Africa country
  profiles: Djibouti* 282
*Eastern Africa regional

*studies: trends and
  interrelationships in
  food, population, and
  energy in eastern
  Africa: a preliminary
  analysis* 285
Eastern Europe 393
Ebola fever 123
ECA (Economic
  Commission for
  Africa) 391
Eckstein, Susan 210
École Normale
  d'Instituteurs 342
ecology
  change in northeast
    Africa 115, 292
  factors in the
    rejection of a fish diet
    300
  historical change in the
    Horn 115
  impact on Afar
    cross-cousin marriages
    164
  impact on society 115
*The ecology of malnutrition
  in eastern Africa and
  from countries of
  western Africa;
  Equatorial Guinea, the
  Gambia, Liberia,
  Sierra Leone, Malawi,
  Rhodesia, Zambia,
  Kenya, Tanzania,
  Uganda, Ethiopia, the
  French Territory of the
  Afars and Issas, the
  Somali Republic and
  Sudan* 118
*The ecology of survival:
  case studies from
  northeast African
  history* 115
economic aid 95
*Economic and social
  development plan,
  1982-1984* 296
*Economic and social
  situation prior to the
  plan 1982-1984* 296
*Economic aspects of Cuban
  involvement in Africa*
  210

Economic Commission for
  Africa *see* ECA
*Economic history of
  Ethiopia, 1800-1935* 99
*Economic progress
  impeded by refugees*
  307
The Economist
  Intelligence Unit 304
economy 3, 7, 12, 48, 51,
  96, 166, 308, 314
  Afar 158
  Africa 306
  agriculture and fishing 4
  Anglo–French rivalry in
    Ethiopia 264
  apprenticeships in the
    informal economic
    sector 294
  Arab interests in
    protecting petroleum
    shipping 216
  banking and monetary
    systems 4, 251
  between World Wars I
    and II 86
  bibliographies 398-400
  British perceptions of
    economy, between
    World Wars I and II
    86
  business conditions 304
  business conditions in
    Ethiopia 304
  business conditions in
    Somalia 304
  characteristics of
    employment in the
    informal economic
    sector 294
  commercial importance
    of the Afar triangle
    183
  comparison with the
    Ethiopian economy
    179
  comparison with the
    Somali economy 179
  cost of living 4
  creation of small
    enterprises toward
    revitalization of the
    employment market
    121

189

195

197

Gulf Cooperation Council
see GCC
Gulf of Aden 30, 32, 34, 38, 140, 260, 262, 263
Gulf of Tadjoura 27, 32, 35, 41, 48, 86, 94
Gulf War 211

H

hafat malabo 343
hagiography 322, 337
Haig-Thomas, David 62
Haile Mariam Mengistu see Mengistu, President Haile Mariam
Haile Wolde Mariam see Mariam, Haile Wolde
Hamad La'Ade see La'Ade, Hamad
Hamilton, David 220
Hancock, Graham 4
Handbook of International Trade and Development Statistics 393
handicrafts 102
Hanks, Robert J. 211
Hansen, Art 138
Hantaan fever 123
Harar 43, 45, 78, 96
Harbeson, John W. 283
Harbow, Vincent 98
Hared, Ismael Guedi 259
Harfang Publications 15
Hargeses 353
Harmonics 346
Harmoniques 346
Harringtin, Captain J. L. 43
Harvey, Joan M. 381
Hasan, Sayyid Mahammad Abdille 345
Hassan Gouled Aptidon see Aptidon, President Hassan Gouled
Hassan Sheikh Mumin see Mumin, Hassan Sheikh
Haud region 332
Hauquin, J. P. 20
Hayward, Richard J. 365, 373

Health: the children of Balbala 243
Healy, Sally 176
heatstroke 109
heello 328
Heellooy heellellooy: the development of the genre heello in modern Somali poetry 328
Heine, Bernd 359
hella yar yar 343
Helland, Johan 154
Her majesty, the khat 9
d'Héricourt, Charles Rochet 55, 194
Hersi, Ali Abdirahman 87
Hersi, Mohammed see Mohammad, Hersi
Hess, Robert L. 88, 254, 311, 371
Heudebert, Lucien 48
Hijaz 198
Hindlip, C. Allsop 49
Histoire de Djibouti: des origines à la république 97
Histoire sommaire de la Corne Orientale de l'Afrique 79
Historical aspects of genealogies in northern Somali social structure 157
Historical dictionary of Ethiopia 75, 103
Historical dictionary of Somalia 75, 103
history 1, 3, 12, 13, 14, 16, 74-107, 118, 282, 310, 386
Afar 200
Africa 76, 89
agriculture 289
Arabic oral histories 200
Arabic writings 83, 200
arms trade in the Horn of Africa 100
bibliographies 398-400
border with Ethiopia 240
border with Somalia 240
chronology of events (1839-1977) 194
circumcision of women 152

colonialism 78
conflict in the Horn 232, 242
cultural ties with Ethiopia 103
Cushitic languages 350
Cushitic prehistory 350
Dervish nationalist movement 345
development efforts 6
diplomacy in the Horn 90
Djibouti–Addis Ababa railroad 94, 261
East Africa 83, 98
economic development 259
economic ties with Ethiopia 103
economy of Ethiopia (1800-1935) 99
economy of the Horn 99
Ethiopia 9, 103, 225, 347
Ethiopia prior to Islam 204
Ethiopian and Eritrean independence movements 215
Ethiopian quest for access to the sea 214
ethnic groups 10
ethnic ties with Ethiopia 103
external relations 10
fish consumption in Africa 300
Franco–Djiboutian relations 84
French colonialism 8
French Foreign Legion 189
French writings 83
Greek writings 83
health care 124
historiography of the Horn 87
Horn of Africa 75, 79, 87, 89, 103, 233, 310, 347
independence 2, 74
independence movement 166
Indian Ocean, 107
infibulation of women 152

208

pharmacology of 125,
129
physiological problems
of chewing 110, 119
production of 110
rail transport from
Ethiopia 122
rate of usage 119
role in the economy 129
role in the political
economy of northeast
Africa 110
role in the society of
northeast Africa 110
role of education in
curbing consumption
129
role of religious
institutions in curbing
consumption 129
seen as major health
problem 129
social aspects of 110
social effects of chewing
119
social problems of 119
Somalia 110, 125
southern Africa 125
statistics of consumer
use 122
Tanzania 125
Yemen Arab Republic
125
*Khat: pharmacognostical
aspects* 125
Khedive, Egypt 64
Ki-Zerbo, J. 89
Killion, Thomas Charles
174
Kingdom of al-Habasha
200
kinship system 164
Kitchen, Helen A. 167
Kloos, Helmut 291
Kobusiewicz, Michael 292
Konstant, Antoine 52
korsiyya 325
Krzyzaniak, Lech 292
kukta 165

L

La'Ade, Hamad 336
laale 343
Labahn, Thomas 78, 187,
312, 324, 330, 365
labour, 8, 174,282
Lagarde, Léonce 48, 77
Laitin, David D. 175
Lake Abbé 4, 12, 36
Lake Assal 3, 4, 12, 17, 23,
48, 58, 62
Lambert, Henri 106
Lamberti, Marcello 365,
404
Landor, A. Henry Savage
53
Langguth, H. R. 20, 34
de Langle, Fleuriot 77
language 75, 348-80
Afrikaans 363
Amharic 315, 351
Amharic grammar 351
Amharic vocabulary for
addictive substances
126
Arabic 322, 369, 376
Arabic loan-words in
Somali 380
Arabic script and
educational progress
357
Arabic script used in
Somali language 376
Arabic words relating to
Islam 203
Bantu 363
bibliographies 363, 398,
399, 400
Boni 359
comparison of Afar and
Issa 162
Cushitic languages 350,
359
Cushitic–Somali
similarities 365
dictionaries for
sub-Saharan African
languages 363
'Dimis and Reedo'
orthography 373
Dirayta 365
distribution of language
in the Horn 349

English 324
English–Somali
dictionary 379
English–Somali
phrasebook 361
Ethiopia 349, 359, 363
evolution of the Sam
languages 359
grammar of sub-Saharan
African languages
363
history of the Cushitic
languages 350
history of the Sam
languages 359
Horn of Africa 309, 310,
349
impact of Arabic loan-
words on Afar
vocabulary 370
impact of Arabic loan-
words on Somali
vocabulary 370
impact of French loan-
words on Afar
vocabulary 370
impact of French loan-
words on Somali
vocabulary 370
Interior Africa 363
Italian 324, 374
Kenya 349, 359
Khoisan 363
Latin script used in Afar
language 372
Latin script used in
Somali language 357,
376
linguistic approach to
self-determination 176
lowland East Cushitic
359
macro-Somali 359
Malayo-Polynesian 363
map of language
distribution 349
multilingualism 369
Oromo vocabulary for
addictive substances
126
Osmanic script 357, 376
phonological
assimilation of Arabic
into Somali 380

213

military contd.
  Western security
    problems with oil and
    mineral access in the
    Horn 211
*Military powers: the
  League of Arab States:
  Djibouti, Somalia,
  Sudan, Egypt and
  Ethiopia* 179
Milukas, Matthew 277
mineral resources 259, 394
mining
  statistics 392
*The mini-republic of
  Djibouti* 305
*The mini-republic of
  Djibouti: problems
  and prospects* 74
Ministère de la Santé
  Publique, Direction de
  la Santé Publique 122
Ministère de l'Éducation
  Nationale, de la
  Jeunesse, des Sports
  et de la Culture *see*
  ENJSC
Ministère des Travaux
  Publics de
  l'Urbanisme et du
  Logement 297-99
Ministère du Commerce,
  des Transports et du
  Tourisme 384
Ministère Français des
  Relations Extérieures
  31
Ministry of Agriculture
  and Rural
  Development 293
Ministry of Foreign Affairs
  81, 251
Ministry of Italian Africa
  88
Ministry of National
  Education, Youth,
  Sports and Culture *see*
  ENJSC
Ministry of Public Health
  129
*Minorités et gens de mer en
  Océan Indien, XIXe-
  XXe siècles: table
  ronde IHOPM,*

*CHEAM, CERSOI,
  ACOI, Sénanque
  1979, GRECO-Océan
  Indien* 163
missionaries 201
MLD (Liberation
  Movement of
  Djibouti) 173
*Modern and traditional
  aspects of Somali
  drama* 319
*The modern
  English–Somali phrase
  book* 361
*Modern Ethiopia from the
  accession of Menelik II
  to the present:
  proceedings of the fifth
  international
  conference of
  Ethiopian studies Nice,
  19-22 December 1977*
  311
*The modern history of
  Ethiopia and the Horn
  of Africa: a select and
  annotated bibliography*
  405
*A modern history of
  Somalia: nation and
  state in the Horn of
  Africa* 91
*The modernization of
  Somali vocabulary,
  with particular
  reference to the period
  from 1972 to the
  present* 353
Mogadishu 236, 321
Mohamed Khalief Salad
  see Salad, Mohamed
  Khalief
Mohamed Mahdi *see*
  Mahdi, Mohamed
Mohamed Nuuh Ali *see*
  Ali, Mohamed Nuuh
Mohamed Said Samatar
  see Samatar,
  Mohamed Said
Mohammed Haji Moqtar
  see Moqtar,
  Mohammed Haji
Mohammed, Hersi 374
Moi, President Daniel

Arap 246
Mokhtar, G. 89
de Monfreid, Henri 46, 161
Moqtar, Mohammed Haji
  403
Mordechai Abir *see* Abir,
  Mordechai
Morgan, Edward 95
Morin, Didier 309, 365,
  369-71
mortality
  drought related 291
  famine related 291
  statistics 387
*Mouloud: a perimeter
  becomes village* 243
*Le Mouloud: un périmètre
  devient village* 243
Moumin Bahdon Farah *see*
  Farah, Moumin
  Bahdon
Moussa Ali volcano 28
Moussie, C. 20
Mouvement de Libération
  de Djibouti *see* MLD
Mouvement Populaire de
  Libération *see* MPL
le Movel, J. L. 27
Mozambique 134, 173
MPL (Popular Movement
  of Liberation) 188
Mullen, J. 293
Muller, J. 20, 25, 34
Muller, Robert 162
Mumin, Hassan Sheikh
  324, 335-36
Murray, Jocelyn 16
Murray, Roger 16
museums, 395
music 145, 338
*La musique traditionnelle à
  Djibouti* 338
*Musique traditionnelle de
  l'Afrique noire,
  discographie: Djibouti*
  338
Mussolini, Benito 90
Muteba, Ernest 230
Muuse Haaji Ismaa'iil
  Galaal *see* Galaal,
  Muuse Haaji Ismaa'iil

214

N

Piuzzi, Alfred 37
Plan d'action 281
Plan de développement
    économique et social,
    1982-1984 296
Plan énergique national 279
Plant ecology: reviews of
    research 67
The Plant formations of
    Western British
    Somaliland and the
    Harar Province of
    Abyssinia 67
PMAC (Provisional
    Military
    Administrative
    Council) 176
Poche, Christian 338
poetry
    balwo 328, 331
    buraambur 330
    criticism of Somali
        politics 346
    dervish 344
    dissemination of poetry
        in Somali society 345
    gabay 330-31
    gabay-hayir genre 344
    geeraar 330
    heello 328
    jiifto 330
    role in the Dervish
        nationalist movement
        345
    role in Somali art 344
    scansion patterns in
        Somali poetry 330
    Somali balwo 317
    Somali classical 323, 330
    Somali genres
        characteristics 344
    Somali oral 323, 328,
        331, 344, 365
    Somali oral poetry and
        nationalism 345
    Somali poetry broadcasts
        1963 332
    Somali religious 323
    transmission of in Somali
        society 345
Poinsot, Jean-Paul 10
le Pointe, Henri 102
Poland 93
Political and economic

uncertainties continue
    to plague the Gouled
    regime 307
Political and military
    limitations and
    consequences of
    Cuban policies in
    Africa 210
Political conflict on the
    Horn of Africa 219
political parties 84
political prisoners 108
politics 5, 48, 304, 305, 396
    Afar agreements for
        creating an Afar state
        183
    Afar attempts at union
        with Ethiopia 183
    Afar political structures
        158
    Afar–Issa rivalry 184
    Africa 303, 306
    Anglo–French rivalry in
        Ethiopia 264
    Antigua and Barbuda
        168
    Arab interest in political
        stability 216
    bibliographies 399-400
    biographies of political
        personalities 188
    breakdown of the
        political system 184
    British perceptions of
        politics, between
        World Wars I and II
        86
    claims for Somali self-
        determination in
        Ethiopia 206
    comic strips satirization
        of government policies
        308
    consolidation of national
        unity following
        independence 256
    constitutional bases of
        executive power 181
    control over Afar
        subgroups by the
        Tadjoura sultanate
        165
    cosmology 81
    creation of an Afar state

and pacification of
    Eritrea 183
creation of political
    parties 84
criticism of President
    Hassan Gouled
    Aptidon's ethnic
    favoritism 171
Cyprus 168
Dervish nationalist
    movement 345
development of workers'
    organizations in
    Ethiopia 174
dilemmas of solving the
    refugee problem 135
domestic politics 308
domination of politics by
    Issas 128
elections 84, 95, 396
elimination of foreign
    threats by President
    Hassan Gouled
    Aptidon 171
end of French rule
    (1977) 91
eradication of public
    health problems 120
Eritrea conflict 232
Eritrean independence
    movements 228
Ethiopia 103, 198, 304,
    306, 347
Ethiopian domestic
    politics 225
Ethiopian political
    economy 174
Ethiopian socialism 283
Ethiopian socialism and
    Eritrean independence
    215
Ethiopian–Somali
    recognition of
    independence 213
ethnic politics 188
ethnic relations 2
ethnic rivalry 81
evolution of Ethiopian
    internal politics 264
executive power 188
Fiji 168
Franco–Ethiopian
    treaties 55
French influence in

218

222

society contd.
Islamic society 203
Issa social organization
162
nomadic Afar societies
162
nomadic Issa societies
162
northeast Africa 115
role of contracts in
Somali clanship 177
role of nutrition 118
role of Somali clanship
in the lineage system
177
role of traditional
artistry in 343
role of women in Somali
society 214
sedentary Afar societies
162
sedentary Issa societies
162
social organization of
pastoral nomads 286
social organization of the
Tadjoura sultanate
165
social settings for Somali
drama 335
social transformation in
Somalia 175
*Society and culture in the
riverine region of
southern Somalia* 333
Society of the Study of
Eastern Africa *see*
SEAO
La soco af Somaaliga 354,
378
soils 67, 289
Soleillet, Paul 46, 77
Soliman, A. K. 123
Somali 149, 155, 156, 159,
160, 175, 176
circumcision 152
clan divisions 157, 177
coast 44
comparative
odontological study of
149
conquest of the Horn 137
custom of circumcision
109, 112

customs of infibulation
109
deportation 130
detention 130
early migrations 142
human rights
deportations of Somali
residents 130
infibulation 112, 152
metrical and
morphological
characters of teeth 149
migrations 137, 139-40
migrations in the Horn
140
nomads in Kenya 178
pastoral nomad
settlement 138
political harassment of
130
refugees 128, 206
rejection of fish diet 300
religious folktales 337
repartition 94
segmentary lineage
system 156
social organization 158
society 53
Soviet literature on 402
studies in humanities 312
studies in natural
sciences 312
territories 45
traditions 94
travel guide 355
veneration of Sufi saints
322
wood engravings 333
Somali Civil War 128, 143,
305
*The Somali coasts: an
account of the T. A.
Glover Senegal-Somali
expedition in the
Somalilands and
Eritrea* 41
*The Somali conquest of the
Horn of Africa* 140
Somali customs 112
Somali Democratic
Republic *see* Somalia
*The Somali dilemma:
nation in search of a
state* 231

The Somali dispute 212
Somali folktales 337
Somali games 334
Somali grammar 354
Somali grammar 378
Somali Institute of
Development
Administration and
Management. *see*
SIDAM
Somali language 312, 315,
323, 349, 359, 369
abstract nouns 380
accent modification 360
accent placement 360
adjectives 377, 380
adverbs 380
Arabic loan-words in 380
bibliographies 329, 377,
404
dialects of 404
dialogues 354
English–Somali
dictionary 379
English–Somali medical
phrasebook 374
English–Somali
phrasebook 361
expansion of
orthography since
1972 348
French–Somali
dictionary 367, 375
French–Somali lexicon
368
grammar 354-55, 365,
374, 377-78
greetings 354
impact of Arabic script
357
impact of French
administrative
terminology on 370
impact of French loan-
words on vocabulary
370
impact of Latin script
357
impact of post-1972
modernization of 376
irregular verbs 366
lexical modernization of
353
Maay dialect 365

233

237

Map of Djibouti

This map shows the more important towns and other features.

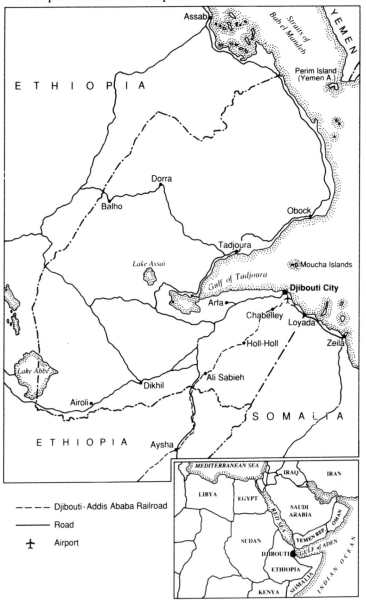